Modern Dreams
An Inquiry into Power, Cultural Production, and the Cityscape in Contemporary Urban Penang, Malaysia

T0338807

Beng-Lan Goh

Modern Dreams
An Inquiry into Power, Cultural Production, and the Cityscape in Contemporary Urban Penang, Malaysia

SOUTHEAST ASIA PROGRAM PUBLICATIONS
Southeast Asia Program
Cornell University
Ithaca, New York
2002

Cornell Southeast Asia Program Publications
640 Stewart Avenue, Ithaca, NY 14850-3857

Studies on Southeast Asia No. 31

Printed in the United States of America

ISBN 0-87727-730-3

Cover: Photo of commercial center by Beng-Lan Goh. Photo of Kampung Serani residents by Salma Khoo-Nasution. Cover design by Judith Burns, Publications Services, Cornell University.

TABLE OF CONTENTS

Acronyms

ABIM	Malaysian Islamic Youth Movement
ASB	Amanah Saham Bumiputera
ASN	Amanah Saham Nasional (National Unit Trust Investment Scheme)
CAP	Consumers' Association of Penang
DAP	Democratic Action Party
FIC	Foreign Investment Committee
HDAM	Housing Developers' Association Malaysia
KLCC	Kuala Lumpur City Center Project
KLSE	Kuala Lumpur Stock Exchange
MARA	Majlis Amanah Rakyat (Council of Trust for Indigenous Peoples)
MCA	Malaysian Chinese Association
MIC	Malaysian Indian Congress
NDP	New Development Policy
NECC	National Economic Consultative Council
NEP	New Economic Policy
NITA	National Information Technology Agenda
NLC	National Land Code
PAS	Pan-Malaysia Islamic Party
PDC	Penang Development Corporation
PEA	Penang Eurasian Association
PERDA	Penang Regional Development Authority
PERNAS	Perbadanan Nasional Berhad (National Corporation)
PHT	Penang Heritage Trust
RM	Ringgit Malaysia (Malaysian Dollar)
RPGT	Real Property Gains Tax
T&CPA	Town and Country Planning Act
UDA	Urban Development Authority
UMNO	United Malays National Organization

TABLES

ACKNOWLEDGEMENTS

This book originated, in part, from the doctoral dissertation I completed a t the Department of Anthropology, Monash University, Australia. Its completion owes much not only to my family, but to friends, colleagues, and teachers I have met in moving from Penang to Melbourne, New York, and, most recently, to Singapore. I owe my deepest gratitude to my supervisors—Joel S. Kahn and Kenneth Young—whose steadfast intellectual support and insightful criticisms direct the original writing of this book. Their engagement in Southeast Asian history, culture, and politics has contributed immensely to my attempts to bring together local knowledge and the questions of the national and the modern, and the interactions of the local and the global.

Many other scholars helped shape my thinking in this book. My revision of major portions of the book was enabled by a most rewarding stint as a Postdoctoral Fellow at the International Center for Advanced Studies, New York University, in a year-long seminar on Cities and Nations organized by Tom Bender and Harry Harootunian. It was through my association with, and learning from, an extraordinary group of scholars at the Center that I was able to go beyond my own thinking on cities and nation: Barbara Abrash, Peter Carrol, Alev Cinar, Jordana Dym, Camilla Fojas, Steven Gregory, Kanishka Goonewardena, Najib Hourani, May Joseph, Rebecca Karl, Abidin Kusno, Karl M. Miller, Timothy Mitchell, Leo Rubinfien, Michael Peter Smith, Daniel Walkowitz, Gwendolyn Wright, Maha Yahya, Marilyn Young, and Xudong Zhang.

My deep gratitude is also owed to Tom Bender, Lisa Drummond, Abidin Kusno, Alev Cinar, Wendy Mee, and Wong Soak Koon for reading part of the revised manuscript in its early and later stages, and offering feedback and valuable suggestions. My revision has equally benefited from the sharp insights of Liu Hong and two anonymous readers who supported this project. I am indebted to Deborah Homsher at Cornell Southeast Asia Program Publications for her patience and support of this project, and to Mary Donnelly and Erick White for their meticulous copyediting.

Besides the International Center for Advanced Studies at New York University, I would like to thank three other institutions from which I received financial assistance for my research and study: the Australian Development Assistance Bureau (now AUSAID) for a Merit Scholarship; Monash University for a Graduate Scholarship; and the Center of Southeast Asian Studies at Monash University for a Travel Grant for my fieldwork.

I shall never forget friends and colleagues in Malaysia whose comradeship and support have been invaluable to me throughout the years: Rohana Ariffin, Chan Lean Heng, Lucille Dass, Foong Kin, Otome Hutheesing, Cynthia Joseph, Khor Yoke Lim, Lekha Lehman, Loh Kok Wah, Pauline & Kntayya Mariappan, Maznah Mohamed, Molly Nyet Ngo Lee, Johan Saravanamuttu, Tan Sooi Beng, Janet Wong May Chin, Wong Soak Koon, Yen Siew Hua, and Zainab Wahidin.

My thanks are also due to many others whom I have met elsewhere who have in one way or another encouraged this scholarship at various stages: Brett Hough, Nerida Cook, Kris Diemer, Frank Formosa, Lucy Healy, Julianne Long, Ramanie Kunanayagam, Michael Ling, Judith Nagata, Nina Patawaran, Pamela Sayers, Ross Shenan, Sharmini Sherrard, Helen Soemardjo, Maila Stivens, Arlene Torres, Juliet Yee, and Mieko & Masaru Yoneno. My colleagues at the Southeast Asian Studies Program at the National University of Singapore have helped me in many ways and I would like to thank them.

Finally, this book is dedicated to the residents of Kampung Serani, without whose generous assistance this book would never have been written. I hope that this book will stand as a tribute to their struggle.

CHAPTER ONE

INTRODUCTION

This book investigates the cultural politics of cityscape transformation through a case study and macro analysis of the city of Georgetown, Penang. The case study documents a fourteen year battle against eviction by the residents of an "urban *kampung*" located in Pulau Tikus, an increasingly fashionable site for condominiums and modern commercial centers.[1] A predominantly Portuguese-Eurasian or *orang Serani* village, the residents were the ground tenants of the Roman Catholic Church.[2] In 1980, the Church entered into a joint venture with a local property development company to convert the village land into shop-houses and terrace houses. However, the severe mid-1980s economic recession delayed the redevelopment of the site. It was only in 1992 that redevelopment recommenced. By this time, the company had been taken over by an Indonesian domestic joint venture capital company, and—in line with the current construction trends in Malaysia—the development was redefined as a commercial center and a condominium project. Before any construction could proceed, the buildings of Kampung Serani first had to be demolished and its inhabitants moved out.[3] Consequently, it was at this time that the conflict between the residents, the Church, and the developer escalated.

The crux of the conflict lies in the close historical ties between the Church and the village community. The villagers were widely perceived as the descendants of a group of Portuguese Eurasians who settled with some Portuguese priests in the vicinity of Kampung Serani in the early 1800s. As the pioneer settlement of Portuguese Eurasians in Penang, Kampung Serani was the nucleus and the site of great attachment for this ethnic group. Not surprisingly, the plans for its redevelopment met with strong opposition from residents. They began by reclaiming the Portuguese-Eurasian heritage and identity of the site to contest their eviction. In the midst of negotiations, the Penang Eurasian Association (PEA), whose leaders are elite members of the community, stepped in to assume the role of mediator in the conflict.

Since the mid-1980s, the PEA has actively engaged in the construction of a distinct Eurasian culture and identity centered on their Portuguese heritage. This project has been fuelled by the national debate over Portuguese-Eurasian identity and claims to Malayness within this identity. In the course of their mediation, the PEA leaders not only reworked the residents' discourses in line with this national discourse, but introduced new arguments based on the importance of Eurasian

---

[1] *Kampung* is the Malay word for village. "Urban *kampungs*" are essentially enclaves of traditional village houses made of wood and zinc often found in juxtaposition to "modern" urban buildings.

[2] *Orang Serani* is another term used locally to refer to Eurasians.

[3] Kampung Serani is the name of the village studied.

contributions to modern education in Malaysia. The Association used these claims successfully to win a heritage house as compensation from the developer and the Church, while the villagers were evicted.

This book argues that we can only understand the cultural politics and the accompanying spatial transformations in the Kampung Serani conflict by reference to the larger processes of modernity in Malaysia. I contend that cultural dynamics rooted in the contest over changing notions of nation, ethnicity, and class connect urban processes to recent economic restructuring and identity reconstructions in the push to turn Malaysia into a fully industrialized country by the year 2020. The urban terrain, as a vital site for the expression of a "modern society," is not only an important locale where these contests are played out, but more importantly, the locus where emerging ethnic identity discourses and various cultural visions of modernity actively reconstitute urban space. This book will illustrate how the categories of nation, ethnicity, and class turn out to be the fertile ground for refashioned identities for the state as well as its citizens. Recent constructions of the categories of nation, ethnicity, class, and new urban built forms, express a profound ambivalence over ideas about the postcolonial and the colonial, East and West, new and traditional, Islam and Malay, and class and ethnicity. As much as this unsettled modernity is a reflection of a similar indecisive stance at the level of the state, it is also the outcome of a condition of constant flux, contestation, and negotiation over the meaning of modernity by various non-state actors and institutions. These cultural dynamics, and the broader social-structural and spatial processes within the push to modernize Malaysia, informed the positions and responses of the actors in the Kampung Serani conflict, which in turn shaped the politics of the conflict and modified the eventual redevelopment design. Modernity in Malaysia, as this book will demonstrate, is defined by contradictory claims, making impossible one homogeneous or coherent meaning for modernity. Despite the state's dominant power, a top-down vision of modernity cannot be implemented. Local identities, conceptions of place, and ways of life, such as the ones that emerged in the Kampung Serani conflict, can reinterpret and resist the state's vision of development and its concomitant cultural forms, leading to multiple and continuous redefinitions of the modern through various mediums such as ethnicity, class, and urban space. State power is never definitive as people's identities are never constituted monolithically from one source but rather are always formed within a network of multiple and conflicting representations and contexts.

Through this analysis of the case of Kampung Serani, this book argues that the Malaysian experience of modernity cannot be understood merely in terms of the transforming power of capitalism nor state hegemonic practices. Rather, it must be understood in terms of collective struggles by citizens and rooted in the social and cultural dynamics that constrain as well as enable them to derive power, class, and cultural status from their positions within the nation-state's modernizing practices. These findings suggest that a meaningful comparison between modernities must take into account the internal social-structural and cultural arrangements within which notions of the modern are translated and made anew, as well as the ways in which these processes intersect and interact with each other across time and space.

DESCRIPTION OF FIELDWORK

I was a postgraduate student at the Department of Anthropology, Monash University, Australia, when I undertook this research. I carried out my fieldwork in Penang, Malaysia, from March 1993 to February 1994 and revisited the field for two weeks in August 1994. I was born in Penang, and studied, worked, and lived there for the majority of my life. As such, my fieldwork was not an experience of "going out there" but rather a return home. I combined both ethnographic and sociological approaches to study a diverse range of subjects. Besides members of the Kampung Serani community, respondents included Church authorities, PEA leaders, members of the broader Eurasian community in Penang, property developers, condominium and apartment dwellers, various local state authorities, politicians, non-governmental groups, academics, lawyers, bankers, and a *feng shui* master.[4] In addition to my primary research, I used a large variety of secondary sources to document the current political, economic, and socio-cultural processes occurring both within the state and at the national level.[5]

My fieldwork in Kampung Serani was not my first contact with the residents. In 1984, while working as a cadet reporter, I had written a feature article on their plight.[6] My interest was rekindled while working on my research proposal. Remembering the Kampung Serani case, I wrote to Paul (pseudonym), the *kampung* spokesperson whom I met in 1984 and received an enthusiastic reply. He became my "patron" during my fieldwork and introduced me to the other villagers. I did not live in Kampung Serani, but instead spent my weekends there when most of the residents were home. I also paid frequent visits to the village during the week to catch up with the latest developments before setting out for other research engagements. My research on the *kampung* residents is based on my field notes and the transcripts of recorded interviews with them.

Some time after I began my fieldwork in Kampung Serani, a former colleague at the university in Penang provided me with a desk in her office.[7] This became my base in making contact with the other subjects of my study. I began by making two lists of respondents: the first was comprised of groups and individuals directly related to the Kampung Serani conflict (such as the Church, the PEA, and the developer); the second consisted of people indirectly connected to it (such as local authorities, other property developers, and community groups in Pulau Tikus).

I was particularly cautious in how I approached the Church and the PEA as the hostilities between them and the *kampung* residents were at their worst during my fieldwork. I realized that tact and sensitivity were called for if I wanted to get their views on the matter. I knew from experience that the Church authorities might refuse to comment on the matter.[8] Direct reference to the Kampung Serani conflict in my approach would risk having my request turned down. I therefore

---

[4] *Feng shui* literally means "wind and water" and is the practice of Chinese geomancy.

[5] I employed many major newspapers—*The Star; New Straits Times; Straits Times; Aliran* (a periodical of social critique); *Property Malaysia* (a publication of the Housing Developers' Association Malaysia); and *Malaysian Business*. I also referred to various government reports such as: *Penang Development Corporation Reports; Penang Investment Reports; City Council Reports; Economic Reports; Property Market Reports;* and the various *Malaysia Year Books*.

[6] The article appeared in the *National Echo*, November 3, 1984, pp. 28-30.

[7] I would like to thank Ms. Hah Foong Lian for her generosity in giving me this space.

[8] See *National Echo*, November 3, 1984, p. 28.

referred to my interest in the Penang Portuguese-Eurasian community and the significance of their relation to the Catholic Church to request an interview with a priest who had earlier served the Pulau Tikus parish, a Catholic Brother, and a committee member of the Church's Justice and Peace Commission. When approaching the PEA, I discussed my interest in Eurasian heritage and identity with two executive committee members pinpointed by the residents as active participants in the conflict. However, I only managed to interview one of the two committee members who is also the local "expert" on Eurasian history. I was turned down by the other who insisted that the former's opinion was representative of the views of the Association. I also carried out informal discussions regarding the matter with two other sub-committee members of the Association. In addition, I interviewed members of other Eurasian communities in Penang to get their views on the Kampung Serani conflict and the recent invocations of Portuguese-Eurasian heritage and identity in the country.

Property developers constituted another major subject group. This move was prompted by my conviction that developers were a major force in shaping the social landscape of modern Penang and that an understanding of these dynamics would help me analyze the circumstances of the Kampung Serani conflict. My first step was to compile a comprehensive list of property developers active in Penang. I did this by a number of methods: procuring the membership list of the Penang Branch of the Housing Developers' Association Malaysia (HDAM)[9]; documenting newspaper advertisements and articles on property development companies and their projects; visiting construction sites to note companies involved; and collecting information on property development companies at local property fairs. In this way I also gathered background information on each of the selected companies. I gave priority to companies with projects in the Pulau Tikus area, but also included companies active in other parts of Penang Island.

I experimented with smaller companies by making telephone calls to request interviews with their directors or managers.[10] However, this method was problematic as I needed to repeatedly explain the nature of my research as my calls were screened before being passed on to the appropriate persons. Another hindrance was the respondents' apprehension over the nature of my interview. After a few attempts, I decided to make my interview requests through formal letters instead (see Appendix A).[11] These letters essentially explained the aims of my research and the expected length of time needed for the interview. I also enclosed a set of interview questions along with each letter (see Appendix B). I pursued these requests with a follow-up phone call.[12] This method worked well and I stuck to it for the rest of my fieldwork.[13]

Nonetheless, the construction boom during my fieldwork meant that property

---

[9] It is not compulsory for property developers to be a member of the HDAM. In 1993, the Penang Branch of the HDAM had a total of forty-nine members.

[10] I managed to get two interview appointments by this method.

[11] My respondents ranged from company directors, property managers, marketing personnel, planners, architects, and engineers working in these companies.

[12] Of the letters I sent out, four companies declined my interview requests while many of the rest responded promptly—even before I could make my follow-up call to them.

[13] An exception to this process was when I used the opportunity at a Property Fair to make direct requests for interviews with two companies.

developers were at their busiest and to get an hour of their time proved extremely difficult. It was not only common to have my appointments cancelled or rescheduled at the last minute, but I also faced frequent telephone interruptions during these interviews. In the latter part of my research I asked respondents to make the interview appointment after office hours. This proved to be successful, and in a few cases the interviews lasted for almost three hours.[14] Using the same method, I approached the company involved in the Kampung Serani conflict and brought up the case during the course of my interview. Overall, I managed to get interviews with twenty property development companies. My success in getting the cooperation of property developers was to an extent enabled by my position as a Malaysian Chinese since all of the property developers that I interviewed were of Chinese descent, although half of these companies had Malay partners. My status as a student of anthropology also helped as many property developers were fascinated that their line of work could be of interest to a social researcher.

I interviewed a *feng shui* master due to a recommendation from one of these developers as I discovered that developers used the services of *feng shui* experts in the process of constructing and promoting their projects. I wanted to understand the logic behind the preoccupation with *feng shui* in the property development industry and its implications for urban politics as a whole. I also interviewed six condominium and apartment dwellers, of whom three were living in the Pulau Tikus area, to further understand consumer response to the developers' conception of a modern lifestyle.

To obtain a comprehensive picture of urban development in Penang Island, I conducted interviews with the Director of the Planning Department of the Majlis Perbandaran Pulau Pinang (the Penang City Council), the Chief Engineer with the Penang Water Board, officers at the Penang Development Corporation (PDC), and the Road Transport Department. I also conducted searches at the Penang Land Office and the Registrar of Companies. Besides state authorities, I interviewed members of a Malay community living in another *kampung* enclave in Pulau Tikus, the Penang Heritage Trust movement (an urban conservation group), lawyers, politicians, and academics.

REPRESENTATION, SELF-REFLECTION, AND SENSE

I often found myself in a somewhat contradictory position while researching, writing, and rewriting this book during a span of years that coincided with a journey from Malaysia to Melbourne, Australia, New York, and finally to the city-state of Singapore. Academic debates on the production of knowledge situate me differently depending on where the debates are held. Am I a Malaysian studying Malaysia, a student from a Western university studying the non-Western, a Southeast Asian scholar in a Western center, or a Malaysian sojourner in a neighboring country?[15] I am of course all of these, and this has challenged me to evaluate the different debates on the production of knowledge from my own

---

[14] In most cases, these appointments started just before office hours ended. All interviews took place at the offices of these companies with one exception, where the interview was conducted at the coffee-house of a hotel in Georgetown.

[15] I consider Australia, where I was based when carrying out this research, as the West.

perspective as I sojourned between these societies in the course of completing this project.

As a Malaysian, I am conscious of the critical reception many Western accounts of Malaysian society and culture have met with in Malaysian academic circles. Such critical responses are part of a generalized critique of colonialism and Orientalism within Malaysia. In fact, the critique of "Western hegemony" is not confined to the academy; it is prevalent in the rhetoric of Malaysia's political leaders.[16] I am concerned by what I perceived to be a growing "hegemonic" sway that the critique of the West has attained in Malaysia. In a climate of increasing "political correctness" and postcolonial sensitivity, it appears that some Malaysian scholars and politicians, as they negotiate their social positions in the world, are also susceptible to the risk of evoking Orientalist categories and the perils of "Othering" in their desire to express their autonomy or cultural difference. However, my time spent as a student of anthropology in Australia, as a research scholar in New York, and as an academic in Singapore also compelled me to address the problem of social comparisons between the East and the West. Many times I have been frustrated by meaningless comparisons in which the developmental experiences of a non-Western country, such as Malaysia, are judged against categories and meanings from the West. I am aware that the practice of establishing the West as the norm against which to judge all other experiences is not necessarily confined to the West. It is equally prevalent in Southeast Asia, albeit camouflaged in different forms. In Malaysia, a reverence of everything Western persists despite the veneer of a strong anti-West rhetoric. My experience of Singaporean society reveals the opposite, at least on the surface levels. In this city-state, the West is often publicly embraced despite endeavors to imagine an Asian modernity distinct from the West's experience. A desire to be accepted into the developmental hierarchies and normative framework of the West remains a significant facet of Singaporean society whereby achievements often only become meaningful when verified by, or set against, norms predetermined by the West.

My own experience of having lived in both the so-called "East" and "West" has taught me that the world is really an interdependent whole, that material and cultural processes within a society are never just confined within that society's national territorial boundaries. Rather, what is inside in a given society is inevitably entwined with, and predicated upon, the outside. As such, I felt a need to seriously address the problem of the East-West binary in my work in order to bring about a clearer understanding and comparison of societies that can transcend this dichotomy. Inevitably, these personal orientations helped shape my theoretical inclinations and trajectory while writing and rewriting this book. I felt that it was imperative for me as a Malaysian scholar to think seriously about the Orientalist challenge in the production of knowledge and the representation of my own society—a society which is fraught precisely because of the apparent tensions between East and West, the colonial and the postcolonial, the local and the global.

I was first exposed to ideas about reflexivity and debates over the anthropologist's role in constructing ethnographic accounts as a student of anthropology in Australia.[17] My exposure to these debates over textual

---

[16] See Chapter Three for further details.

[17] A more elaborate discussion on the crisis of representation in anthropology is provided in Chapter Two.

representation made me aware of the importance of rhetoric and power in my research and writing, as well as in my representation of my society. My academic experience both in New York and Singapore made me appreciate the warnings of postcolonial theorists of the appeal and problems of using "non-Western" culture to critique the West when the non-West is intricately bound up with originally Western regimes of knowledge and modes of representation. Although I found these debates useful, my experience of the effect of nationalist sentiments in the production of knowledge in Malaysia alerted me to the importance of another issue: the need to consider the broader social, political, and moral relations in my research analyses.

Consideration of the broader political and socio-cultural milieu calls into question the assumption of a naturalistic identification or mutual understanding among Malaysians. Othering the West has led some Malaysian academics to overstate the positional affinity between Malaysians. In this research, I have been particularly cautious not to assume any necessary correspondence between my research subjects and myself. Consequently, when I approached the Kampung Serani residents at the outset of my fieldwork, I was sensitive to the differences between us in terms of ethnicity, culture, and experiences, despite the fact that we shared a similar class background. I was aware that these differences would inevitably influence my interpretation of the events even though my ethnographic account would try to be faithful to their experiences and views of the conflict. I was aware that as an observer I could never fully capture, understand, nor represent what it meant to them to be uprooted from their homes and community.

Furthermore, I had to deal with several ethical concerns arising from my fieldwork, which further unsettled any easy identification between myself and the residents. Firstly, I was conscious of the injustice of the situation where, by virtue of being a researcher, I gained a voice to speak about the conflict, while those personally involved were effectively silenced. Secondly, I realized that the academic language of this thesis, as well as my efforts to make sense of their experiences at a more theoretical level, may be too removed from the "local site" for my thesis to be meaningful to the residents. Finally, I was actively aware that their loss was in one sense my gain. I would ultimately benefit, in the form of professional accreditation, from the telling of their stories. However, as I learned more and more about the complexity and the diversity of the issues and forces involved in the conflict, I became convinced that this conflict was not an isolated case, and that there was a need to theorize and analyze this local conflict in order to make sense of the broader processes which set in train similar dynamics throughout Malaysia.

My decision to combine ethnography with sociology was in part prompted by my desire to locate my ethnographic project within the historical, political-economic, and cultural processes that are local yet tied to national and global systems. This motivation is shaped by both theoretical and personal concerns over the question of how the meaning of modernity turns on the question of difference and comparison. In my opinion, a meaningful understanding of the modern experience must consider both external and internal forces of history, economics, politics, and culture that shape configurations of cultural difference, as well as their impact on people's lives, social realities, and coping mechanisms as they struggle to make meanings and exert some control over their lives. My research findings pointed to a poignant link between the cityscape, constructions of ethnic and cultural identity, and the diverse visions of modernity in Malaysia at both official and everyday levels of experience. Following from this, my research focused on two themes: the intensity of political, social and cultural divisions among various urban groups amidst rapid modernization, and the nationalist aspiration for modernity and international recognition; and the relationship between these divisions and the changing cityscape. Finally, I must reiterate that this book should only be read as one possible interpretation, for which I alone am ultimately responsible, of these events. My only hope is that by placing the Kampung Serani residents' views and experiences at the core of my analysis, this book can at least serve as a tribute to their fourteen-year long struggle.

CHAPTER OUTLINE

As stated earlier, the aim of this book is to explicate the fundamental forces behind the transformation of modern Malaysian society through an analysis of the Kampung Serani conflict. In order to accomplish this task, this book must identify the local relations of power and cultural struggle operating in the conflict, as well as locate these relations within the broader processes of modernity in Malaysia. With this in mind, I have organized my discussion in the following manner.

Chapter Two explores recent conceptualizations of modernity that have redrawn a center-periphery model so as to envision these relations as interconnected and dependent phenomena. This undermines a view of this relationship as hierarchical or unidirectional, making possible the conceptualization of the global and the local as simultaneous processes without privileging one over the other. I discuss recent studies of Southeast Asian modernities that have taken up this theoretical challenge to understand non-Western modernities in their own terms and with reference to their own priorities. Such studies reveal the interplay between specific historical and cultural contexts and the great range of modern forms and ideas thus generated, endowed with local, if contested, meanings. I propose an anthropological theoretical framework that combines both power and practice approaches to uncover how cultural difference is produced, transformed, and sustained within historical contexts and under the aegis of various agencies. I make two arguments. Firstly, I argue for the need to frame modernity through a critical discussion of the multiple, shifting, and contested cultural discourses over what is modern and the institutional and individual practices that produce them. Secondly, I argue that we recognize the centrality of internal, prior, or on-going social structural and cultural dynamics in mediating the production, conversion, and translation of modern ideas and forms in the experience of modernity.

Chapter Three extends discussions of Malaysian modernity to highlight the conceptual challenges raised by the issues of nation, ethnicity/culture, and class. I argue that there is a need to understand both the origin of the system of cultural signification of the nation, and the mediating institutions, types of agencies, and privileged sites in which cultural and ethnic forms are produced, appropriated, and contested. I argue that a combination of discourse and practice approaches can provide the greatest insights into what enables and inhibits the actions of social actors as well as the complexities of this social action and its effects on society. My arguments on the tensions surrounding nation, ethnicity/culture, class, and modernity in contemporary Malaysia are substantiated with reference to concrete examples of current transformations. I suggest that an important dimension of the experience of modernity in Malaysia is realized through transformations in the city/urban terrain. The wider scene of development and urban struggle suggests that the Kampung Serani conflict over urban growth is not an isolated incident but is, rather, representative of other cultural and spatial struggles that have emerged in response to Malaysian modernization.

Chapter Four contains the details of the Kampung Serani conflict as recounted by my primary informants and introduces the local players directly involved in the conflict, that is, the *kampung* residents, the Penang Eurasian Association, the landowner (the Roman Catholic Church), and the property development companies. This chapter identifies the configurations of culture and history that arose from the conflict and lays the foundation for my analysis of their intertwinement with national and global forces of economic, political, and cultural identity formation in contemporary Malaysia.

Chapter Five presents the ethnographic narratives of the *kampung* residents and explores their perceptions and responses to the conflict throughout the struggle. In particular, this chapter describes how the villagers reconstructed their personal, cultural, and historical relationship to the *kampung* in response to the changing circumstances of the conflict. In doing so, I hope to disclose important internal dynamics, long-standing personal meanings, and on-going power politics amongst the *kampung* residents that mediated their perceptions, experiences, and responses as they struggled to protect their families and communities from the upheavals of modern life and urban development.

Chapter Six illustrates the way in which leaders of the Penang Eurasian Association drew upon both a national debate on the status of the Portuguese Settlement in Melaka and regional claims regarding the contribution of local Eurasians to modern education in Malaysia to construct a rhetoric of a unique Portuguese-Eurasian identity. The Association used this discourse as political leverage to get their demands for a "heritage house" met and to dissipate opposition from the villagers. The chapter argues that this ability to manipulate broader ideas about Portuguese-Eurasian identity (made possible by the shifting meanings of Malayness in contemporary Malaysia) lent additional legitimacy to the Association's argument and to their claim to represent the Penang Eurasian community in Penang.

In Chapter Seven, I discuss the impact of cultural and spatial politics in Penang resulting from the national push for modernization on the position of the Church and the Penang Eurasian Association. Specifically, I argue that the Church's decision to redevelop Kampung Serani and the Penang Eurasian Association's urgent desire to own a "heritage house" to exhibit Eurasian cultural identity were directly related to increased pressure on land and the rise of identity politics in the Pulau Tikus area.

Chapter Eight considers the responses of the two property developers in the Kampung Serani conflict from the point of view of the exigencies of the property development sector. I argue that the fortunes of the property development industry, and the particular agenda of the companies involved, shaped the developers' responses, which in turn contributed to the outcome of the conflict.

Chapter Nine concludes with an evaluation of the empirical evidence presented in the book to argue that Malaysian modernity should not be understood merely in terms of the transformative power of capitalism nor as a top-down process of state domination. Rather, it should be understood as an everyday experience of tumultuous change that inevitably makes possible conscious agency and the formation of cultural identity. My analysis of the Kampung Serani conflict demonstrates the analytical significance of local power struggles when rethinking modernity. These local conflicts provide a context in which we can best observe the active processes of the conversion, negotiation, and translation of modern ideas and forms as ordinary people struggle against the external impositions and initiatives of the modern within the complex nexus of micro, national, and global forces of transformation.

CHAPTER TWO

SOUTHEAST ASIAN MODERNITY RECONSIDERED

What appears to characterize late twentieth century modernity—whether Southeast Asian or Western—is the concern with the issue of cultural identity and difference. This historical period marked by a world increasingly integrated into a global capitalist economy has not produced rationalistic, future-oriented advanced capitalistic societies as previously supposed.[1] Rather, the outcome has been the twin process of capitalist expansion and increasing global cultural replication on the one hand, and the rise of unique configurations of nationality, ethnicity, tradition, and cultural authenticity on the other. Scholars have been perplexed by the dualistic formulations of modernity, sometimes also presented as the simultaneity of the past and the present, or the co-existence of the West and the East, or the universal and the particular. This dualism of contemporary modernity has called into question any unproblematic divide between tradition and modernization, past and present, the West and the non-West, and fundamentally challenged a post-Enlightenment idea of historical progress as the unilinear unfolding of time and experience whereby the Western mode of time and being is the norm against which all other experiences are judged. The multiple cultural formulations of modernity in the contemporary world suggest that "modernity" as experienced in the West is no longer the natural and only destination for all other modernities.

In line with this development, historians are among those who have taken up the critique of the authority of Western history.[2] Correspondingly, there is a growing body of literature across various disciplines that attempts to theorize modernity from the margins of the West and outside the limits of the West. In part, this development has been spurred by poststructuralist and postmodernist critiques

---

[1] The classical conceptualization of modernity views modernization as an evolutionary progression towards rationalistic, future-oriented, advanced societies. For a discussion on the theme of modernity in the works of Marx, Weber, and Durkheim, see Charles Lemert, ed., *Social Theory: The Multicultural Classic Readings* (Boulder, CO: Westview Press, 1993), pp. 35-135; and Anthony Giddens, *The Consequences of Modernity* (Cambridge: Polity Press, 1990), pp. 1-16. See also David Frisby, *Fragments of Modernity: Theories of Modernity in the Work of Simmel, Kracauer, and Benjamin* (Cambridge: Polity Press, 1985) for views of other classical theorists. For a brief history on the origins and evolutionary use of the term modernity, see Philip Cook, *Back to the Future* (London: Unwin Hyman, 1990), pp. 2-35.

[2] See for example Hayden V. White, *MetaHistory: The Historical Imagination in Nineteenth-Century Europe* (Baltimore: Johns Hopkins University Press, 1973); Prasenjit Duara, *Rescuing History from the Nation: Questioning Narratives of Modern China* (Chicago: University of Chicago Press, 1995); and Harry Harutoonian, *History's Disquiet: Modernity, Cultural Practice and the Question of Everyday Life* (New York: Columbia University Press, 2000).

of monolithic theories and metanarratives of modernity. The poststructuralist concern to uncover the power/knowledge processes under which the world/culture presents itself as real has expanded into an active critique and deconstruction of the premises and knowledge claims of the West. Edward Said is arguably one of the most influential thinkers to emerge from this line of thought. Said's *Orientalism* framed world history in terms of geo-politics by arguing that the division between the East and the West, and the representations of each, were produced in the historical encounter of imperialism.[3] In turn, the postmodernist repudiation of metanarratives and revolution against meaning and representation have contributed to an increasing rejection of the assumed primacy of the category of the "West," its history and culture.[4]

While a deconstructive turn poses a danger in making all theories partial and local, some scholars have instead harnessed its liberating dimensions to rework theory from the margins rather than succumbing to a total dissolution of subject-positions and a paralysis of comparisons often associated with deconstructive approaches. The studies that I have in mind are those characterized by the need to scrutinize Western narratives of the modern, particularly in terms of their exclusionary and hierarchical discourses which obliterate complex genealogies of the modern within the West, and subordinate alternate narratives of the modern outside the West, into a linear narrative structured by the principle of human reason and capitalist rationality.[5] This does not mean however that the rethinking of modernity requires an abandonment of Western history and theory. Rather, the aim is to call into question existing conceptions of Western modernity to find a way to transcend the East-West or universal-particular binary in order to bring about a more meaningful understanding, comparison, and translation across different modernities.

Paul Gilroy's *Black Atlantic* is concerned precisely with a formulation of a theory of Euro-American modernity from the viewpoint of a marginalized people—the black diaspora—to unsettle the conception of Euro-American modernity along with its territorial and cultural assumptions.[6] In his historical study of migration and cultural expression within the African diaspora of nineteenth and early twentieth-century Europe and the Americas which was wrought by slavery and imperial conquest, Gilroy challenges the idea that modernity is solely the achievement of white Euro-American bourgeois society. Arguing that a genealogy of modernity must take into account slavery and colonialism, Gilroy suggests that blacks in the West are integral to the unfolding of modernity and, in fact, are the

---

[3] Edward Said, *Orientalism* (London: Penguin Books, 1991).

[4] For an elaborate discussion of the poststructuralist and postmodern critiques of the primacy of Western history and culture, see Robert Young, *White Mythologies: Writing History and the West* (London and New York: Routledge, 1990), pp. 11, 19-20.

[5] Anthony Giddens is one of the theorists of modernity who conceptualizes modernity as a "Western" project and views capitalist modernity as a Western phenomenon before its expansion beyond the boundaries of the West. See Giddens, *Consequences of Modernity*, pp. 174-175. An analysis and critique of the Western experience of modernity is found in Marshall Berman, *All that is Solid Melts into Air: The Experience of Modernity* (New York: Verso, 1983). For a critique of Berman's analyses, see Perry Anderson, "Modernity and Revolution," *New Left Review* 144 (1984): 96-113.

[6] Paul Gilroy, *The Black Atlantic: Modernity and Double Consciousness* (Cambridge, MA: Harvard University Press, 1993).

archetypal bearers of modernity.[7] Gilroy's study illuminates how modernity is inevitably a transcultural, international, diasporic, and hybrid formation that arose in part from the interstitial position of blacks as a people lodged between the local, the national, and the global/universal.[8]

Other scholars have similarly questioned the assumption of a homogenous West. Joel Kahn, for instance, points out that Western modernism has been "multicultural" from its inception. He shows how an expressivist discourse on cultural difference and alterity emerged in the form of a general critique of techno-rationalist, bureaucratic, and evolutionary modernism during the nineteenth century in Europe.[9] Ann Stoler has also contributed to this debate by showing that modern forms and practices did not necessarily originate within the boundaries of the West.[10] In her work on colonial practices in the Dutch East Indies, Stoler shows how the emergence of a bourgeois identity in the Netherlands was the result of racial practices of Dutch colonialists endeavoring to distinguish themselves from the mixed-blood population and the "poor whites" in the colonies. In relocating the emergence of modern forms of identity in the colonies instead of Europe, Stoler's work demonstrates the importance of the colonial project in constituting the modern experience. Several other scholars such as Paul Rabinow, Anthony King, Timothy Mitchell, and Gwendolyn Wright have also shown how techniques, practices, and institutions of urban planning and architecture associated with the West were first developed or experimented with in the colonies.[11]

Indeed, social scientists and historians have, for a long time, sought to grapple with the origins of modern consciousness and its exclusive association with the West. A case in point is Donald Lach's *Asia in the Making of Europe* which appeared in 1965.[12] In this four-volume book, Lach demonstrates that non-European/Asian elements have a place in the making of artistic and intellectual ideas in Europe. The book paints a complex story of the making of Europe by detailing how Renaissance ideas in the West were not wholly constituted from within the spatial and cultural realms of the West, but were instead informed by ideas and knowledge gathered from the Western encounter with Asian civilizations. The idea that modern consciousness did not originate in the West alone might also be inferred from Benedict Anderson's remarkable book, *Imagined Communities*, as several scholars have pointed out.[13] In this book, Anderson suggests that the first truly modern nationalism developed in the various creole-led independence movements throughout the Americas in the latter half of the

---

[7] Gilroy, *Black Atlantic*, p. 221.

[8] Ibid., p. 127.

[9] Joel S. Kahn, *Culture, Multiculture, Postculture* (London, Thousand Oaks, and New Delhi: Sage Publications, 1995), pp. 10-15.

[10] Ann Stoler, *Race and the Education of Desire: Foucault's History of Sexuality and the Colonial Order of Things* (Durham: Duke University Press, 1992).

[11] Paul Rabinow, *French Modern: Norms and Forms of the Social Environment* (Cambridge, MA: MIT Press, 1989); Anthony King, *Global Cities: Post-Imperialism and the Internationalisation of London* (London and New York: Routledge, 1990); Timothy Mitchell, *Colonising Egypt* (Cambridge: Cambridge University Press, 1988); and Gwendolyn Wright, *The Politics of Design in French Colonial Urbanism* (Chicago: University of Chicago Press, 1991).

[12] Donald F. Lach, *Asia in the Making of Europe* (Chicago: University of Chicago Press, 1965).

[13] See Neil Lazarus, *Nationalism and Cultural Practice in the Postcolonial World* (Cambridge: Cambridge University Press, 1999), p. 129.

eighteenth and the first half of the nineteenth centuries rather than in Europe.[14] For Anderson, while the nationalisms of Western Europe may have, in some instances, prefigured the development of nationalisms in the new world, their allegiances were to the *ancien regime*. It was in the Americas that a populist version of imagined communities of nation-states, common citizenship, and popular sovereignty emerged, later developed in Western Europe, and then spread to Eastern Europe and elsewhere in the world. More recently, Perry Anderson makes a somewhat similar argument in his critique of postmodernism by suggesting that the idea of modernism and postmodernism were first conceptualized in the distant world of Latin America and not in Europe as would be expected.[15] According to Perry Anderson, "modernismo" was a term coined in 1890 by a Nicaraguan poet in proclaiming Latin American writers' cultural independence from Spanish literature.[16] What is more, he argues that the idea of postmodernism appeared in the interstitial world of Latin America around the 1930s, before its appearance in England or America.[17]

If the origins of the modern can no longer be associated solely with the West, then it might no longer be meaningful to speak of modernity in terms of the language of original and copy or first and late-comer. Neither would it make sense to take the Western narrative of modernity as the normative standard against which to understand all other non-Western modernities, although their histories may be intertwined. Critics argue that a privileging of the Western narrative of modernity would render the efforts of non-Western people—along with their notion of autonomy—and their new categories and meanings of the modern as insignificant—or worse, as simply derivative. Instead, such meanings should force a rethinking of the conceptions and categories of "modernity" itself. Recent attempts at developing theories of modernity relevant to non-Western cases insist that a recognition of the non-West as a producer of knowledge and theory must take the multiple histories and cultures at work in the world as parallel to existing "theories" rather than as mere responses to universal forms.[18] They have suggested

---

[14] Benedict Anderson, *Imagined Communities: Reflections on the Origin and Spread of Nationalism*, revised edition (New York: Verso, 1991), pp. 47-65.

[15] Perry Anderson, *The Origins of Postmodernity* (London and New York: Verso, 1998).

[16] Ibid., p. 3.

[17] Ibid., pp. 1-6.

[18] Some scholars, particularly those who draw on insights from "postcolonial criticism"—a genre of writing that examines the exclusionary and ambivalent practices of colonialism—have refused to conceptualize modernity predicated on Western-derived concepts or priorities. Instead, they have worked towards recovering peripheral or subaltern histories and experiences of the modern. By focusing on local conditions and agency, yet fully cognizant of the larger global forces at work, these scholars argue that modernity can only be understood through a re-conceptualization that takes into consideration multiple social agents in complex interactions which integrate the center and the periphery. Some examples of this kind of intellectual pursuit can be found in the works of Gyan Prakash, "Writing Post-Orientalist Histories of the Third World: Indian Historiography is Good to Think," in *Colonialism and Culture*, ed. Nicholas B. Dirks (Ann Arbor: University of Michigan Press, 1992), pp. 66-104; Naoki Sakai, *Translation and Subjectivity: On 'Japan' and Cultural Nationalism* (Minneapolis: University of Minnesota Press, 1997); Dipesh Chakrabarty, "Postcoloniality and the Artifice of History: Who Speaks for 'Indian' Pasts?," in *A Subaltern Studies Reader, 1986-1995*, ed. Ranajit Guha (Minneapolis: University of Minnesota Press, 1997), pp. 263-294; Fernando Coronil, *The Magical State: Nature, Money, and Modernity in Venezuela* (Chicago: University of Chicago Press, 1997); Lila Abu-Lughod, ed., *Remaking Women: Feminism and Modernity in the*

that tropes such as "translation, hybridization, and even dislocation" might be more useful for comprehending non-Western modernity than the existing notions of "imitation, assimilation (forced or attempted), or rejection."[19] In keeping with such orientations, scholars have endeavored to approach the making of modernity in non-Western societies in their own terms and priorities in order to highlight the immense differences in the way in which narratives of the modern can take form in different cultural and historical contexts. This is not to say that these studies ignore the global flows of capital, goods, people, and culture that are associated with modernity. Rather, they have gained a new understanding towards the relations between centers and peripheries that underwrite modernity—that is, the currents that determine modernity do not flow only in one direction. The divergent manifestations of modernity that emerged in different parts of the world are seen as interconnected and dependent phenomena. The global and the local are seen as simultaneous processes without privileging one over the other. Thus, what's local and specific is also global and comparative.[20]

Here, particularly, the Southeast Asian quest for modernity—characterized by the greater role of the state in disciplining capital as it adopts rules of technical rationality from the West while recovering "traditional" elements of culture—provides grounds for a theorization of non-Western modernity from local perspectives. Recent studies have largely explored Southeast Asian modernity against the backdrop of nation-state formation, anti-colonial/imperial nationalism, and globalization. In line with larger theoretical developments, these scholars have called for a need to eschew a Western- and capitalism-centered view of modernity to focus on the specific economic, cultural, and national interests within which these societies make their own modernities after their own priorities. Increasing attention is placed on local histories, cultures, and structures, and their relations with national and global forces to understand the different unfolding of the nation, rationality, and capitalism in ways that may embrace, reproduce, translate, as well as transform Western forms. To make my point, I will briefly discuss three debates that emerged from these new approaches to understand the cultural transformations of Southeast Asian modernity.

First, in seeking to explain Southeast Asian modernity, some studies assert that a conception of modernity in terms of the workings of capitalism and the spread of Western forms and ideas cannot fully bring out what it means to be modern for Southeast Asians. These studies recognize capitalism as a powerful force of change responsible for aligning Southeast Asian modernity with Western forms of the modern, but insist that the social relations underlying capital are always cultural. The works of Adrian Vickers and Michel Picard on Balinese modernity are

---

Middle East (Princeton: Princeton University Press, 1998); Henrietta L. Moore, ed., *The Future of Anthropological Knowledge* (London and New York: Routledge, 1996); Aihwa Ong, "Anthropology, China and Modernities: The Geopolitics of Cultural Knowledge," in *The Future of Anthropological Knowledge*, pp. 60-92; and Marilyn Ivy, *Discourses of the Vanishing: Modernity, Phantasm, Japan* (Chicago: University of Chicago Press, 1995).

[19] Abu-Lughod, *Remaking Women*, p. 18.

[20] For an argument on the theoretical contribution of local knowledge in critique of the pervading universalism in Western social sciences that exclude or obliterate forms of rationality and modes of experience outside the time-space of the West, see Henrietta L. Moore, "The Changing Nature of Anthropological Knowledge: An Introduction," in *The Future of Anthropological Knowledge*, pp. 1-15.

specifically concerned with recuperating the cultural agency and history of the Balinese people to show how local agents translate and find similarities with universal ideas of the "modern" rather than act as "passive recipients of Western initiatives."[21] However, they are careful to show that emergent modern forms are not to be understood in terms of the survival of cultural forms and practices relevant to former times. Rather, their studies highlight the fundamental issues of power and cultural production operating under modern conditions within Balinese society. They show that there is no one single form of the modern for the Balinese, but that discourses of the modern are part of a set of power relations in which some are more authorized to act than others. Vickers contends that Balinese cultures, like other Southeast Asian cultures, have a long history of translating and making outside forms new and local. He suggests that the universal ideas of the "modern" only came to be accepted and translated in Balinese society precisely because there were local precedents and experiences of the Balinese version of the *"moderen."*[22] Picard's study demonstrates that the Balinese notion of being modern involves a sense of holding on to tradition in which the category of religion/*agama* or the sacred is integral, as the Balinese people endeavor to gain control of their lives amidst the rapid forces of tourism and change.[23] Recent volumes that attempt to develop a theory of the rise of the new middle class in modern Southeast Asia have also endeavored to understand this class through historical and cultural perspectives on class and power rather than via a narrow political-economic reading of the phenomenon.[24] If ordinary people struggle to establish control over the intrusion of global forces on their lives, so do the nation-states of Southeast Asia. A volume on *Asian Forms of the Nation* examines how the development of nations in the region was shaped by their individual pre-national histories.[25] The argument here again is not to recuperate cultural essentialism or primordialism, but rather to assert the historical experiences and cultural priorities of societies that invariably influence the contemporary forms and narratives of the nation and their contestations.

This in turn connects with a second type of study that seeks to denaturalize and historicize the nationalist formulations of the modern by showing how they are created from a complex intersection between colonial ideas and knowledges and their postcolonial effects. These studies are influenced by postcolonial theoretical

---

[21] Adrian Vickers, ed., *Being Modern in Bali: Image and Change*, Yale University Southeast Asian Studies Monograph 43 (New Haven, CT: Yale University Southeast Asian Studies, 1996), p. 6.

[22] Ibid. (emphasis in original).

[23] Michel Picard, *Bali: Cultural Tourism and Touristic Culture* (Singapore: Archipelago Press, 1996); and Michel Picard, "Cultural Tourism, Nation-Building, and Regional Culture: The Making of a Balinese Identity," in *Tourism, Ethnicity, and the State in Asian and Pacific Societies*, ed. Michel Picard and Robert E. Wood (Honolulu: University of Hawaii Press, 1997), pp. 181-214.

[24] See Michael Pinches, ed., *Culture and Privilege in Capitalist Asia* (London and New York: Routledge, 1999); Richard Robison and David Goodman, eds., *The New Rich in Asia: Mobile Phones, McDonalds and Middle-Class Revolution* (London and New York: Routledge, 1996); and Richard Tanter and Kenneth Young, eds., *The Politics of Middle Class Indonesia*, Monash Papers on Southeast Asia No. 19 (Clayton, Victoria, Australia: Centre of Southeast Asian Studies, Monash University, 1990).

[25] Stein Tonneson and Hans Atlov, eds., *Asian Forms of the Nation* (Richmond, VA: Curzon Press, 1996).

approaches that explore how colonial categories of race and culture return, in renewed forms, in the postcolonial era.[26] Abidin Kusno's recent study that seeks to foreground an active relationship between post-Independence architecture and colonial and postcolonial social effects in Indonesia is an example of this line of enquiry.[27] Focusing on the particular histories and cultures of Indonesia, Kusno shows how the discourses of colonial architecture and urban planning continue to influence the politics of time and space in postcolonial Indonesia. In addressing the interconnections between past and present, Kusno demonstrates how the production of architecture and space is constituted by the cultural politics among various groups of individuals and political and social reformers when ignoring or representing the empire. In contrast to postcolonial theorists who presume that colonialism displaced indigenous cultures, Kusno's work demonstrates how colonial cultural frameworks become the productive ground for the reworking and reproduction of new ideas of the modern in the postcolonial era. In addition, he observes that modern architectural discourses in Indonesia are not necessarily constructed vis-à-vis the West alone, but are also produced in relation to other regional forces from the neighboring countries of Southeast Asia. A volume edited by Aihwa Ong and Michael Peletz that explores the reworking of gender in Southeast Asian modernity has equally endorsed the need to uncover the webs of knowledge, power processes, and cultural politics created from the intersection between the ideologies of globalization, postcoloniality, and nationalism.[28]

Third, there is a group of studies that explore the workings of state hegemony and power in the making of new subjects in the Southeast Asian pursuit of modernity. It has been noted that the projects of modernity in Southeast Asia involve not only state attempts to transform the economy but also to construct new identities for their citizenry.[29] Some studies have pointed to the contested nature of these national projects of modernity. While recognizing the power of various Southeast Asian nation-states in shaping, representing, and enforcing their economic and cultural formulations of modernity, these studies also seek to emphasize the historical complexity of social formations in these societies to show that state hegemony is always more fragile than it appears, as there are always aspects of people's lives and practices that are never wholly subject to any regimes of control. Two volumes—*Modernity and Identity: Asian Illustrations* and *Southeast Asian Identities: Culture and the Politics of Representation in Indonesia, Malaysia, Singapore, and Thailand*—demonstrate just how state-sponsored programs of modernity in Southeast Asia often involve the political and cultural domination of some groups over others within complex intersections of national and

---

[26] For an example, see Phyllis G. L. Chew and Anneliese Kramer-Dahl, eds., *Reading Culture: Textual Practices in Singapore* (Singapore: Times Academic Press, 1999).

[27] Abidin Kusno, *Behind the Postcolonial: Architecture, Urban Space and Political Cultures in Indonesia* (London and New York: Routledge, 2000).

[28] Aihwa Ong and Michael G. Peletz, eds., *Bewitching Women, Pious Men: Gender and Body Politics in Southeast Asia* (Berkeley: University of California Press, 1995).

[29] See Maila Stivens and Krishna Sen, eds., *Gender and Power in Affluent Asia* (London: Routledge, 1998); Alberto Gomes, ed., *Modernity and Identity: Asian Illustrations* (Bundoora, Victoria: La Trobe University Press, 1994); Joel S. Kahn and Loh Kok Wah, eds., *Fragmented Vision: Culture and Politics in Contemporary Malaysia* (Sydney: Allen & Unwin, 1992); and Joel S. Kahn, ed., *Southeast Asian Identities: Culture and the Politics of Representation in Indonesia, Malaysia, Singapore and Thailand* (Singapore: Institute of Southeast Asian Studies, 1998).

global forces of economic modernization. This has resulted in the resurgence and revivalism of ethnic identities in the region as marginalized groups and classes construct different identities in order to create a constituency to further their own interests in their struggles against economic, political, and cultural domination.[30] Southeast Asian modernity, as the contributors to the volumes show, is strongly characterized by national integrationist policies, but the drive to uniformity based on a dominant ethnic culture has resulted in disunity and a new resuscitation of traditional forms and the revivalism of ethnic identities within a nexus of local, national, and global tensions.

From the above discussion we can see how recent studies, seeking to give agency to local agents by uncovering their specific cultural contexts and priorities, try to better understand the ways in which modern forms and ideas are produced, imbued with local meanings, and contested in modern Southeast Asia. The issue that preoccupies these inquiries is that of nation-state formation, and in particular the processes of economic and cultural modernization that attempt to construct new subjects and subjectivities. Against this backdrop, pressing questions emerge centered on the need to denaturalize and historicize the ways in which ideas and forms of the modern come about and are made meaningful and authoritative, as well as resisted, within the complex nexus of the local-national-global. These interrogations, as we know, are primarily motivated by the aim to effect a theoretical disengagement from Western narratives of the modern.

The study of Southeast Asian modernity as a historically and culturally specific problem, therefore, appears to me as a cultural anthropologist to be directly related to the concerns of anthropology. If culture is a site of difference under modern conditions, then there is an urgency for us to understand how differences are produced, transformed, and sustained within concrete cultural and historical contexts and under the aegis of various types of agency. Using ethnographic and macro investigations, this book makes two specific interventions in debates on Southeast Asian modernity. The first concerns insights into the actual circumstances and detailed histories of individuals and their shifting relationships with state and historical practices in order to understand how people perceive, construct, cope with, and are affected by contemporary changes around them. The second relates to the centrality of internal social-structural and cultural dynamics in mediating the production, conversion, and translation of modern ideas and forms in the experience of modernity. An anthropological approach foregrounds context-sensitive narratives, thereby making possible a more historically grounded and culturally centered appreciation of the modern condition. Here recent developments in cultural anthropology—associated with more contemporary understandings of human agency and social transformation in contemporary social theory—provide a framework for an investigation into the Malaysian experience of modernity.

---

[30] For accounts of how gender and class have become important sites for the reworking of the modern in the Southeast Asian context, see Stivens and Sen, eds., *Gender and Power in Affluent Asia*; Aihwa Ong, "State versus Islam: Malay Families, Women's Bodies and the Body Politic in Malaysia," *American Ethnologist* 17,2 (1990): 258-276; Laurie J. Sears, ed., *Fantasizing the Feminine in Indonesia* (Durham: Duke University Press, 1996); and Saskia E. Wieringa, "Sexual Metaphors in the Change from Sukarno's Old Order to Suharto's New Order in Indonesia," Working Paper Series No. 23 (The Hague: Institute of Social Studies, 1996).

ANTHROPOLOGICAL CLAIMS AND THEIR POSSIBILITIES FOR THE STUDY OF SOUTHEAST ASIAN CULTURES

In a review of anthropological studies of Southeast Asia, John Bowen suggests that the "ubiquity of publicly displayed cultural forms" in the region poses a distinctive attraction for anthropologists working in the interpretive tradition.[31] The interpretive perspective, which draws largely on the ideas of Boas and Weber, is characterized by the analysis of culture through publicly accessible forms and the meanings inscribed in them by various social actors. The figure most associated with the interpretive tradition is Clifford Geertz whose fieldwork encounters in Indonesia are legendary.[32] Geertz provided several significant contributions to the interpretive study of culture. Geertz was largely concerned with the efficacy or autonomy of culture. His contribution lies in his definition of culture as a set of publicly accessible forms which freed it from earlier assumptions of culture as sets of values "locked inside people's heads."[33] To Geertz, public forms are the sources of knowledge for members of a society and can be interpreted and read by outsiders such as the anthropologist.[34] This, in effect, turns all forms of social action and material culture into possible objects of study since they are now the very character of culture rather than expressions of it.[35]

While Geertz's work has provided much impetus to the development of the interpretive tradition in the anthropology of Southeast Asia, at least three aspects of his work have come under increasing criticism in light of newer theoretical developments both within and outside anthropology over the years. First, Geertz's framework has been criticized for its narrow focus on the internal logic of symbols and meanings which offers no explanation of the connections between culture and action: the processes that mediate the way people think, experience, and act upon their world.[36] Second, the Parsonian influence in the Geertzian framework which leads to viewing culture as an internally coherent cultural system structured by a single ethos and worldview has come under attack for ignoring power dimensions and other forms of differences within societies.

---

[31] John Bowen, "The Forms Culture Takes: A State-Of-The-Field Essay on the Anthropology of Southeast Asia," *Journal of Asian Studies* 54,4 (1995): 1048. Recent scholarship has increasingly questioned the study of Southeast Asia as a cultural area in light of increasing globalization and transnational practices that unsettle clear divisions between the local, the national, and the global, as well as challenge notions of the ubiquitous power of Southeast Asian states. For a review of these works, see Mary Margaret Steedly, "The State of Culture Theory in the Anthropology of Southeast Asia," *Annual Review of Anthropology* 28 (1999), pp. 431-454.

[32] For example, see Clifford Geertz, *The Religion of Java* (Chicago: University of Chicago Press, 1960); Clifford Geertz, *Agricultural Involution* (Berkeley and Los Angeles: University of California Press, 1963); Clifford Geertz, *Negara* (Cambridge: Cambridge University Press, 1980); and Clifford Geertz, *Local Knowledge: Further Essays in Interpretive Anthropology* (New York: Basic Books, 1983).

[33] Sherry B. Ortner, "Theory in Anthropology since the Sixties," in *Culture/Power/History: A Reader in Contemporary Social Theory*, ed. Nicholas B. Dirks, Geoff Eley, and Sherry B. Ortner (Princeton, NJ: Princeton University Press, 1994), p. 374. See also Bowen, "The Forms Culture Takes," p. 1049.

[34] Ortner, "Theory in Anthropology since the Sixties," p. 374.

[35] Ibid.

[36] Ibid., pp. 375-377.

Lastly, Geertz has been criticized for his unreflexive stance in promoting a form of authentic culturalism that claims objective knowledge about other cultures.

Consequently, the interpretive approach to the study of Southeast Asian cultures has undergone significant changes since the dominance of Geertz's approach. The treatment of culture as public forms, the emphasis that social actors impute meanings to objects, and the insistence that meanings can be read by outsiders continue to inform numerous contemporary anthropological studies of Southeast Asia. There is, however, a new emphasis on power and reflexive considerations. Bowen has noted the increasing tendency among anthropological studies of the region to treat cultural forms as giving rise to the creation of multiple and conflicting meanings by differently situated actors, irreducible to any internally coherent wholes. This development is part of a more critical anthropology that has emerged following postcolonial and postmodern critiques of dominant conceptions of culture. In the following discussion I want to draw out the theoretical possibilities of a more critical anthropology that have emerged from this development. In particular, I want to draw on recent debates about power and agency to develop a framework through which to analyze the processes involved in translating and transforming cultural meanings.

The critique of anthropology's links to the foundationalism of Western knowledge claims has raised unresolved questions concerning anthropology's authority in the production of knowledge. Ethnography—anthropology's methodology of producing knowledge—has come under severe attacks in recent years.[37] The traditional anthropological goal of achieving an understanding of other non-Western cultures as coherent, meaningful, discrete, and integral systems has been criticized for reifying and orientalizing other cultures and as implicated in the constitution and maintenance of anthropology's authority.[38] This development has led to a self-critique among anthropologists that has largely centered on the issue of ethnographic writing in knowledge production. This debate over reflexivity has created much controversy within anthropology and has raised a multitude of questions about ethnographic practice that anthropologists are tackling in various ways today.[39] For its part, the attention to

---

[37] For early thoughts in the debates over the crisis of representation in anthropology, see James Clifford and George E. Marcus, eds., *Writing Culture: The Poetics and Politics of Ethnography* (Berkeley: University of California Press, 1986); George E. Marcus and Michael M. J. Fischer, *Anthropology as Cultural Critique: An Experimental Moment in the Human Sciences* (Chicago: University of Chicago Press, 1986); Richard G. Fox, ed., *Recapturing Anthropology: Working in the Present* (Santa Fe, New Mexico: School of American Research Press, 1991); John and Jean Comaroff, *Ethnography and the Historical Imagination* (Boulder, CO: Westview Press, 1992); and Moore, ed., *The Future of Anthropological Knowledge*.

[38] James Clifford, *The Predicament of Culture: Twentieth-Century Ethnography, Literature, and Arts* (Cambridge, MA: Harvard University Press, 1988), pp. 92-114.

[39] These debates are concerned with the reflexive manner by which anthropologists construct cultures. Among other things, this has led to experimentation with various modes of interpreting culture. For example, see Kevin Dwyer, *Moroccan Dialogues* (Baltimore: Johns Hopkins University Press, 1982); Jean-Paul Dumont, *The Headman and I* (Austin, Texas: University of Texas Press, 1978); Paul Rabinow, *Reflections on Fieldwork in Morocco* (Berkeley and Los Angeles: University of California Press, 1977); and Marcus and Fischer, *Anthropology as Cultural Critique*. For critical appraisals of the reflexive trend, see Joel S. Kahn, "Towards a History of the Critique of Economism: The Nineteenth-Century German Origins of the Ethnographer's Dilemma," *Man* 25,3 (1990): 108-128; Joel S. Kahn, *Constituting the Minangkabau: Peasants, Culture and Modernity in Colonial Indonesia* (Providence, RI: Berg

textual/representational practices in this reflexive turn has led to a more complex understanding of the processes of objectification and the construction of otherness in anthropological writings. It has forced anthropologists to face squarely the politics and ethics of their representations. Importantly, there is now a recognition of partiality and positionality in the anthropologist's construction, interpretation, and representation of cultures.

However, as some scholars have rightly pointed out, the politics of otherness is not reducible to the politics of representation alone.[40] The issue of power does not enter the anthropological project only at the moment of representation but exists in a variety of ways across anthropological research.[41] A narrow preoccupation with only textual representation bypasses some of the more important epistemological issues of fieldwork and ways of explaining why people come to see and constitute themselves as culturally different.[42] Accordingly, many scholars have worked towards acknowledging this problem. Creative experimentation with methodological strategies has changed conventional methods of ethnography, bringing about new critical approaches in cultural analysis. What appears to characterize the present theoretical moment is an eclectic mix of theoretical approaches. In recent years ethnographers have increasingly borrowed ideas from outside the discipline (as others have similarly appropriated ideas from anthropology) in an increasing rapprochement between the humanities and the social sciences.[43] Among other things, this development has brought to the fore critical reflections on the issues of power, resistance, and social action in analyses of the cultural. I locate the project of this book within two sets of interrelated debates that have emerged from this development.

First, I refer to the debates that have highlighted the interrelations between culture, power, and resistance. After almost two decades of critique, there is now a clear shift away from an essentialist view of culture as a unitary entity of shared meanings to a view of "[c]ulture as emergent from relations of power and domination, culture as a form of power and domination, [and] culture as a medium in

---

Publishers, 1993), pp. 6-20; Lila Abu-Lughod, "Writing Against Culture," in *Recapturing Anthropology*, pp. 137-162; Steven P. Sangren, "Rhetoric and the Authority of Ethnography: 'Postmodernism' and the Social Reproduction of Texts," *Current Anthropology* 29,3 (1988): 405-435; and Ong, "Anthropology, China and Modernities," pp. 61-62.

[40] See for example, Akhil Gupta and James Ferguson, eds., *Culture, Power, Place: Explorations in Critical Anthropology* (Durham: Duke University Press, 1997); Abu-Lughod, "Writing Against Culture"; and Moore, "The Changing Nature of Anthropological Knowledge: An Introduction," pp. 1-15.

[41] Gupta and Ferguson, *Culture, Power, Place*, p. 46.

[42] In a growing frustration with the narrow preoccupation with textualist strategies in the bid to overcome the problem of domination in anthropological knowledge production, some scholars have turned to a search for new ethnographic epistemologies. For example, see Abu-Lughod's call for an "ethnography of the particular" to bring closer the language of everyday life and the language of ethnographic texts in "Writing Against Culture," pp. 149-157; Aihwa Ong's call for a "contrapuntal anthropology" that deploys a political de-centering away from viewing the world from a Western vantage point to include perspectives from the non-West in "Anthropology, China and Modernities," pp. 84-86; and Joel S. Kahn's demands for the insertion of concrete socio-historic conditions in anthropological analyses in *Constituting the Minangkabau*, pp. 12-21.

[43] See Terence J. McDonald, ed., *The Historic Turn in the Human Sciences* (Ann Arbor: University of Michigan Press, 1996).

which power is both constituted and resisted."[44] This contemporary orientation recognizes that culture is more fragmented than unitary and that the production and reproduction of culture is always embedded in multiple and unequal interactions of power, domination, and resistance within a given society. It comes about as a result of a new understanding that power pervades all levels of society and exists in relation to resistance. This understanding of power is largely attributed to the influence of Foucault's theory of "discourse."[45]

The Foucauldian notion of "discourse" is primarily concerned with the operations of power in "institutional discourses and disciplinary practices" where "technologies" derived from knowledge (particularly scientific knowledge) become new modes of subjugation by defining people as the objects of knowledge. This is based on Foucault's arguments on the emergence of a technology of disciplinary power derived from knowledge for the modern governance of society in Europe between the sixteenth and eighteenth centuries. This technology of power was decentralized from the state into a system of micro-powers that implicated institutional practices of disciplining and normalizing social norms at the everyday level.[46] Foucault argues that knowledge generates power by constituting people as subjects and then governing these subjects through this knowledge. This argument also highlights that power exists as a relation in the sense that "[w]here there is power, there is resistance."[47] Foucault's hermeneutics reveal the ways in which social and cultural transformations become constituted in their present form, as forces that make individuals subjects of certain cultural categories and images. Importantly, Foucault's theory emphasizes that the forces of control and dependence of knowledge exist externally as well as internally within individuals, binding them to their own identity by a kind of self-knowledge that they believe to be true about themselves.[48] Consequently, anthropologists have borrowed the notion of discourse from Foucault to focus on the complex, shifting, and contested meanings over time and at particular social locations that constitute culture and its particular effects on people's lives, social realities, and identities.[49] Anthropological studies of postcoloniality in particular have drawn on the Foucauldian notion of discourse to analyze culture as a colonial object and mode of knowledge and its political and historical consequences on postcolonial societies.[50]

While Foucault's theory of discourse provides for the ubiquity of complex relations of power, culture, and resistance in society, there is however little room in it for the conscious, expressive, or political efforts of the social actor. Culture is

---

[44] Dirks et al., eds., *Culture/Power/History*, p. 6.

[45] Ibid., p. 7.

[46] Michel Foucault, *Discipline and Punish: The Birth of the Prison*, trans. Alan Sheridan (London: Allen Lane, 1977).

[47] Michel Foucault, *History of Sexuality*, vol. 1, trans. Robert Hurley (New York: Pantheon, 1978), p. 95.

[48] See Catherine A. Lutz and Lila Abu-Lughod, eds., *Language and the Politics of Emotion* (Cambridge: Cambridge University Press, 1990), p. 6; Gupta and Ferguson, *Culture, Power, Place*, p. 18.

[49] See Lutz and Abu-Lughod, eds., *Language and the Politics of Emotion*; Dirks et al., eds., *Culture/Power/History*, pp. 4, 7-8.

[50] For example, see Nicholas B. Dirks, ed., *Colonialism and Culture* (Ann Arbor: University of Michigan Press, 1992) and Stoler, *Race and the Education of Desire*.

still seen as an expression of a systemic force rather than the individual or actor. This, in part, has been attributed to the particular strand of French post-structuralism practiced by Foucault. In the French poststructuralist thinking, the subject is decentered and thought to have "no internal coherence" nor "autonomous existence" to enable the act of recovering self-knowledge.[51] In view of this shortcoming, for my purposes here I turn to another set of debates that endeavor to create a theoretical space for the "intentional" actor.

The second cluster of debates concerns a body of diverse studies that endeavor to show how conscious practices of social actors are constrained as well as empowered by cultural dynamics. These debates offer more sophisticated analyses of how social actors create culture, are constrained by it, yet have the capacity to change and reinterpret culture in their own meaningful terms.[52] These eclectic approaches are loosely grouped under an idiom known as "practice."[53] The development of the practice framework is associated with four major works. These are: Pierre Bourdieu's *Outline of a Theory of Practice*, Anthony Gidden's *Central Problems in Social Theory*, Michel de Certeau's *The Practice of Everyday Life*, and Marshall Sahlins's *Islands of History*.[54] Informed by a range of theoretical traditions that span from classic Weberian perspectives, structuralism, phenomenology, critical theory to hermeneutics, practice scholars have endeavored to find an explanation for the structures of domination within a society that can simultaneously integrate both the structural/material and the cultural/ideal dimensions. Practice theorists are primarily concerned with the ways in which the forces of social transformation are internally mediated, not only by social structural orders, but also by cultural patterns. The practice approach accords central place to the actors' intentions and their everyday practices to reveal that social change arises from mundane practices or when traditional strategies fail, and not necessarily from any tumultuous revolution. It emphasizes that social action is most deeply constrained by the highly patterned and routinized behavior central to the systemic production of everyday life, and yet recognizes the instances of purposeful acts where actors change the meaning of existing relationships. At the heart of this argument is its radical insistence on three integrated arguments: "that society is a system, that the system is powerfully constraining, and yet the system can be made and unmade through human action and interaction."[55]

The practice perspective offers a more sophisticated explanation of the production of meaning in social action than is provided by an interpretive perspective. An interpretive approach, which is equally concerned with making sense of the symbols and meanings invested and interpreted by social actors, tends

---

[51] Dirks et al., eds., *Culture/Power/History*, p. 13.

[52] See Ortner, "Theory in Anthropology since the Sixties," pp. 388-401; and Sherry B. Ortner, *High Religion: A Cultural and Political History of Sherpa Buddhism* (Delhi: Motilal Banarsidass Publishers, 1992), p. 11.

[53] Marcus and Fischer, *Anthropology as Cultural Critique*, p. 85.

[54] Pierre Bourdieu, *Outline of a Theory of Practice*, trans. Richard Nice (Cambridge: Cambridge University Press, 1978); Anthony Giddens, *Central Problems in Social Theory: Action, Structure and Contradiction in Social Analysis* (Cambridge: Cambridge University Press, 1979); Michel de Certeau, *The Practice of Everyday Life*, trans. Steven Rendall (Berkeley: University of California Press, 1984); and Marshall Sahlins, *Islands of History* (Chicago: University of Chicago Press, 1985).

[55] Ortner, "Theory in Anthropology since the Sixties," p. 403.

to be overly preoccupied with the internal logics of systems of symbols and meaning, and thus neglects social action.[56] Besides, interpretive approaches—particularly those associated with Clifford Geertz—are problematic in that they tend to subscribe to an essentialist and bounded conceptualization of culture as coherent, authentic, and integrated.[57] Practice theorists have avoided these pitfalls with a more politically informed methodology. The practice approach has also made an important departure from a transactionalist or instrumentalist perspective that assumes that social action is solely motivated by rational and pragmatic considerations.[58] Overall, the practice approach offers a more complex understanding of social action by revealing that social action is most deeply constrained by highly patterned daily behavior without losing sight of the purposeful instances of practice. The essence of the practice approach can be examined via a discussion of Bourdieu's concepts of the *habitus* and Raymond Williams's concept of hegemony.[59]

In Bourdieu's theory, the *habitus* refers to cognitive structures through which people deal with the social world.[60] The social world also has its own structures and the theory of *habitus* seeks to describe a dialectical relationship between the two worlds that is mediated by social practice.[61] According to Bourdieu, people are invested with a series of internalized schemes or "embodied structures" through which they perceive, evaluate, and act in the social world.[62] These internalized structures reflect objective class divisions in the social world.[63] Acquired through the long-term occupation of a position in the world, *habitus* is a form of "embodied history" that has been internalized as "second nature" such that it becomes experienced as natural.[64] The *habitus* enables and limits the actors at the same time. It instills a "practical sense" in which the actor takes on or embodies the

---

[56] Ibid., p. 374.

[57] For a critique of Geertz, see ibid., pp. 375-379; Kahn, *Constituting the Minangkabau*, pp. 21-30.

[58] Transactionalism in anthropology assumes rationality on the part of social actors and analyses social action in terms of individual choice and decision making. For examples of transactionalism in anthropology, see Bruce Kapferer, ed., *Transaction and Meaning: Directions in the Anthropology of Exchange and Symbolic Behavior* (Philadelphia: Institute for the Study of Human Issues, 1976); Fredrik Barth, "On the Study of Social Change," *American Anthropologist* 69,6 (1966): 661-669; and F. G. Bailey, *Strategems and Spoils* (New York: Schocken, 1969).

[59] Pierre Bourdieu, *Distinction: A Social Critique of the Judgement of Taste*, trans. Richard Nice (Cambridge: Cambridge University Press, 1984); Raymond Williams, *The Long Revolution* (Harmondsworth: Penguin, 1965).

[60] A concept related to Bourdieu's theory of *habitus* is the "field." Fields are products of strategies of differentiation and modes of domination within the history of a given society. For instance, an action is never intrinsically economic but comes about from "a field of struggles" that establishes a shared belief that economic exchanges have their own autonomous purposes. In order to analyze the field, the analyst must trace the power relationships and the objective structure of relations as well as the nature of the *habitus* of the actors who occupy the various positions within the field. See Derek Robbins, *The Work of Pierre Bourdieu: Recognizing Society* (Buckingham: Open University Press & Milton Keynes, 1991), pp. 115-176.

[61] Bourdieu, *Distinction*, p. 17.

[62] See Pierre Bourdieu, *The Logic of Practice*, trans. Richard Nice (Stanford: Stanford University Press, 1990), pp. 54, 56; and Bourdieu, *Distinction*, p. 468.

[63] Bourdieu, *Distinction*, p. 468.

[64] Bourdieu, *The Logic of Practice*, p. 56.

identities and social categories within which he/she grows up.[65] Therefore, the "intentional" actor in Bourdieu's theory is never fully strategizing but is profoundly and systematically patterned through habitual behaviors, judgement schemes, or a particular class ethos. In making this point, Bourdieu calls attention to the daily routines that people perform over and over again in their lives and in social interaction. These learned habits or deeply ingrained dispositions are based upon and embody the rules and principles that organize a system as a whole. It is on this basis that people are never totally free to act. Their hopes and desires are more or less in line with the limits of the objective possibilities associated with their worlds.[66]

However, the property of an enacting and acting *habitus* can also be empowering as it functions as a form of "accumulated capital" that gives the individual a sense of "relative autonomy" over external determinations.[67] The actor, Bourdieu insists, is always "a world within the world."[68] This is because the *habitus* is a constantly changing structure that is adapted by individuals who are constantly changing in the face of the contradictions in which they find themselves. *Habitus* can also be a collective phenomenon as people sharing similar positions in society tend to share a *habitus*. Precisely because of the varietes of *habitus* that exist in the social world, actors are never determined solely by the structures of the social world. Thus, while the *habitus* may constrain thought and choice, it does not determine action. People always deploy identities in contradictory ways because people's identities are the products of participation in contradictory situations rather than the result of any intrinsic nature.

This lack of determinism in Bourdieu's work sets his theory above both the reductionism of much mainstream structuralism and the unbounded possibilities of meaning construction posed by performative theorists.[69] The *habitus* is structured by the social world but is also able to structure the social world at the same time. As Bourdieu puts it, the *habitus* is "the system of structured, structuring dispositions, ... which is constituted in practice and is always oriented towards practical functions."[70] Bourdieu's elaboration of the *habitus* highlights the fact that people's responses and adaptations are never simply ad hoc nor solely motivated by interest or pragmatism. Instead, people's actions are governed by deeply ingrained and systemic patterns and value schemas that are embodied within particular social and symbolic forms that constitute a given system.[71]

---

[65] Ibid., p. 68.

[66] Bourdieu uses the term "doxa" to explain this instillation of a sense of limit on one's desires. See Dirks, et al., eds. *Culture/Power/History*, p. 13; Bourdieu, *The Logic of Practice*, p. 68.

[67] Bourdieu, *The Logic of Practice*, p. 56.

[68] Ibid., p. 56.

[69] The postmodernist turn has led some theorists to see identity in "performative" terms, that is, subjectivity is made and remade within its patterns and articulations where the sense of self is always slipping away, fragile, and ever fragmenting. For an example of this approach, see Judith Butler, *Gender Trouble: Feminism and the Subversion of Identity* (New York and London: Routledge, 1990) where she extends the limits of subjectivity to argue that a "gendered self" does not exist at all; that self is a series of performances.

[70] Bourdieu, *The Logic of Practice*, p. 52.

[71] Ortner, "Theory in Anthropology since the Sixties," p. 392.

Bourdieu, however, gives little attention to history.[72] His theory tends to treat action in terms of relatively short-term moves and decision making and does not look into how meanings change over time at particular social locations and at particular historical moments. However, the turn to history in both the human and social sciences has meant that recent anthropological works using practice theory are addressing the issue of the historicity of cultural meanings in their investigations.

In a rather similar vein to Bourdieu's arguments, but paying more attention to acts of resistance and social transformation, Raymond Williams has also made a significant contribution to the understanding of social action or practice.[73] Williams, a leading figure in the British cultural studies movement based at Birmingham University, evokes Gramsci's concept of "hegemony" to define culture as a site of struggle between the forces of resistance of subordinate groups and the forces of incorporation of dominant groups in a given society. Williams's approach is motivated by an effort to go beyond Marxist notions of an economic base determining a superstructure of culture and politics. Williams argues that the base/superstructure dichotomy gives the impression that culture is a set of symbols, when it is more properly understood as a set of practices. He insists that both base and superstructure coexist within the world of culture itself. Williams uses the Gramscian understanding of hegemony to refer to a condition in which a dominant class does not merely rule but leads a society by winning the consent of subordinate groups through a process of moral and intellectual leadership.[74] Hegemony is never total but always multiple, contradictory, and contested. Williams argues that people are never wholly subject to the forces of power and influence because they always construct their own sense of position and experience in society. Meaning structures are formed and negotiated by competing groups within society. Williams uses the terminology "structure of feeling" to refer to the articulations between experiences of daily life and larger systems and the insidious expressions of ideology. Williams's conception of hegemony frees culture and society from being understood as merely fixed forms or states. Rather, the experiential, personal, and sentimental dimensions of all of life's domains, while structured, are also inherently social and political.

In Williams's theory of hegemony, imposed cultural forms must always be reworked, altered, and transformed in this process. Culture as a form of social practice must always be understood in terms of its relationship to domination and subordination. For Williams, culture is not simply imposed by the elite nor does it spontaneously emerge from below. Rather, culture is the site of perpetual negotiation, of mixed- and counter-intentions, both from "above" and from "below." Subsequently, borrowing from Williams and the British cultural studies movement, anthropologists have appropriated the idea of the shifting and incomplete nature of hegemony, with its implication of culture as contested, contingent, and a terrain marked by resistance and incorporation, into their ethnographic analyses.

The themes explored in these debates about discourse and social practice often complement and overlap each other. Each approach endeavors to understand the

---

[72] Ibid., p. 396.

[73] Williams, *The Long Revolution*, p. 64.

[74] See Antonio Gramsci, *Selections from Prison Notebooks*, ed. and trans. Quintin Hoare and Geoffrey Nowell-Smith (London: Lawrence and Wishart, 1971).

ubiquity of the operations of power in society and their effects on social action. The Foucauldian notion of power operates in institutional discourse and disciplinary practices. Among the practice theorists, however, power is inscribed in the "logic of practice" in everyday life.[75] The politically informed dispositions in these two approaches mean that culture is no longer accorded the degree of coherence associated with the classical conception of culture.[76] Both approaches are characterized by the refusal to make distinctions between ideas and practice, text and the world, culture and structure, or the material and the ideal. Both debates recognize the play of multiple, shifting, and competing ideas in society and are concerned with their practical effects. In addition, the practice approach offers an actor-centered and systemic focus that links the consciousness of social actors with political and economic transformations. It throws new light on the internal processes of cultural mediation, reinterpretation, and transformation by showing that social action is political, deeply rooted in everyday practices, and culturally patterned, but can also potently alter cultural meanings and impact on society and history. A recuperation of the "purposeful" actor is possible due to the recognition that the system has very powerful and determining effects on people, yet there are always emergent and residual possibilities located in people's experiences, passions, and aspirations to effect changes in society.

The significance here is that "discourse" and "practice" approaches to social action and social transformation have the potential to bridge the gap between culturalist and materialist or political economic analyses of society. Their emphasis on the integration of structure and culture renders the construction of culture and political economy as mutually constitutive processes; the material and the cultural are two sides of the same coin, so to speak, that must be understood in relation to each other and never separately. Together, these approaches form a framework that integrates the issues of power, culture, and structural forces in explaining social action. Even more crucial, it allows a theoretical space for the "purposeful" actor to recognize the disparate knowledge, experiences, and passion in people that, partially, empower them to construct, transform, and resist the world around them in accordance with their own priorities and perspectives. Such a framework takes seriously a social actor's intentions and interpretations of various experiences, symbols, and categories, and treats them as mutually constitutive of the social structures and social practices that reproduce, as well as transform, society.

FRAMING MALAYSIAN MODERNITY THROUGH CULTURAL DISCOURSE AND SOCIAL PRACTICE

In light of the above discussions, the challenge of this book is to conceptualize the interactions between the larger political, economic, and socio-spatial forces in contemporary Malaysia as well as the subjective agency of the actors in the Kampung Serani conflict without reverting to arguments of essentialist or instrumentalist cultural practices. I am concerned with how the actions, visions, and constructed identities of the Portuguese-Eurasian actors in the Kampung Serani conflict were inseparable from the conditions under which the broader discourses of

---

[75] Dirks et al., eds., *Culture/Power/History*, p. 17; and Bourdieu, *Distinction*, p. 180.

[76] See Abu-Lughod, "Writing Against Culture," p. 147.

nation, ethnicity, class, and progress were generated, regimented, and negotiated through institutional and everyday practices in contemporary Malaysian society. A practice framework provides a means to trace the interconnections between the actions, dreams, and identities of the actors in the Kampung Serani conflict and the specific structural and cultural arrangements operating at both the macro- and the micro-levels in the push to modernize Malaysia. In particular, the recognition of the "intentional actor" allows me to take into consideration the disparate knowledge and experiences of people that, in part, enable them to construct and make meaningful worlds out of the conditions in which they are embedded.

This book frames the experience of modernity in Malaysia through a critical discussion of the multiple, shifting, and contested cultural discourses over nation, ethnicity, and class in Malaysia and the institutional and individual practices that produced them. In this way, modernity becomes a problem of the social actor and society. My analysis of the diverging cultural constructions in the Kampung Serani conflict interrogates the discursive operations of power, structural, and cultural dynamics at the macro/national and the micro/conflict levels. At the broader level, I want to show how the discursive discourses of nation, ethnicity, and class embedded in the Malaysian aspiration for modernity create linkages with colonial categories as well as generate new forms of subjection and exclusionary practices. Here, I want to highlight how the new schemas of nation, ethnicity, and class in the Malaysian quest for modernity had differentiating impacts on particular groups and individuals depending on their class, ethnicity, geographic location, and so on. Some groups and individuals stood to gain official recognition while others lost out, some gained new opportunities while others were subject to new contradictions and obstacles. These larger national discourses and practices had subsequent impacts at the micro-levels of social action. As I argue, they had constitutive and material impacts on the socio-spatial realities, aspirations, and political identities of the actors in the Kampung Serani conflict because they posed particular sets of contradictions, problems, and opportunities to the actors involved, forcing them to respond and react to the changing circumstances. Here, my analyses have a twofold goal. On the one hand, I explore how the experiences, actions, and cultural arguments of the actors in the Kampung Serani conflict were differentiated and dependent on their class locations, their ethnic backgrounds, and their access to social, cultural, and political resources. On the other hand, I establish a distance between the actors' predisposed cultural configurations and their intentions by locating individual and collective experiences as part of larger social and cultural webs—the "multiple *habitus*" of Bourdieu or the "structure of feeling" of Williams, if you will—in which people's identities can never be totally predetermined as they always possess enough personal meanings, experiences, desires, and histories to reorganize, transform, or challenge the world around them.

On the basis of this analytical framework, the next six chapters examine the responses of the players in the Kampung Serani conflict in terms of how historical, material, and cultural forces operating at both the micro- and macro-and levels constrained as well as posed opportunities for them, and how their particular responses combined to shape the cultural politics and spatial outcomes of the conflict.

CHAPTER THREE

NATION, ETHNICITY, CLASS, AND THE CHANGING CITYSCAPE IN MODERN MALAYSIA

For many observers of Malaysian society, 1969 is a turning point in Malaysian social history. It marks the beginning of increasing state power in Malaysian social and cultural life that was necessitated by fluid social, political, and cultural conditions in the newly independent country. The turbulence began with the 1969 racial riots, revealing discontent among local ethnic groups, particularly the Malays, over the nation-building project.[1] The newly independent nation-state had inherited from British colonial rule a plural society, segregated along racial and occupational lines. Colonial rule and economics had left Malays concentrated in the traditional peasant economy, while Chinese and Indians were recruited to work in tin mines and rubber estates, respectively. A laissez faire development policy during the early Independence era only exacerbated the problem of Malay underdevelopment when compared to the Chinese and Indians, who became more integrated into the capitalist economy. The revelation of strong animosity between various ethnic groups in the 1969 riots brought to light the crisis of decolonization, nation-building, and development in the modern Malaysian nation-state. It was in response to this social discontent that a top-down project of reimagining the future of the nation-state was formulated, one which saw a greatly expanded and more interventionist role for the Malaysian state.

The New Economic Policy (NEP), a twenty-year-long affirmative action policy founded on a mixture of rationalist and ethnic arguments, proposed a reemphasis of the privileged position of the Malays as the solution to achieve national unity. Such a policy redistributed economic wealth, largely from the Chinese and to an extent from foreign investors, to the predominantly Malay *bumiputeras*. From the outset, its aim was to create a Malay business community. Its target was increasing the Malay share of corporate capital from 2.4 percent in 1970 to 30 percent in 1990.[2] The period after 1969 saw rapid modernization; the NEP provided the major impetus for growing state intervention and public sector expansion as the government embarked on an ambitious plan to accelerate economic growth via industrialization and urbanization in the name of Malay development. Central to

---

[1] The riots broke out in the streets of Kuala Lumpur following a highly charged federal election in which issues of language and education were fought along ethnic lines.

[2] The *bumiputera* proportion of share capital rose to 19.3 percent in 1990 versus that of the Chinese which grew from 27.2 percent in 1970 to 44.9 percent in 1990. See Edmund Terence Gomez and K. S. Jomo, *Malaysia's Political Economy: Politics, Patronage and Profits* (Cambridge: Cambridge University Press, 1997), p. 179.

this modernizing project was, of course, the goal of distributing economic wealth to the Malays, in particular to create a Malay business class, through a form of social control which differentiates the Malays (*bumiputeras*) from the non-Malays (non-*bumiputeras*). This political commitment to wealth redistribution along ethnic lines gave rise to ethnically based policies as well as ethnic tensions in the Malaysian experience of capitalist development. The political obligation to ensure a greater share of wealth ownership among the Malay community led to a variety of government interventions that established the web of interconnections between political and business actors which remains a strong feature of Malaysian economic activity. State intervention also created ethnic rivalry as Malay capitalists, backed by the state, emerged as strong challengers to Chinese capital during the 1980s.

This phase of modernization was accompanied by bids to forge a National Cultural Policy as well as to find alternative models of modernization from those of the West. State attempts to formulate a National Cultural Policy based on Malay culture were initiated in the early 1970s but met with strong opposition from non-Malay communities who sought equal representation in the policy. Continuous challenges from other ethnic groups made it impossible to reach a resolution over whose culture should be represented in the national culture, and the state began to withdraw from this endeavor by the mid-1980s in order to focus instead on a developmentalist rhetoric. Economic development and material growth became the new public policy emphasis as the government, then under the Mahathir administration, began an ambitious program of infrastructural and economic development under the aegis of "Looking East." The Look East policy, designed to emulate Japan's industrialization and work ethic, was implemented in 1981 when Dr. Mahathir Mohamed became the Prime Minister. As part of this policy, various schemes to promote a more direct relationship between Japan and Malaysia in terms of investment, education, training, and technological exchange were established. The introduction of the concept of "Malaysia Incorporated" in 1983 to promote cooperation between the government and the private sector in the service of the national interests was equally inspired by a similar concept of "Japan Incorporated." Incidentally, the Look East policy resulted in a spate of infrastructural growth that was largely dependent on Japanese technology. Not surprisingly, Malaysia emerged as the country with the largest orders for Japan's construction exports in 1982.[3]

Nevertheless, by the late 1980s, the NEP's ethnically determined political ideology came under critical pressure from a growing and increasingly diverse society. Government regulation had led to the development of patronage networks, which gave rise to what has come to be known as "money politics"—the close relationship between business and politics, especially in the channeling of state economic resources and protection to individuals, groups, and private companies, particularly those associated with the United Malays National Organization (UMNO), the dominant party representing Malay interests in the National Alliance.[4] In the context of growing political and business entwinement, the struggle for political and economic power eventually led to increasing divisiveness

---

[3] *The Japan Economic Review*, April 6, 1982, p. 14.

[4] See Edmund Terence Gomez, *Politics in Business: UMNO's Corporate Investments* (Kuala Lumpur: Forum, 1990).

within the Malay political leadership. This divisiveness was epitomized by the UMNO split in 1987. As the dominant party representing the Malays and the leading partner in the Barisan Nasional (National Alliance) government, the split in UMNO was thus symbolic of growing differences within the Malay community.[5] Some scholars view the political feud within UMNO as a struggle for political and economic power in the context of the increasing integration of politics and business.[6] Others, instead, trace the cause of this political discord to the contrasting cultural visions between different fractions within UMNO.[7] Under the Mahathir government, there has been a significant policy shift away from direct state sponsorship of Malay business interests, along with a government push to encourage Malay capitalists to be more independent from the state. This shift has created tensions and strains within the Malay polity, resulting in a constant oscillation between more liberal policies and more protectionist policies.[8] In addition, growing tension and disaffection within the Malay community over different views about democratic principles and government authoritarianism has been observed.[9]

The split in Malay leadership is not the only divisive factor amongst the Malays. The resurgence of Islam in the early 1980s has also fragmented the Malay community. In the 1970s, Islam was taken as a unifying, and to an extent a "primordial," essence of Malay identity. However, Islam became involved in a widespread global religious struggle in the 1980s that could no longer be contained within the framework of Malay nationalism. The Malaysian government and UMNO, the very powers supposed to safeguard Malay interests, were increasingly challenged by the Muslim community for not being Islamic enough. Islamic groups have challenged the Malaysian Constitution, the NEP philosophy that grants a privileged position to the Malays over Others, and even Malay culture (*adat*) as un-Islamic.[10] Consequently, while Islam acted as an integrative bastion of Malay

---

[5] The immediate cause of this split was the 1987 UMNO elections, in which a fraction (known as "Team B," led by Razaleigh, the former Finance Minister) opposing Mahathir's camp (Team A) contested the validity of the party elections in court. The court ruled UMNO was an illegal party because it had contravened sections of the relevant acts governing societies in Malaysia. The reaction of the Mahathir camp was to register a new UMNO.

[6] See Harold Crouch, "Authoritarianism, Money Politics and Modernity," in *Fragmented Vision: Culture and Politics in Contemporary Malaysia*, ed. Joel S. Kahn and Loh Kok Wah (Sydney: Allen & Unwin, 1992), pp. 32-33.

[7] Khoo Kay Jin, "The Grand Vision: Mahathir and Modernization," in *Fragmented Vision*, pp. 65-67.

[8] The Malaysian government's planned redistribution of economic wealth to the Malay—or more correctly, *bumiputera*—communities is well known. This aim was embodied in the NEP. Its goals were to a) make the ethnic distribution of the workforce in each sector similar to that of the population as a whole, and b) increase the *bumiputera* share of corporate sector ownership from 2.4 percent in 1970 to 30 percent in 1990. In July 1991, the NEP was replaced by the New Development Policy (NDP). Under the NDP the 30 percent corporate equity rule for *bumiputeras* has been relaxed.

[9] See Khoo Kay Jin, "The Grand Vision: Mahathir and Modernisation," pp. 44-76; and Johan Saravanamuttu, "The State, Authoritarianism and Industrialisation: Reflections on the Malaysian Case," *Kajian Malaysia* 2 (1987): 43-75.

[10] See Hussin Mutalib, *Islam and Ethnicity in Malay Politics* (Singapore and New York: Oxford University Press, 1990); K. S. Jomo and Ahmad Shabery Cheek, "Malaysia's Islamic Movements," in *Fragmented Vision*, pp. 79-106; and Chandra Muzaffar, *Islamic Resurgence in Malaysia* (Petaling Jaya: Fajar Bakti, 1987).

identity in the 1970s, the 1980s saw it creating divisions among the community itself.[11]

Along with these political and cultural changes within the Malay community, there have also been widespread political and cultural transformations among other communities in contemporary Malaysia. Malay fragmentation within the context of a growing economy and differentiated society by the late 1980s created a space for other ethnic groups to assert their specific interests and to challenge the government on grounds ranging from civil liberties to the NEP itself.[12] For instance, other ethnic groups, like the Kadazans in Sabah, as well as non-ethnically based groups, such as artists and feminists, have similarly asserted their specific interests and identities.[13]

Within this picture of deep political and cultural divisions amidst intense development, industrialization, and urbanization, the New Development Plan (1991-2000) and Wawasan 2020 (Vision 2020) were launched in 1991. The New Development Plan (NDP) is a medium-term policy in line with the Outline Perspective Plan 2 and the Sixth Malaysia Plan (1991-1995), while Vision 2020 provides long-term objectives. NDP places more emphasis on attacking hard-core poverty, gives more attention to the rapid development of a *bumiputera* and industrial community, stresses growth led by the private rather than the public sector to achieve restructuring, and focuses attention on human resource development to achieve the country's growth and distributional objectives. Formulated and implemented at the height of Malaysian economic confidence, Vision 2020 is ambitious in scope. It expects Malaysia to achieve the status of an "industrialized" country by 2020 by accelerating industrialization and modernization. Launched by Prime Minister Mahathir in a speech entitled "Malaysia: The Way Forward," Vision 2020 makes an explicit commitment to the forging of a "Malaysian Nation" (*Bangsa Malaysia*) transcending ethnic identities and loyalties, a strategy which greatly encouraged the non-Malays, who responded enthusiastically.

---

[11] Among the government's responses to the Islamic threat was its implementation of Islamization policies and efforts to win over some of its Islamic critics. One successful example of this absorption of critics is the former Deputy Prime Minister, Anwar Ibrahim—formerly a known government critic representing the Malaysian Islamic Youth Movement (ABIM)—who joined the Mahathir administration in 1982. See Crouch, "Authoritarianism, Money Politics and Modernity," p. 31, and Hussin Mutalib, *Islam and Ethnicity in Malay Politics*, pp. 134-139. Upon entering the Mahathir administration, Anwar swiftly rose to the position of Deputy Prime Minister until his downfall in 1998. In view of Anwar's background and influence in Islamic activism, some analysts believe that the charges of sodomy against him and his subsequent indictment, after he was deposed as Deputy Prime Minister, were particularly potent in discrediting his reputation among the Islamic community. See *Aliran Monthly* 18,8 (1998); 18,9 (1998); 20,1 (2000).

[12] See Lim Lin Lean and Chee Peng Lim, eds., *The Malaysian Economy at the Crossroads: Policy Adjustment or Structural Transformation* (Kuala Lumpur: Malaysian Economic Association and Organisational Resources, 1984).

[13] Kadazans are the largest indigenous group and the "definitive people" of the state of Sabah in East Malaysia. For details of counter-hegemonic movements in Malaysia, see Loh Kok Wah, "Modernisation, Cultural Revival and Counter-Hegemony: The Kadazans of Sabah in the 1980s," in *Fragmented Vision*, pp. 225-253; Maila K. Stivens, "Perspectives on Gender: Problems in Writing About Women in Malaysia," in *Fragmented Vision*, pp. 202-224; and Tan Sooi Beng, "Counterpoints in the Performing Arts of Malaysia," in *Fragmented Vision*, pp. 282-306.

The euphoria of rapid economic growth, modernization, and enthusiasm for the future came to a sudden halt at the end of 1997 with the economic crisis set off by the falling Malaysian Ringgit, under the domino effect of the sudden collapse of the Thai baht. The rapid decline of the Malaysian Ringgit saw the overturning of years of economic liberalization when Dr. Mahathir Mohamad announced the imposition of strict currency controls in Malaysia on September 1, 1998 in a bid to save the Malaysian economy from total collapse. The sacking of Anwar Ibrahim as the Deputy Prime Minister on charges of sodomy, treason, and sedition the very next day worsened the situation and set off unprecedented widespread civil unrest in Malaysian society. A Reformasi (Reformation) Movement, backed by Malaysians of all ethnic groups but with predominantly Malay support, emerged and called for social and political reforms in the country. This movement eventually led to the establishment of the Barisan Alternatif (Alternative Alliance), a coalition of opposition parties which contested the Barisan National (National Alliance) in the 1999 General Elections. While the National Alliance won 102 out of the 144 seats that they contested (twenty more seats than required to maintain a two-thirds majority), the results of the 1999 election revealed significant shifts in ethnic politics and voting practices. For the first time in the history of the country, political opposition shifted into the hands of the Malays, with the Parti Islam SeMalaysia (PAS) or the Pan-Malaysia Islamic Party leading the opposition front.[14] Malay support for UMNO eroded significantly as it only managed to win 48.6 percent of the vote in constituencies with more than two-thirds Malay voters, compared to 60.8 percent in the 1995 General Elections.[15] In addition, although the National Alliance won the majority of seats, they only managed to win 54 percent of the total votes, compared to the 65.2 percent obtained in the 1995 Parliamentary General Elections. These transformations suggest that Malaysian society is on a threshold of radical political and social change.

We can surmise from the above developments that Malaysian modernization is strongly associated with a particular nationalist ideology that lends legitimacy to the state to engage in a program of social and cultural regulation. As a result, the quest for modernization is centrally implicated in ethnic differentiation, creating a situation in which ethnic and class hierarchies in modern Malaysian society are the direct product of state regulative practices more than of capitalist progress. Entwined with the project of nation building, economic and social modernization only exacerbates and reconfigures ethnic and cultural identities in the Malaysian context. If the nation is the site for the production of cultural difference in modern Malaysia, then there is an imperative for us to understand many important questions: where does the system of cultural signification of the nation come from; how is it produced; how has it changed from the past; and what are its powerful consequences for society, economy, and politics? In addition, what are the mediating institutions, agencies, privileged sites, and cultural forms that shape and reshape the processes of national identification? It is to these questions that we will next turn.

---

[14] In the 1995 General Elections, PAS obtained 18 percent more of the popular votes in the seats it contested. See *Aliran* 19,10 (1999): 1-7.

[15] Ibid.

NATION, ETHNICITY/CULTURE, AND CLASS IN MALAYSIAN MODERNITY: CONCEPTUAL CHALLENGES

The foundation of the Malaysian nation-state rests on political claims to "Malayness." The newly independent Malaysia emerged in the name of the Malays who, for various historical and cultural reasons, were defined as indigenous people and accorded with special status in the transference of power from the British rulers.[16] Malay nationalist leaders who led the drive towards Malaysia's independence compromised their nationalism with an appeal to the immigrant peoples to make their homes in Malaysia. Under this cooperation, it was conceded that the Malaysian Constitution would recognize the sovereignty of the Malay Sultans and the special status of the Malays as indigenous people, while citizenship rights—either by birth or by fulfilling requirements of residence, language, and taking an oath of loyalty—were given to immigrant groups. Thus, independence saw the elevation of the Malays into a nation or *bangsa* (defined as race or nation) which formed the distinct cultural core of Malaysia. Other immigrant groups were accorded with a legalistic definition of citizenship or *warganegara*. A Malay is defined in Article 160 (2) of the Malaysian Constitution as "one who professes the religion of Islam, habitually speaks the Malay language, [and] conforms to Malay custom." In addition, Malay identity is also confirmed by the endowment of special *bumiputera* status and privileges. *Bumiputera* literally means "son of the soil" and Malays are the definitive *bumiputeras* of Malaysia, forming the largest of the three officially designated *bumiputera* groups.[17]

This legal and racialized definition of Malayness is nonetheless a colonial product that emerged in the late nineteenth century under the influence of a racial ideology of inherent biological and cultural differences.[18] Prior to this period, the term "Malay" had a more ambiguous usage. It referred to a range of objects, such as: an ethnic community, a cultural system, a society with a distinctive social history, as well as both royalty and their subjects in the Malay Peninsula, Sumatra, and the surrounding islands in the Malay archipelago.[19] The extension of the term Malay to the surrounding areas of Peninsula Malaysia indicates that the term carried with it both local and regional connotations. It was only around the 1900s that a territorially bound and racialized notion of the Malay race (or *bangsa*) emerged,

---

[16] The Federation of Malaya gained independence from Britain on August 31, 1957. On September 16, 1963 the Malaysian nation-state was proclaimed, with the alliance of the territories of Sabah, Sarawak, and Singapore. Subsequently, Singapore left the alliance in 1965, following opposition from the People's Action Party to the terms of the constitution.

[17] Other *bumiputera* groups are: the *orang asli* (referring to the small, scattered groups of aborigines found mainly in Peninsula Malaysia), and the Malay-related groups (referring to the ethnic groups found in the states of Sabah and Sarawak). See Malaysia, *Malaysia Year Book 1992-1993* (Kuala Lumpur: Berita Publishing Sdn. Bhd, 1992), p. 73. For a list of these groups, see Article 161A (7) of the Malaysian Constitution.

[18] Charles Hirschman, "The Making of Race in Colonial Malaya: Political Economy and Racial Ideology," *Sociological Forum* 1,2 (1986): 330-361.

[19] See Mohamed Aris Othman, *The Dynamic of Malay Identity*, Monograph No. 7 (Faculty of Social Science and Humanities, Universiti Kebangsaan Malaysia, 1983); Syed Husin Ali, *The Malays: Their Problems and Future* (Kuala Lumpur: Heinemann Educational Books [Asia] Ltd., 1981); and Sharon Siddique, "Some Aspects of Malay-Muslim Ethnicity in Peninsula Malaysia," *Journal of Contemporary Southeast Asia* 3,1 (1981): 76-87.

influenced by European ideas on the "natural" identification between "race," nation, and territory, as Malays struggled to define their world and identity in response to the European colonial presence and the increasing arrival of Chinese and Indian immigrants in Malaya.[20]

Indeed, the conceptions of Malay identity in postcolonial Malaysia continue to oscillate between fluid and rigid notions of Malayness. A number of studies have explored the shifting conceptions of Malayness within the context of Malay nationalism and its impact on ethnic and cultural configurations in modern Malaysian society. By and large, these studies have been influenced by Benedict Anderson's seminal work, *Imagined Communities*, which takes the nation as a discursive phenomenon represented as a unitary and transcendental domain rather than a natural linguistic, geographical or racial entity.[21] These studies have sought to denaturalize the concept of the Malaysian nation by pointing to the relations of power and domination that authorize some cultural representations, while impeding others, in the struggle for a unitary definition of the nation. A number of commentators on Malaysian society have taken up the challenge of understanding contemporary cultural configurations in terms of the politics of Malay nationalism in a rapidly modernizing and globalizing Malaysia.[22]

Tensions created by global Islamic forces on Malay nationalism and its impact on political and social development in Malaysia are themes taken up by Hussin Mutalib. He argues that the reassertion of an Islamic ethos since the 1970s in Malaysian society has created identity tensions within the Malay community as its members become more aware that they are both Malays and Muslims. He argues that the turn to a more pristine Islam, which rests on a more universalistic conception of Muslim brotherhood/sisterhood, or *ummah*, rather than on a particularistic identification of Malay communalism, has created new priorities for and perspectives on society and politics that have at certain times challenged the tenets of Malay nationalism. The tension between nationalism and religion led to increasing Islamization policies on the one hand, and growing challenges against the Malaysian Constitution, the supremacy of federal laws, the power of the

---

[20] Historians have noted the long history of trade and migration of people between the Malay archipelago and the Indian subcontinent, the Arab world, China, Japan, and Europe. See Anthony Reid, *Southeast Asia in the Age of Commerce, 1450-1680*, vol. II (New Haven and London: Yale University Press, 1993). Some historians have argued that proto-nationalist writings in Malaya were strongly shaped by British and European ideologies through both direct incorporation of these ideas from Western writings and indirect borrowing from the ideas of Egyptian reformers. See Anthony C. Milner, *The Invention of Politics in Colonial Malaya: Contesting Nationals and the Expansion of the Public Sphere* (Cambridge: Cambridge University Press, 1994), Chapter 9.

[21] According to Anderson, the logic and construction of the nation is imagined in view of the fact that members of the nation can never get to know most of their fellow members, yet they hold in their minds an image of communion or a shared past. Anderson argues that this imagination of the nation is enabled by the spread of print capitalism. See Benedict Anderson, *Imagined Communities: Reflections on the Origin and Spread of Nationalism*, revised edition (New York: Verso, 1991).

[22] An early work by William Roff shows how Malay nationalism during the pre-World War II era was divided into at least three main streams of thought which reflected the differing cultural and social orientations of Malay elite groups at that time. See William R. Roff, *The Origins of Malay Nationalism* (Kuala Lumpur and Singapore: University of Malaya Press, 1967).

Sultans, and even the philosophy of the New Economic Policy, on the other.[23] Hussin Mutalib rejects interpretations that accord Malays and their political parties a central role in shaping Malaysian political and social life. Instead, he asserts that it is the politics of Malay identity, wrought from an uneasy fusion between Islam and Malay ethnic sentiments, which fundamentally shapes Malaysian politics and society.

Clive Kessler problematizes the refashioning of Malay nationalist ideals as products of a disjunctive modernity in which Malay culture and "tradition" play a stabilizing role in an otherwise disruptive modernization.[24] Using Hobsbawm and Ranger's arguments concerning "invented tradition," Kessler argues that the recuperation of "tradition" in current Malaysian nationalism is not a survival of the past or an outcome of its continuing unfolding but is instead a construct—an artifice which is fashioned from customary or antique elements yet is essentially new, modern, and contemporary.[25] He also observes that the shifts in the Malay conception of Malayness are accompanied by current anomalies in the official definition of Malay identity. For example, he points out that there are now Muslim Malays, such as the Acehnese immigrants, who are not *bumiputeras* and that there are Malay *bumiputeras*, such as certain *orang asli* (aboriginal) groups, who are not Muslims.[26]

Furthering this argument, Joel Kahn treats cultural and spatial reconfigurations in recent Malaysian society as a specifically middle-class project that is bound up with Malay nationalism and global culture. Observing a trend in the reconstruction of Malay identity among the new middle classes as they seek to play down the role of Islam while emphasizing symbols of "traditional" Malay culture—such as aspects of Malay court, aristocratic, and *kampung* life—Kahn argues that these discourses are part and parcel of contemporary world culture despite their repudiation of global or Western political and cultural orders.[27] He argues that the disjunctive nature of cultural flows will continue to emerge as long as Malaysia attempts to challenge the imposition of global or Western forms.[28] These shifts in the imagery of Malayness are not necessarily mere ideal imaginings, but have concrete consequences, as they can also be inscribed onto urban space and built forms as various groups struggle for recognition in Malaysian society. Kahn shows how nostalgic discourses of Malay *kampung* culture or "tradition" are helping to create a neo-modern urban form typified by the reproduction of *kampung* architecture as various social actors appropriate these imaginings and inscribe them onto urban space. Muhammad Ikmal Said adds to the debate on the middle class's role by arguing that an increasingly similar lifestyle

---

[23] Hussin Mutalib, *Islam and Ethnicity in Malay Politics*, p. 165.

[24] Clive S. Kessler, "Archaism and Modernity: Contemporary Malay Political Culture," in *Fragmented Vision*, p. 135.

[25] Ibid., pp. 134, 140. See Eric Hobsbawm and Terence Ranger, eds., *The Invention of Tradition* (Cambridge: Cambridge University Press, 1983).

[26] Kessler, "Archaism and Modernity," p. 139.

[27] Joel S. Kahn, "Class, Ethnicity and Diversity: Some Remarks on Malay Culture in Malaysia," in *Fragmented Vision*, pp. 157-178.

[28] See also Joel S. Kahn, "Culturalizing Malaysia: Globalism, Tourism, Heritage, and the City in Georgetown," in *Tourism, Ethnicity, and the State in Asian and Pacific Societies*, ed. Michel Picard and Robert R. Wood (Honolulu: University of Hawaii Press, 1987), pp. 99-127.

and consumer culture among this group has produced changes in Malaysian ethnic nationalism. Taking the more favorable acceptance of the Chinese Lion Dance in contemporary Malaysian society as an example, he argues that the commercialization of ethnic cultural practices, particularly in the tourist industry, has led to a depoliticization of ethnic practices.[29]

Highlighting that, since its onset, Malay nationalism has never been homogenous at either the elite or the popular level, Shamsul instead points to the importance of subaltern resistance to hegemonic discourses about the nation in constituting modern social and cultural life in Malaysia.[30] Drawing on some of the controversies over the history of Malay nationalism,[31] Shamsul argues for the need—via the concept of "nations-of-intent"—to look at the production of ethnicity as a terrain of exchange between the socially powerful and the socially marginalized. Defining "nation-of-intent" as an idea of a nation that still needs to be constructed, he argues that Malaysia is characterized by a situation of "one-state, many nationalisms," thus his conception of "nations-of-intent."[32] He emphasizes the prevalence of competing nations-of-intent among both elites and the general populace. He cautions that the current dominant definition of *bumiputera* identity is but one among many nationalist identifications within the *bumiputera* community.[33] Thus, Shamsul sees the new concept of "Bangsa Malaysia" in Vision 2020 as yet another conscious effort to foster a new nationalist ideology in anticipation of Malaysia's fully industrialized status. Inevitably, this new imagining of the nation has become a contested site as both *bumiputera* and non-*bumiputera* groups struggle to find a middle ground between authoritative and popular conceptions of nationhood. In step with this argument, Timothy Harper points to a nationalism that is no longer dependent on a Malay cultural foundation but is instead based on new notions of common Malaysian citizenship.[34] Basing his arguments on the recently emergent concepts of the New Malay or *Melayu Baru*, the "New Malaysian" and so on under Vision 2020, Harper interprets these

---

[29] Muhammad Ikmal Said, "Malay Nationalism and National Identity," in *Malaysia Critical Perspectives: Essays in Honour of Syed Husin Asli*, ed. Muhd Ikmal Said and Zahid Emby (Kuala Lumpur: Persatuan Sains Sosial Malaysia, 1996), pp. 34-73.

[30] Shamsul A. B., "Nations-of-Intent in Malaysia," in *Asian Forms of the Nation*, ed. Stein Tonnesson and Hans Antlov (Richmond, VA: Curzon Press, 1996), pp. 323-347.

[31] Historians have long argued that, from its onset, Malay nationalism has never been homogenous. An early study by William Roff shows how Malay nationalist orientations prior to the Second World War were shaped by social and educational differences between three elite core groups. See William Roff, *The Origins of Malay Nationalism*. Ariffin Omar, however, argues that race and nationalism are two different forces in Malaysian history. He contends that an imagined Malay community never developed into an embracing nationalism that united the various Malay communities when the Malaysian nation-state was established. He argues that the Malays maintained separate state identities and lived under the various rules of Sultans of "*kerajaan*" (government), even with the establishment of newly independent Malaya in 1957 and the formation of Malaysia in 1963, following the incorporation of Singapore, Sabah, and Sarawak. See Ariffin Omar, *Bangsa Melayu: Malay Concepts of Democracy and Community, 1945-1950* (Kuala Lumpur: Oxford University Press, 1993).

[32] Shamsul A. B., "Nations-of-Intent in Malaysia," p. 328.

[33] Ibid., p. 354.

[34] See Timothy Norman Harper, *The End of Empire and the Making of Malaya* (New York: Cambridge University Press, 1998), pp. 371-378.

developments as evidence of the declining relevance of Malay cultural nationalism.

Adopting a postcolonial take on nationalism, C. W. Watson problematizes ethnic and cultural configurations in contemporary Malaysia by arguing for their inextricable involvement with Western regimes of knowledge and modes of cultural representation.[35] In an essay designed to explore the construction of the post-colonial subject in Malaysia, Watson argues that the constructions of race and ethnicity which accelerated after the mid-1970s were shaped by a "second wave of decolonization" involving Malay intellectuals who struggled against the aristocratic elite to represent the interests of the Malay peasantry and other marginal groups who were formerly under-represented in the conception of the nation.[36] He views the construction of the Malay subject during the 1970s as a contested site of post-colonial debate which oscillated between endorsing and refuting the idea of Malay identity created under colonialism. Highlighting UMNO's book, *Revolusi Mental*, and Dr. Mahathir's controversial book, *The Malay Dilemma*, Watson shows how the endeavor to free Malays from colonialist knowledge is fraught with difficulty because the very act of rejecting colonialist ideology demonstrates the internalization of these same beliefs. He argues that this type of decolonization politics was prevalent until at least the early 1980s, as attested by policies such as Look East, Malaysian Incorporated, Buy British Last, and the increasing turn to the Asian-values debate.[37] Watson argues that a rupture from the colonial past occurred in the 1990s when nationalist rhetoric took on a futuristic dimension. Epitomized by the launching of Vision 2020, which aspired to signal Malaysia's place in the world as a fully industrialized country, this global orientation resulted in an increasingly influential ethic of commercial values and practices with regards to ethnic and cultural conceptions.

Watson predicts that in the near future ethnic and cultural configurations in Malaysian society will most likely focus more on postmodernist consumers than postcolonial subjects.[38] This prediction is endorsed by Raymond Lee, a Malaysian sociologist, who similarly views a postmodern culture, shaped by the increasing commercial interests of transnational companies and Western consumer patterns, as a potential threat to ethnic nationalism and the project of modernization in Malaysia.[39] Nevertheless, these quick conclusions about a rupture with the colonial past in recent ethnic configurations might be premature. This is because colonial ideas about race and ethnicity remain the very foundational categories that serve the interests of nationalists and ordinary people, even though definitions of ethnicity have taken on some new dimensions. Obviously, Malaysians still move and work within these categories. Given this scenario, it is perhaps more pertinent to conclude that the emergence of "the middle class" as a new social category could potentially disrupt the colonial category of "race" or "ethnicity" in the future.

---

[35] C. W. Watson, "The Construction of the Post-Colonial Subject in Malaysia," in *Asian Forms of the Nation*, pp. 297-322.

[36] Ibid., p. 305.

[37] Ibid., p. 319.

[38] Ibid., pp. 319, 321.

[39] Raymond L. M. Lee, "Modernity, Anti-Modernity and Post-Modernity in Malaysia," *International Sociology* 7,2 (1992): 153-171.

Other scholars, such as Michael Peletz and David Banks, have endeavored to show just how the larger nationalist discourses about Malay identity are enforced, policed, negotiated, and/or contested in everyday life in Malaysian society. In his study of the Malay experience with the rationalization of identity and religious practices, Peletz shows how the Malaysian state, via local agents such as the police and religious leaders, has strengthened distinctions between ethnic boundaries by policing the expression of Islamic symbolism.[40] His study demonstrates the potency of everyday disciplinary practices via the control of religious expressions that serve to rationalize differences and boundaries between Malays and non-Malays in contemporary Malaysian society. Banks's work, in contrast, highlights the everyday negotiations about, and changing conceptions of, Malayness via a textualist approach.[41] He shows how Malay literature and various other Malay writings have been instrumental in changing popular conceptions of Malay identity. To take just one example, Banks highlights how the image of the Malay village, or *kampung*, has changed from a symbol of Malay backwardness to an idealized repository of pristine Malay culture and values. Other scholars such as Maila Stivens and Aihwa Ong have problematized gender as a site for the reworking of nationalist imaginings.[42] They argue that the symbols of nationalism are not gender-neutral. Rather, national imaginings are always implicitly or explicitly based on gendered notions. Thus, they argue that struggles over the meaning of modernity must be understood in terms of the contested interrelationship between changing notions of nation, ethnicity, and class.

To summarize, recent studies have highlighted that ethnic and cultural patterns in modern Malaysian society must be understood within the context of the interaction between the particularities of its history, the cultural politics of nationalism, and processes of economic modernization and globalization. They point to a series of conflicting cultural representations shaped by the tensions emerging from the interplay of Malay communalism, Islam, class differentiation, anti-colonial sentiments, gender, and global modernity. By posing these insights, these studies have opened up for investigation the relationship between human agency, history, and local, national, and global forces in shaping ethnic and cultural politics in contemporary Malaysia. They share a common concern to reconcile the relationship between dominant and subordinate cultural practices when examining the complex interaction between local, national, and global forces operating in contemporary Malaysian society. Nevertheless, these studies have yet to adequately address the relationship between the social actor and culture, nor have they fully examined the complexities of peoples' cultural responses to their changing social environment. Troubling questions over the conditions, processes, and motivations that enable social actors to remake cultural meanings, or to transcend and resist existing material and symbolic orders, remain unanswered. In addition,

---

[40] Michael G. Peletz, "Sacred Texts and Dangerous Words: The Politics of Law and Cultural Rationalization in Malaysia," *Comparative Studies in Society and History* 35,1 (1993): 66-109.

[41] David Banks, *From Class to Culture: Social Conscience in Malay Novels Since Independence*, Yale University Southeast Asian Studies, Monograph No. 29 (New Haven: Yale University Southeast Asian Studies, 1987).

[42] Maila Stivens, "Theorising Gender, Power and Modernity in Affluent Asia," in *Gender and Power in Affluent Asia*, ed. Maila Stivens and Krishna Sen (London: Routledge, 1998), pp. 1-34; Aihwa Ong, "State versus Islam: Malay Families, Women's Bodies and the Body Politic in Malaysia," *American Ethnologist* 17,2 (1990): 258-276.

these studies tend to assume that social action is predominantly shaped by the rational pursuit of material or symbolic power. Nevertheless, more often than not, people act only when compelled to because they find themselves in a bind or challenged by sudden opportunities. As such, in charting the relationship between culture and human action, it is imperative to not only understand how existing material and symbolic processes shape, dictate, or obstruct people's lives and perceptions, but also the possibilities that they pose. In addition, social action is also often more complex than is usually presented in these studies. Any individual's act of opposing or remaking cultural meanings is to an extent limited by the objective conditions of his or her socialization, as well as by on-going dynamics within groups. Thus, it is equally necessary for us to grasp the complex dimensions of social action in order to understand how people transform their identities as they struggle to protect or change their social and cultural worlds when faced with structural forces that impinge on their lives.

In light of the above discussions, the challenge in analyzing the Kampung Serani conflict is to trace how the interaction between the larger historical and material forces in contemporary Malaysia and the subjective agency of the involved parties molds the events and cultural dynamics of the Kampung Serani conflict. Here, an anthropological approach that combines "discourse" and "practice" approaches to social action is useful, because it provides more adequate insights into the relationship between the social actor and culture. Such a theoretical framework not only recognizes that systemic collective processes have a very powerful and determining effect on people, but also realizes that emergent and residual possibilities within people—in their experiences, passions, and dreams—also produce changes in society. Consequently, this framework enables us to chart how material and symbolic processes, operating within and without groups or individuals, shape and limit people's lives, perceptions, and actions. More specifically, my analysis will chart the interconnections between the production of a distinct Portuguese-Eurasian identity in the Kampung Serani conflict and wider constructions of a distinctive "indigenous" Portuguese-Eurasian identity, while also locating these interconnections within the context of a shifting cultural politics of Malay nationalism. Specifically, I will identify the various historical, material, and symbolic resources behind Portuguese-Eurasian identity and examine how these resources were appropriated, reworked, and contested by local groups in response to the events of the Kampung Serani conflict. In recuperating the agency of the social actors involved, attention will be paid to highlighting prior and contemporary material and symbolic dynamics within the groups involved to better understand their priorities, choices, and responses. My findings will emphasize how the new configurations of nation, ethnicity and class in Malaysian society must be understood in terms of how people purposefully and actively struggle within the context of deeply constrained and patterned behavior to reimagine public meanings. These cultural politics, I will demonstrate, have particular consequences for the nature of urban experience and can effectively transform the urban landscape.

Using my own research findings, I want to further explore the debates around the changing discourse of nation, ethnicity/culture, class, and modernity during the recent push to modernize the country in line with Vision 2020. I argue that an important dimension of the experience of Malaysian modernity is found in the city/urban terrain when these cultural discourses of modernity are appropriated by the state and various social actors and inscribed onto modern urban built forms as these actors pursue their own vision of a future Malaysia.

VISION 2020—GRAND NARRATIVE OF MODERNITY

To understand why Vision 2020 is so significant, we need to consider the circumstances under which it was formulated and implemented. Vision 2020 was launched in February 1991 during the heyday of Malaysia's economic confidence. It coincided with a period of intense development, industrialization, and urbanization beginning in the late 1980s. It is not surprising, therefore, that Vision 2020 is ambitious in scope, and expects Malaysia to achieve the status of an "industrialized" country by the year 2020 through a strategy of accelerating industrialization, growth, and modernization. Launched by Prime Minister Mahathir in a speech entitled "Malaysia: The Way Forward," Vision 2020 sets twin goals for a future Malaysia. First, it calls for the development of a more competitive, and scientifically and technologically proficient, economy with strong industrial links. Second, it envisions the forging of a culturally and morally excellent Malaysia.[43] This modernist vision prescribes the following:

Malaysia should not be developed only in the economic sense. It must be a nation that is fully developed along all the dimensions: economically, politically, socially, spiritually, psychologically and culturally. We must be fully developed in terms of national unity and social cohesion, in terms of social justice, political stability, system of government, quality of life, social and spiritual values, national pride and confidence.[44]

Mahathir's sense of nationalism, his ideas about national development, and his adroitness in mobilizing Malay nationalist sentiments have been well documented.[45] According to Mahathir, progress for the Malays will come via

---

[43] Vision 2020's main objectives are to establish: a united, peaceful, integrated, and harmonious nation; a secure, confident, respected, and robust society committed to excellence; a mature, consensual, and exemplary democracy; a "fully moral" society with citizens strongly imbued with spiritual values and the highest ethical standards; a culturally, ethnically, and religiously diverse, liberal, tolerant, and unified society; a caring society with a family-based welfare system; an economically "just" society with inter-ethnic economic parity; and a "fully competitive," dynamic, robust, resilient, and prosperous economy. The policy also envisages more competitive, market-disciplined, outward-looking, dynamic, self-reliant, diversified, adaptive, technologically proficient, and knowledgeable human resources, as well as low inflation, an exemplary work ethic, and a strong emphasis on quality and excellence.

[44] Mahathir Mohamed, "Malaysia: The Way Forward." Speech delivered at the Inaugural Meeting of the Malaysian Business Council, Kuala Lumpur, February 28, 1991 (Kuala Lumpur: Malaysian Business Council, 1991).

[45] Mahathir's political career began with his infamous and controversial idea that it is essential to change Malay/*bumiputera* values and behavior for Malaysia to develop. These assumptions were still present in the 1980s when he formulated the Look East Policy during the early years of his leadership, a policy emphasizing that the Malays should copy Japanese work ethics and attitudes. For details, see Khoo Boo Teik, *Paradoxes of Mahathirism: An Intellectual Biography of Mahathir Mohamed* (Kuala Lumpur: Oxford University Press, 1995); Hussin Mutalib, *Islam and Ethnicity in Malay Politics*; Shaharuddin Maaruf, *Malay Ideas on Development: From Feudal Lord to Capitalist* (Singapore: Times Books International, 1988); and Mahathir Mohamed, *The Malay Dilemma* (Singapore: Asia Pacific Press, 1970).

industrialization and urbanization.[46] In fact, Malaysia has experienced tremendous growth in both these sectors for the past decade or so. There is no doubt that urbanization and industrialization will remain vital areas of growth under Malaysia's current modernization projects. There are, however, three significant new directions in Vision 2020. Firstly, Vision 2020 is intended to provide for an all-encompassing view of modernization. Its vision is not confined to the economic sector but extended to cover political, cultural, and spiritual dimensions. Secondly, its objective is to push Malaysia into the ranks of the newly industrialized countries by the end of the century. This latter objective is clearly an attempt to improve Malaysia's position in the world. It can thus be interpreted as a mobilization of nationalist pride vis-à-vis the world. In line with these objectives, the Malaysian government implemented several grand modernization plans, such as the National Information Technology Agenda (NITA), which focuses on the vital role of science and technology in shaping Malaysia's future as a global information society with a fully industrialized status.[47] Thirdly, Vision 2020 marks a shift from the New Economic Policy by making growth, modernization, and industrialization national priorities, while giving less emphasis to ethnic redistribution goals. Importantly, Vision 2020's explicit commitment to the forging of a "Malaysian Nation" (Bangsa Malaysia), transcending ethnic identities and loyalties, greatly encouraged the non-Malay community in Malaysia, who responded enthusiastically to the re-imagining of the nation. The commitment to a "Malaysian Nation" is a sign of liberalization, an opening up of the nation to other ethnic groups apart from the Malays. Inevitably, this step implies a concomitant relaxation of the definition of Malay identity, since the nation and Malayness are interrelated categories.

Despite these new departures, Vision 2020 has not abandoned the commitment to wealth redistribution along ethnic lines. This was reflected in a recent controversy over a press statement by a Chinese businessman who, in his capacity as the deputy chairman of the National Economic Consultative Council (NECC), spoke about proposals on lowering the Malay quota in certain industries.[48] His remarks sparked adverse reactions among the Malay political and business community, leading to the public reassertion by the Prime Minister, Dr. Mahathir, that the Malaysian government "will not back down, not even by one step, in defending the Malays. . ."[49]

As in the past, Vision 2020 is still strongly aligned with state-implemented policies and reforms that reflect the government's own vision of the future. The

---

[46] Kit G. Machado, "Japanese Transnational Corporations in Malaysia's State Sponsored Heavy Industrialization Drive: The HICOM Automobile and Steel Projects," *Pacific Affairs* 62,4 (1989-1990): 508.

[47] Under the NITA, information communication technology is recognized as the engine of growth within all sectors of the Malaysian economy. For studies on information technology in Malaysia, see Wendy Mee, "Envisaging a Malaysian Information Society: A Nationalist Utopia?," (PhD Dissertation, LaTrobe University, 1999).

[48] This controversy arose when, during an interview granted to the *Far Eastern Economic Review*, Mr. David Chua, the deputy secretary-general of the Associated Chinese Chamber of Commerce and Industry Malaysia, suggested that the NECC wanted to see increased liberalization and competition in Malaysian society based on merit. The NECC was established in 1999 and charged with formulating the country's economic policy for the Eight Malaysia Plan. The NECC panel comprises representatives from the government, private sector, political parties, and social organizations.

[49] *The Straits Times*, August 18, 2000, p. 41.

government's vision, however, does not go unchallenged, and the implementation of these dominant views often sets off debates and disputes as these ideas are appropriated, reworked, or challenged by different groups. One arena of ideological contestation occurs around the debates over new sources of collective identification for the new Malaysia.

DIVERGENT CULTURAL IDENTITIES

Since the launch of Vision 2020, a series of propaganda exercises disseminated by the local media and government campaigns have attempted to convince Malaysians that Malaysia's rapid economic growth and dramatic urban transformation signal the dawn of a new and vibrant era. Perhaps the most notable of these endeavors was when, for the first time in the country's history, Malaysians heard the national anthem—the *Negaraku*—played to a faster tempo during the National Day Parade in 1993. The decision to speed up the tempo of the national anthem was issued by the Parliamentary Secretary in the Prime Minister's Department who specifically sought to explain the decision in terms of keeping up with the nation's changing aspirations.[50]

An active identification and inculcation of appropriate cultural values for Malaysians on the part of the government also characterizes this period. By the mid-1990s, the country was engulfed by a new slogan, "Malaysia Boleh" or "Malaysia Can," aimed at instilling self-confidence and grandiose dreams into Malaysians. Under this slogan, a series of highly publicized feats by ordinary Malaysians unfolded: the conquest of Mount Everest, a successful solo sailing quest around the world, as well as a number of individual and collective Guinness World Record stunts. This "can-do" frenzy was also accompanied by a nationwide rhetoric urging citizens to fight a number of newly identified social problems seen to be part of "yellow culture" from the West. These are the social problems of *lepak*, or loafing, among school children, and *bohsia* or *bohgian*, the problem of underage sex among girls or boys, respectively. Politicians, military officers, and Islamic and community leaders were among those who initiated a nationwide effort in the 1990s to eradicate these social ills.[51]

Inevitably, this period saw an escalated rhetoric against the West and Western values. The "Othering" of the West is not new in Malaysian society. A main proponent of the anti-West rhetoric is none other than the Prime Minister, Dr. Mahathir Mohamed. His controversial book, *The Malay Dilemma*, published in 1970, represents an early critique of the West. In this book, Mahathir advocates the overcoming of Malay backwardness via the overturning of the British colonial mentality, policy, and economy.[52] Likewise, *The Challenge*, a collection of essays

---

[50] See *The Star*, May 4, 1993, p. 1. This move was followed by the Chief Minister of Penang State announcing a similar plan to change the beat of the Penang State Anthem so as to reflect the people's enthusiasm and dynamism in bringing the state to a higher level of progress.

[51] Efforts to eradicate loafing activities include the following: a suggestion by the Malaysian Defense Ministry to hold discipline-oriented camps for loafers, and a joint effort among the northern states in Peninsula Malaysia, that included village heads, voluntary agencies, and resident associations, to hold psychological warfare programs for youths to fight against the loafing problem. See *New Straits Times*, January 10, 1994, p. 1.

[52] Ironically, through his intention to overcome Malay backwardness by calling for the politics of intervention in order to create a Malay capitalist class, Mahathir may be interpreted as

written in the 1970s, denotes another attempt to reject the Western model of modernization. Here, Mahathir argues that the West is afflicted by a "perversion of values" and he promotes instead a progressive form of Islamic modernization as an alternative developmental model.[53] During the 1990s, Mahathir's anti-West rhetoric constituted a common feature of Malaysian social life. This time, the rhetoric became focused on the hypocrisy and double standards of the Western world regarding issues of press freedom and democracy. An instance of this critique occurred upon his return from the forty-eighth United Nations General Assembly in 1993, when Mahathir launched an attack on the "biased and unfair nature" of Western media in "blacking out anything good the South has to say."[54] In the same year, Mahathir also attacked media magnate Rupert Murdoch's take-over of Hong Kong Star TV claiming that it was another attempt by the Western media to "undermine Asian interests."[55] During the 1993 National Day celebrations, Mahathir used the Bosnia-Herzegovina issue to point to the discrepant standards of the West with regards to human rights.[56] The anti-West rhetoric reached a peak that same year during the torrent of "West bashing" in the local media over Malaysia's conflict with Australia after its Prime Minister, Paul Keating, used the word "recalcitrant" in referring to Mahathir, who absented himself from the Asia-Pacific Economic Cooperation (APEC) meeting in Seattle.[57] This anti-West rhetoric continues into the twenty-first century. In the country's first National Day celebrations of the new millennium, the Prime Minister again warned Malaysians that "foreign powers were still bent on recolonizing the country."[58]

All this is not to suggest that Mahathir's anti-Western convictions are not problematic, nor that they are passively endorsed by Malaysian society. Nevertheless, a relentless tirade against the West, whereby elements of local cultural values and beliefs are valorized as ideal alternatives for the future, constitutes a critical component of Malaysia's national project of modernization. Malaysians are constantly told not to duplicate Western styles and practices but instead to strive to maintain high moral values based on Malaysian "culture," Islam, and "tradition." Here, the village (*kampung*) emerges as a favorite site for the idealization of culture and morality. As mentioned earlier, a number of scholars have noted a greater appreciation for *kampung* culture in recent Malaysian society.[59] This nostalgia for the *kampung* can perhaps be better put in perspective if we consider that rapid Malay urbanization has seen the migration of

---

having essentially validated and reproduced colonial stereotypes and racial prejudices concerning the "lazy native."

[53] Mahathir Mohamed, *The Challenge* (Petaling Jaya: Pelanduk Publications, 1986), p. 91.

[54] *The Star*, October 3, 1993, pp. 1, 3.

[55] *New Straits Times*, August 4, 1993, p. 2.

[56] *The Star*, August 31, 1993, p. 1.

[57] For examples, see *The Star*, December 5, 1993, p. 1; *New Straits Times*, December 5, 1993, p. 13; *New Straits Times*, December 6, 1993, p. 6; *New Straits Times*, December 7, 1993, pp. 1, 2; *New Straits Times*, December 9, 1993, p. 1.

[58] *New Straits Times*, August 31, 2000, p. 36.

[59] Banks, *From Class to Culture*; and Kahn, "Class, Ethnicity and Diversity," p. 31.

Malays from villages into cities under various government programs.[60] Despite their role in the migration, the government has contributed to this nostalgic mood in its launch of a national Kampungku (My Kampung) project in 1991. The aim of the Kampungku project is to preserve traditional Malay villages in order to showpiece them as living "museums," so that the younger generation will know how their ancestors lived.[61] In the launching of one of the Kampungku projects in the state of Perak, Dr. Mahathir called on Malaysians to strive for high moral values, akin to those found in village culture, in order to achieve the goals of Vision 2020. He explained that, "The Kampungku programme is not asking everyone to stay in villages but to uphold the village culture which is good."[62]

Amidst the preoccupation with "change" and "newness," the Malaysian political elite became engaged in a heated debate over new ethnic images and identifications. Sometime in 1991, Dr. Mahathir Mohamed started the ball rolling by introducing and popularizing the use of the term "Melayu Baru," or the "New Malay."[63] The term refers to a community of Malays who have experienced both mental and cultural reformation, and now possess:

> a culture suitable to the modern period, capable of meeting all the challenges, able to compete without assistance, learned and knowledgeable, sophisticated, honest, disciplined, trustworthy and competent.[64]

In calling for the realization of the "New Malays" during the 1992 UMNO General Assembly, Dr. Mahathir reiterated that the "new culture" can be "ours" but "we must raise our effort to make ourselves into people who are able to take their appropriate place in this modern world."[65] This culturalist revamp of Malayness gained even more attention after 1993 when members of a dominant faction within UMNO, who see themselves as archetypal "New Malays," decided to call themselves the Wawasan (Vision) team during party elections.[66] The "New Malay" concept is used differently among various elements of the Malay

---

[60] The total urban population classified as Malays rose from 19 percent in 1947 to almost 40 percent in 1980. Various federal government agencies such as the Urban Development Authority (UDA) and MARA (Council of Trust for the Indigenous People) were set up to ensure Malay participation in urbanization and industrialization.

[61] The first project was started in the state of Negeri Sembilan, followed by Selangor in 1992 and then another in Perak in 1993. The third Kampungku project was launched by the Prime Minister himself. See *The Star*, July 23, 1993, p. 1.

[62] *The Star*, July 23, 1993, p. 1.

[63] See Shamsul A. B, "Orang Kaya Baru: Origin, Construction and Predicament of Malay Noveaux Riche" (Working Paper for Workshop on Cultural Constructions of Asia's New Rich, Asia Research Centre, Murdoch University, July 8-10, 1995), p. 18.

[64] See Khoo Boo Teik, *Paradoxes of Mahathirism*, p. 335. During the formulation of the New Economic Policy at the peak of "capitalistic nationalism" among the dominant Malay elite, the youth wing of UMNO published a book titled *Revolusi Mental* (Mental Revolution) which emphasized the need for mental reformation among Malays in order to realize their political powers for the successful pursuit of Malay capitalism. It has been suggested that this book, as well as Mahathir's infamous *Malay Dilemma* , can be regarded as documents of Malay political capitalism See Shahruddin Maaruf, *Malay Ideas on Development*, pp. 138-139.

[65] Ibid.

[66] This faction was headed by Datuk Seri Anwar Ibrahim who was vying for the seat of the Vice-President in UMNO. He was later appointed Deputy Prime Minister.

community, with significant differences observed between Malay intellectuals, politicians, middle classes, and the business community.[67] Malay intellectuals and politicians are, in general, more anxious to find continuities with the past and Islam, while Malay middle classes and corporate figures display much more nonchalance in the recasting of Malayness as a symbol of progress.[68]

As the construction of Malayness is predicated on the construction of its "Others," it is not surprising that the repositioning of Malay identity produces resonances among other ethnic identities in the country. Other partners in the National Alliance (Barisan Nasional) endorsed the construction of a series of "new" identities that, they argued, best suited the new era.[69] For instance, the Malaysian Chinese Association (MCA) took the opportunity during its forty-fourth anniversary celebration in 1993 to call for the realization of a Bangsa Malaysia (Malaysian Race).[70] They argued that the term was appropriate in current times as Malaysians, including the Chinese, had undergone a process of "evolution" and had become more Malaysian.[71] The MCA later announced that it was opening its membership to all Malaysians of "Chinese origin," even those bearing non-Chinese names and including those "whose mothers or grandparents were Chinese."[72] In justifying this decision, the party announced that it had received many membership applications from Malaysians of Chinese descent but bearing Thai, Indian, and Kadazan names.[73] This change in membership policy drew a swift response from the Malaysian Indian Congress (MIC) which announced that they had always been open to all Malaysians of "Indian ancestry."[74]

The MCA's "liberalization" of its party membership policy was not unprecedented. This move was in step with UMNO's earlier liberalization of its Malay-only membership ruling, when it extended party membership to certain non-Malay and non-Muslim groups, such as the Thais in the north of Peninsular Malaysia and *bumiputera* groups in Sabah. This UMNO move was made public by Mahathir during his response to the MCA membership policy.[75] (For the first time ever, indigenous groups apart from Malays were allowed to join UMNO in 1992

---

[67] For a Malay politician's view of the characteristics of the "New Malay," see Muhammad Haji Muhd Taib, *Melayu Baru* [New Malay](Kuala Lumpur: ITC Book Publisher, 1993).

[68] Harper, *The End of Empire and the Making of Malaya*, pp. 371-378.

[69] Malaysia's political arena is dominated by the ruling Barisan Nasional, which comprises political parties representing the three major ethnic groups of the country. These are: UMNO (the leading party of the Alliance) for the Malays, the Malaysian Chinese Association (MCA) for the Chinese, the Malaysian Indian Congress (MIC) for the Indians, and the Gerakan, which supposedly represents the various ethnic groups, but has a predominantly Chinese interest.

[70] *The Star*, March 1, 1993, p. 1.

[71] The MCA President made this statement. He specifically called for the sharing of cultures among the different ethnic groups in the country, and the political party made its point by inviting Indian and Malay cultural groups to perform at this celebration. See ibid.

[72] *The Star*, January 16, 1994, p. 1.

[73] See footnote 13 in this chapter for an explanation of the Kadazan people.

[74] *The Star*, January 16, 1994, p. 1.

[75] See *The Star*, January 17, 1994, p. 2.

when UMNO became a political party in the eastern state of Sabah and opened its membership to the indigenous populations in that state.)[76]

The other remaining partner in the National Alliance, the Gerakan party, responded by launching its own vision of the "New Malaysian."[77] Gerakan defined the "New Malaysian" person as someone who possessed a global perspective, pursued science and technology, led an environmentally friendly lifestyle, upheld the extended family system, possessed a good working ethic, and was patriotic.[78]

This fervor among the dominant political parties to rework ethnic identities in response to the country's aspirations for modernity sparked off similar moves amongst some minority groups in Malaysia. In particular, the opening up of the terms of ethnic identity and identification with political parties led to the mobilization of a number of communities around their claims of indigenous or *bumiputera* status. Given the interrelations between Malayness and the endowment of special economic and social privileges in the Malaysian context, the cultural politics of claiming indigenous identity are inevitably intertwined with class aspirations. Malayness is inevitably linked to notions of achieving a "middle-class" status. The two leading claimants in the politics of claiming Malayness were the Portuguese-Eurasians and the Baba Nyonya Chinese communities from Melaka.[79] In 1993, these two minority groups made boisterous claims for *bumiputera* status on the grounds of their long historical presence in Melaka (the symbolic birthplace of Malay civilization). They argued that they were similar to the Malays in terms of culture, tradition, and language. In addition, they seized the opportunity created by the liberalization of UMNO's membership policy to call on UMNO to also allow them to join as party members.[80]

The evocations of Portuguese-Eurasian identity and Baba Nyonya Chinese identity are intricately linked to broader currents within identity and class politics in Malaysia. For the purposes of this book, it is important to show how reconstructions of Portuguese-Eurasian identity within the context of contemporary

---

[76] The UMNO decision to enter into Sabah politics was associated with the federal government's attempt to wrench control from Sabah's opposition party government. For details, see Loh Kok Wah, "Modernisation, Cultural Revival and Counter Hegemony," pp. 225-253.

[77] The party drafted a twenty-five year plan to pursue its vision.

[78] The Gerakan prescribed a total of nine characteristics in its vision of the "New Malaysian." The other sought-after virtues are: an open and liberal attitude towards the learning of languages; creativeness and innovation; and honesty, sincerity, and a compassionate, caring, and sharing nature.

[79] Melaka is believed to have been founded about 1400 and is the place where the history of great Malay power in Malaya began. See Barbara Andaya and Leonard Andaya, *A History of Malaysia* (London: Macmillan, 1982), pp. 35-38. The Portuguese-Eurasian history in Melaka is said to begin in the sixteenth century while the history of the Melakan Baba Nyonya Chinese community dates back to the fifteenth century. For details on the Baba Nyonya community, see Tan Chee Beng, "Baba and Nyonya: A Study of the Ethnic Identity of the Chinese Peranakan in Malacca,"(PhD Dissertation, Cornell University, 1979); and John C. Clammer, *Straits Chinese Society* (Singapore: Singapore University Press, 1980).

[80] For details of the Portuguese-Eurasian claims see Chapter Six. In the case of the Baba Nyonya community, they provided documentary proof that some members of their community had joined UMNO more than twenty-five years previously (*New Straits Times*, March 31, 1993, p. 8). Upon this claim, the Deputy Education Minister issued a statement to highlight the fact that during the early years of independence, the first Prime Minister of Malaysia had offered *bumiputera* status to the Baba Nyonya Chinese community, but they had turned it down. See *The Star*, April 4, 1993, p. 4.

identity and class politics were played out in the Kampung Serani conflict. The politics of indigenousness, class, and modernity not only determined relations between the kampung's residents and the PEA, but also effectively modified the cityscape plans of the kampung site.

As can be observed, recent conceptions of nation, ethnicity, and class constructed in the context of the reworking of subjectivities express a certain ambivalence towards the meanings of modernity. This ambivalence is reflected in the unresolved appeal of the East and the West, the old and the new, the traditional and the modern, ethnicity and class, Islam and Malayness, and the local and the global. These ambivalent discourses, centered around changing notions of ethnicity, class, and modernity, are not merely abstract imaginings but have concrete manifestations when they are appropriated by institutional and social actors and inscribed onto urban space as these actors pursue their own visions of a future Malaysia.

CONCRETE MODERNITIES AND MODERN URBAN CULTURE: REACHING FOR THE SKY

Malaysia's continuing rapid economic growth since the late 1980s has, among other things, effected dramatic transformations in the urban skyline. Two features mark these transformations. Firstly, new building forms have risen up, such as multi-leveled shopping complexes, tower office blocks, luxurious condominiums, resorts, and golf and other recreational clubs. Secondly, there has been a move towards restored, reconstructed, and "reused" construction projects developed around old colonial or heritage buildings.[81] I am not suggesting that changes in Malaysia's cityscape have only occurred during this time period.[82] Indeed just prior to this period, in the early 1980s, the government embarked on a spree of public spending on public infrastructure resulting in a property boom.[83] However, my point of departure is the more recent transformations that have occurred in Malaysian cities since the late 1980s. In my view, city growth in Malaysia prior to the late

---

[81] Some of these "reused" projects are: the former Central Market (now a modern bazaar), the Infokraf building (an exhibition center for Malaysian traditional arts and handicrafts), and two former colonial mansions, Carcosa and Seri Negara (now an exclusive boutique hotel). For details of such transformations in the capital city of Kuala Lumpur, see Robert Powell, *Innovative Architecture of Singapore* (Singapore: Select Books, 1989); S. Vlatseas, *A History of Malaysian Architecture* (Singapore: Longman Publishers, 1990); Chan Chee Yong, ed., *Post-Merdeka Architecture Malaysia, 1957-1987* (Kuala Lumpur: Pertubuhan Arkitek Malaysia, 1987); *International Architect* 6 (1984); and *MIMAR* 26 (December 1987): 64-72.

[82] As some Malaysian architects have already pointed out, European modernist building forms were present in Malaya before the Second World War, usually in the form of public buildings such as schools, administrative offices, courts, and railway stations. Chan Chee Yong, *Post-Merdeka Architecture Malaysia, 1957-1987*, p. 16.

[83] Incidentally, this spate of infrastructural growth was largely dependent on Japanese technology as it coincided with Malaysia's "Look East" policy. See Chang Yii Tan, "Tilting East—The Construction Problem," in *Mahathir's Economic Policies*, ed. K. S. Jomo (Kuala Lumpur: Insan, 1988); and Alasdair Bowie, *Crossing the Industrial Divide: State, Society, and the Politics of Economic Transformation in Malaysia* (New York: Columbia University Press, 1991). One Kuala Lumpur icon built during the property boom of the early 1980s is the Dayabumi Complex. The design of this modern multi-story building incorporated Islamic motifs on its exterior walls and was constructed by the Japanese construction companies Takenaka Komuten and Kumagai Gumi. See Chang Yii Tan, "Tilting East," p. 31.

1980s was most immediately related to the need to expand Malaysia's heavy industry and high-technology resources. Constructions since the late 1980s took a somewhat different turn, as evidenced by the recent fetish for height and magnitude. Indeed, the following observation of a local publication aptly describes this fad:

> This brings us to the national obsession with the tallest, the biggest, the longest, and the widest. In these urban centers, we have witnessed the construction of, for instance, the tallest tower, the highest building, the biggest shopping mall, the longest bridge, etc. All these modern constructions are proudly considered by the country's leadership as physical reminders of the country's tremendous achievements.[84]

Nevertheless, the pursuit of these "modern icons" was not without its hiccups. In 1990, in a bid to have "Asia's tallest condominium" project built in Kuala Lumpur, the local Malaysian authorities together with the Foreign Investment Committee (FIC), which regulates foreign investment in Malaysia, conspicuously speeded up their approval of the project's planning application. The project, however, failed to materialize, as the Tokyo-based property company behind it became entangled in tax scandals back in Japan and had to abandon the project.[85] This experience did not dampen the government's determination, however, as other ventures followed which eventually met with success and much hype.

The first of these successes was the construction of the 421-meter tall Kuala Lumpur Tower, a joint venture project between Syarikat Telekom Malaysia Berhad (the semi-privatized national telecommunications company) and a German company. This tower, completed in 1995, was at that time the third tallest building in the world, but was misleadingly described in the local press as "the tallest structure in the world and capable of providing the state-of-art [sic] telecommunications facilities."[86] On the heels of the Kuala Lumpur Tower project came the construction of the National Science Center, a project by the Public Works Department, which was said to be "the country's first truly intelligent building."[87] "Intelligent buildings" incorporate information technology, automated communication controls, and management systems to allow for more efficient use of resources, increasing comfort and security for their occupants. It seems that height is no longer the sole criterion in the assessment of modern constructions. The "intelligent building" made its debut in the city of Kuala Lumpur in 1992 in the form of a twenty-seven story building.[88] On completion, it was promoted as an "ultra modern" and high-tech building. Subsequently, Kuala Lumpur City Hall announced that it would give priority to the development of such "intelligent

---

[84] *Aliran Monthly* 15,3 (1995): 5.

[85] See Doug Tsuruoka, "Feet of Clay: Japanese Firm Denies Hitches with KL Tower Plan," *Far Eastern Economic Review*, July 26, 1990, pp. 51-52.

[86] The Kuala Lumpur Tower, a RM270 million joint-project, features a revolving restaurant, an observation platform, and a theatre. For details, see *The Star*, September 24, 1993, p. 3.

[87] *The Star*, March 12, 1993, p. 1.

[88] This project was built along Jalan Raja Laut by a member of the Cycle and Carriage Group—the Bintang Kemajuan Limited Company. See *Malaysian Business*, March 1-15, 1992, p. 27.

buildings" to ensure that the city maintained a competitive edge in attracting foreign investors.[89]

Malaysia's dream of having the tallest building in the world was realized with the completion of the 1,457 feet (eighty-eight stories) Petronas Towers. The Towers are owned by the national oil corporation and designed by Cessar Pelli, the Argentine-born architect based in New York who designed Canary Wharf in London.[90] Developed as part of the Kuala Lumpur City Center Project (KLCC), Petronas Tower has twin commercial peaks of stainless steel and glass-clad construction linked by a bridge at the forty-fourth floor. Much attention has surrounded the Islamic motifs in the external design of the towers, motifs designed to reflect the building's cultural and regional identity. The internal floor design of superimposed squares and circles is said to symbolize unity, harmony, and strength.[91] By balancing the state-of-the-art facilities with careful details of Islamic principles and tradition, the building is officially presented as a "true embodiment of the tradition and future of Malaysia" and a "new global symbol for the city and the nation."[92]

Later impressive additions to the Malaysian skyline are the Express Rail Link—the Kuala Lumpur Sentra—and the Multimedia Super Corridor. The Multimedia Super Corridor is a grand modernization plan under the National Information Technology Agenda (NITA) that focuses on the vital role of science and technology in shaping Malaysia's future as a global information society with a fully industrialized status.[93] This project is a fifteen by fifty kilometer corridor that encompasses the KLCC and continues south towards the neighboring state of Selangor to include two "intelligent" cities, Putrajaya (Malaysia's new administrative center) and Cyberjaya (an industrial center for information technology companies), ending at the modern Kuala Lumpur New International Airport (KLIA). The KLIA, which opened in 1998, is a project designed by Japanese architect Kisho Kurokawa (who is also the architect for the Kuala Lumpur Sentra project) and is based on the theme of a "tropical forest" to emphasize the fusion between technology and nature.

Clearly, these constructions point to a growing concern by Malaysian elites to display these modern icons to the world community as much as the Malaysian public. Features such as size, height, and grandiosity are obviously associated with prestige and achievement. The correlation between height and stature in the current Malaysian built environment is perhaps best summed up by the

---

[89] *The Star*, July 29, 1993, p. 6.

[90] The Petronas Towers are supposed to be some twenty feet higher than the Sears Tower in Chicago, which has held the record of tallest building for the past twenty years. See Jonathan Glancey, "Far East Reaches for the Sky," *The Independent*, reproduced in *The Star, Section Two*, July 28, 1994, pp. 3-4.

[91] Indeed, one of the recurring themes in current Malaysian architecture is modern Islamic design. Some examples of these "modern Islamic buildings" are: the Parliament Building, the National Mosque, the Tabung Haji Building (housing the organization that oversees the annual Muslim pilgrimage to Mecca), the Dayabumi Complex, the Selangor State Mosque, and the National Library (which has been described as a futuristic Aztec or Maya temple).

[92] Cessar Pelli, "The Petronas Towers, Kuala Lumpur, Malaysia," in *Progressive Architecture*, March 1995, p. 35.

[93] Under the NITA, information communication technology is recognized as the engine of growth within all sectors of the Malaysian economy.

advertisement for a high-rise condominium project. It reads, "At 500 feet above sea level, you can't help but look down on others."[94]

Amidst these new constructions, there has also emerged a concern over urban conservation, especially of "heritage" buildings. "Heritage" is now a widely heard and used concept in Malaysia's active "heritage" movements.[95] These urban-based movements, comprised largely of professionals and elites, have become a powerful force in urban areas, where they have received widespread support from the public, the government, and the business sector for the conservation of buildings designated as having heritage value. For instance, a credit card company sponsored a "Heritage Trail" project in Melaka. This walking tour charted and described nominated heritage buildings in the city.[96] In addition, the Ministry of Housing and Local Government announced that national conservation legislation would be formulated to ensure the proper preservation of heritage buildings.[97]

The thematization of "heritage" is not merely confined to old buildings; there is an accompanying trend to incorporate heritage elements in new urban projects. Among such projects there has emerged a specific neo-modern urban form in Malaysian urban centers: the reproduction of the Malay *kampung* house. The romanticization of the Malay *kampung* house is evidenced by the reproduction of this vernacular structure in countless miniature models throughout Malaysia—in airports, public spaces, and tourist centers.[98] Some of these reproductions, including the Bank Bumiputera in Kuala Lumpur, utilize reproductions of Minangkabau roofs in their modern urban built forms.[99] In fact, the popular reception of this vernacular structure prompted the Malaysian Institute of Architects in 1993 to submit a proposal to the Ministry of Housing and Local Government recommending a new style of township, the *Kampung-minium*—which is an idealized view of *kampung* living as part of the broader romanticization of the *kampung*.[100] According to the president of the Malaysian Institute of Architects,

---

[94] This advertisement for Gasing Heights in Petaling Jaya, Kuala Lumpur, appeared in *The Star*, July 4, 1993, p. 17.

[95] The national body of the heritage movement is the Heritage Council of Malaysia, which is particularly active in the capital city of Kuala Lumpur. Its chairperson is a well-known Malay business figure and a member of Negeri Sembilan royalty. The council has also organized a series of public seminars throughout the country on Malaysia's architectural "heritage."

[96] An American Express-Melaka Heritage Trail was set up in 1992 and Penang State has now set up a similar trail for the city of Georgetown (see *The Star*, August 17, 1993, p. 10).

[97] *The Star*, July 28, 1993, p. 4.

[98] See discussions on the "Mini Malaysia" project located in the state of Melaka in Kahn, "Culture, Ethnicity and Diversity," pp. 168-170. During my fieldwork, the private company managing the now privatized historical Fort Cornwallis in Penang constructed, in the compound of the fort, a Malay *kampung* house beside a handicraft center and a historical gallery as tourist attractions.

[99] In Malaysia, the Minangkabau people are found largely in the state of Negeri Sembilan.

[100] The Malaysian Institute of Architects, founded in 1967, is a body that organizes the professional architects of the country, promotes education, conducts competitions, advises government agencies, and arranges affiliations with professional organizations in other countries.

Kampung-minium [is] coined from the words *kampung* and condominium [and] will incorporate the best of the *kampung* and condo living. In other words the best of the East and the West.[101]

An advertisement for a condominium project called Kampung Warisan (Heritage Kampung) is evidence of the prominence of the heritage concept.[102]

However, despite the romanticization of the traditional village, there is a noticeable ambivalence towards authentic *kampung* houses situated in urban centers. Ironically, *kampung* houses located within urban centers, such as those found in Kampung Serani, are considered to be an eyesore and deemed to be out of keeping with Malaysia's modern aspirations. Consequently, urban *kampungs* have been destroyed at a swift rate in the name of development and national pride.[103] This ambivalence towards the *kampung* house is reflected in the outward appearance of the "preserved" and "traditional" house. Commentators have noted the elegance of these showpieces.[104] I would add that, in contrast to many existing rural *kampungs*, such showpieces are sanitized and modernized. This gap between reality and representation is noticeable if one looks at the many existing rural *kampungs* around the country. Unlike the model village house, many existing rural houses are architecturally eclectic—even messy—and lack modern sanitation facilities. Many actual villages are in a rather dilapidated condition and have only basic amenities, considered "unmodern" by urban standards. The model *kampung* house has been constructed according to romanticized perceptions and in a way that makes it acceptable for modern consumption. This has an impact on government development plans. For example, the Perlis state government plans to transform older villages in the state into modern housing settlements. According to the Perlis Chief Minister, the objectives of the project are to replace the "wooden style houses" with "modern brick houses and better amenities" in order to "project a modern outlook" which is "an image befitting to the current development trends."[105]

The rush to construct modern icons in the Malaysian cityscape is inevitably accompanied by significant shifts in capital flows into the property development sector. To further understand the complexities of the struggle over a modern urban Malaysia, I will discuss some of the dynamics between capital, the state, and community groups amidst the rapid pace of urban development.

---

[101] See *The Star, Business Section*, February 23, 1993, p. 2.

[102] The advertisement for this project by a wholly owned subsidiary of Eastern & Oriental Limited Company appeared in *The Star*, March 24, 1994 under the title "Back to the good old days." The project features 275 units within five condominium blocks, a clubhouse, *kopitiam* (this is a common Malaysian term for coffee shop), *kedai runcit* (grocery shop), twenty-four-hour security, jogging and bicycle tracks, and so on.

[103] Perhaps another commonly regarded eyesore in the Malaysian urban centers is the squatter settlement. For an interesting case study that attempts to account for the persistence of a squatter settlement in a Malaysian urban center by exploring its connections to industrial capitalism, identity politics, and political patronage in contemporary Malaysia, see Patrick Guinness, *On the Margins of Capitalism: People and Development in Mukim Plentong, Johor, Malaysia* (Singapore: Oxford University Press, 1992).

[104] Kahn "Culture, Ethnicity and Diversity, p. 168; Lim Yee Juan, *The Malay House: Rediscovering Malaysia's Indigenous Shelter System* (Penang: Institut Masyarakat, 1987).

[105] *The Star*, August 29, 1993, p. 13.

A PERPETUAL STATE DILEMMA

In Malaysia, domestic Chinese capital has long dominated the property construction sector.[106] This tendency became even more pronounced after the introduction of the New Economic Policy (NEP).[107] The requirement that Chinese firms incorporate Malay partners under the NEP, coupled with the government's consistent favoring of foreign capital over Chinese capital in the manufacturing sector, has led Chinese firms to take a short-term view of their economic activities and, as a result, many ventured into property construction.[108] Malay capital began to emerge as a powerful rival in the property construction industry only in the 1980s. Malay capital typically took the form of huge public enterprises (now referred to as Non-Financial Public Enterprises, such as PERNAS and the Urban Development Authority [UDA]).[109] In addition, private investment companies affiliated with UMNO, such as the Fleet Group, became equally active in the industry.[110]

The property boom in the late 1980s was marked by increased foreign investment due to economic deregulation policies adopted by the government. This liberalization first began as part of the government's response to the severe economic recession of the mid-1980s. A key feature of this policy shift was the relaxation of foreign equity stipulations under the NEP, and indeed the hallmark of Malaysia's economic growth has been its dependence on foreign capital.[111] Although economic deregulation has mainly resulted in an influx of foreign

---

[106] In the post-Independence era, diversifying into property development almost became a ritual for bigger Chinese businesses. See Tan Tat Wai, *Income Distribution in West Malaysia* (Kuala Lumpur: Oxford University Press, 1982).

[107] For details about the NEP and its successor program, the NDP, see footnote 8 of this chapter.

[108] For example, in 1981, Chinese firms made large investments in tourist and hotel complexes—a total of RM124 million or 27.4 percent of total Chinese investments. See James V. Jesudason, *Ethnicity and the Economy: The State, Chinese Business, and Multinationals in Malaysia* (Singapore: Oxford University Press, 1989), p. 164. Another trend was the spread of assets and activities outside Malaysia. See Nick Seaward, "A Question of Quantifying Investments," *Far Eastern Economic Review*, December 3, 1987, pp. 84-85. An estimated US$12 billion of non-Malay capital was said to have left Malaysia between 1976 and 1985.

[109] PERNAS is said to be one of the most ambitious public enterprises set up to achieve NEP goals. See Khoo Kay Jin, "The Grand Vision," p. 49; and Bruce Gale, *Politics and Public Enterprise in Malaysia* (Petaling Jaya, Selangor: Eastern Universities Press, 1981). UDA is a semi-government enterprise set up under the NEP. It has a main holding company, Paremba, which was sold to UMNO's Fleet Group. See Gomez, *Politics in Business*, p. 95. Paremba's dealings in the property sector are well-known. See Gomez, *Politics in Business*, pp. 40, 93-95.

[110] For details about the merger of UMNO's Fleet Group into Faber Merlin, a property development company, see Gomez, *Politics in Business*, pp. 79-91.

[111] See Linda Y. C. Lim and Pang Eng Fong, *Foreign Direct Investment and Industrialisation in Malaysia, Singapore, Taiwan and Thailand* (Paris: Development Centre of the Organization for Economic Co-operation and Development, 1991), p. 88; and Kamal Salih, "The Malaysian Economy in the 1990s: Alternative Scenarios," in *The Malaysian Economy Beyond 1990: International & Domestic Perspectives*, ed. Lee Kiong Hock and Shyamala Nagaraj (Kuala Lumpur: Persatuan Ekonomi Malaysia, 1991), p. 5. In October 1986, 100 percent foreign ownership was allowed under certain conditions. Prior to that, under the NEP, foreign companies were required to structure their equity so that Malaysian investors held at least 70 percent share, with at least 30 percent *bumiputera* (Malay) equity.

investment into the manufacturing sector, some policies were specifically targeted at stimulating the property development sector by deliberately attempting to encourage the flow of foreign capital into this sector.

While the shift to liberalize foreign investment in the property development industry appeared to signify a declining emphasis on the distributional goals of the NEP on the part of the government, the situation is by no means so clear cut. As mentioned earlier, the political tensions created by the Malaysian state's attempt to step back from direct participation in and protection of Malay capital resulted in an on-going oscillation between liberalization and interventionist policies.[112] My research shows how pronounced this oscillation has been in the property development sector. For example, whenever foreign capital was seen to jeopardize the interests of Malay capital, the government quickly reacted by re-imposing restrictions. This led to a situation in which policies were confused, transitory in nature, and formulated in an almost ad hoc manner. The events discussed below demonstrate the unresolved conflict within the government over the distributional goals of the NEP versus greater liberalization in the promotion of urban growth.

The two main policy areas which best exhibit these rapid and often confusing changes are land legislation and economic policy. Changes to the National Land Code (NLC)—the principal land legislation governing Peninsular Malaysia— reveal these conflicts with regards to land legislation. In Malaysia, foreign ownership of land for agricultural and residential/building purposes has been a nationalist issue since Independence.[113] After much lobbying by various nationalist groups, amendments were made to the NLC to totally prohibit foreign ownership of "agriculture" and "building" land in 1985.[114] However, a year later these amendments were replaced (via Act 658 which came into effect on January 1, 1987) when economic recession led the government to pursue greater liberalization of the economy. Following the liberalization of the NLC, the government allowed 100 percent foreign equity in new hotel and tourist construction projects in 1988. This incentive still applies, although a foreign-owned company is required to restructure its equity such that Malaysians hold at least a 49 percent share (and *bumiputeras* a 30 percent share) after five years from the date of first operation.[115]

These changes led to an unprecedented upsurge in foreign acquisition of urban property in Malaysia.[116] This buying spree was further facilitated by relaxation in

---

[112] See Khoo Kay Jin, "The Grand Vision," pp. 44-76.

[113] See Wolfgang Senftleben, *Background to Agricultural Land Policy in Malaysia* (Wiesbaden: Otto Harrassowitz, 1978), p. 163.

[114] This amendment to the NLC came into effect on March 25, 1985 (via Act 587). However, after appeals by the Bankers Association Malaysia that banks be allowed to create charges and liens on such land to secure collateral, it was amended (via Act 624 which came into effect on September 13, 1985) to allow banks to create charges and liens on these land categories, but it prohibited them to bid in case the land was put up for auction. No prohibitions were ever imposed on foreign ownership of industrial land in the NLC.

[115] See Malaysia, *Economic Report, 1992/3*, Vol. 21 (Kuala Lumpur: National Printing Department, 1992), p. 325. Foreign capital flows into tourism-related infrastructure, such as resorts, theme parks, and golf courses, were also facilitated by the creation of the National Tourism Plan under the Sixth Malaysian Plan (1991-1995). See Malaysia, *Sixth Malaysia Plan, 1991-1995* (Kuala Lumpur: Government Printers, 1991), p. 233.

[116] See *New Straits Times*, September 21, 1989, Business and Finance Section, p. 15; Nick Seaward, "Foreigners on the Lookout for Bargains," *Far Eastern Economic Review*, March 16, 1989, pp. 49-50; Doug Tsuruoka, "Eager Buyers Look for More," *Far Eastern Economic Review*,

the country's exchange controls[117] and the lowering of property transfer taxes under amendments to the Real Property Gains Tax (RPGT).[118] For changes in the RPGT, see Appendix C.

In response to the spate of foreign acquisitions of Malaysian property, media and public concern brought political pressure on the government to clamp down on foreign ownership. The situation in Johore, Selangor, Melaka, and Penang had sparked fears that "Singaporean and Taiwanese investors were devouring a disproportionate share of the [property] market at the expense of bumiputra [sic] (native Malay) competitors."[119] The growing fear that foreign capital was eroding the interests of Malay capital caused the FIC to issue guidelines and impose a series of conditions on all foreign acquisition of property.[120] However, the FIC rulings changed so rapidly that it led to great confusion among developers, bankers, lawyers, and even state governments. (For my documentation of these changes between 1992 and 2000, see Appendix D.)[121]

In 1992, restrictions on foreign ownership were again imposed in amendments to the NLC, amendments which required that foreigners procure prior written approval from respective state authorities before they acquired agricultural and building land (via Act A832/92). Ironically, however, it was at about this time that the FIC eased its hard-line attitude towards foreign purchases of Malaysian

---

March 21, 1990, p. 50; and Kamal Salih, "The Malaysian Economy in the 1990s," p. 51. Official statistics on foreign ownership mainly relate to commercial real estate in cases involving huge acquisitions. In 1988, RM500 million worth of commercial property was bought by foreign investors out of a total volume of transactions valued at RM8.14 billion. See *New Straits Times*, April 7, 1989, p. 1. Figures for the first half of 1989, announced by the Deputy Finance Minister, showed that foreigners only accounted for RM300 million or 5.7 percent of the RM5 billion worth of total property transactions. However, the Minister added that he was aware that the statistics did not reflect the actual situation. See *New Straits Times*, Business and Finance Section, September 23, 1989, p. 11. In Penang, foreign ownership of properties was reported to be at 14.5 percent in 1987. See Malaysia, *Property Market Report, 1987* (Kuala Lumpur: Ministry of Finance, 1987), p. A-54.

[117] In 1986 foreigners were allowed to borrow up to RM10 million from all local sources without permission from the Controller of Foreign Exchange if they obtained 60 percent of credit facilities from locally incorporated financial institutions. But in 1991, Bank Negara (Central Bank) banned all domestic lending by foreigners for property acquisition in Malaysia. See Doug Tsuruoka, "Stake in the Cake: Malaysian Government Split over Foreign-Investment Rules," *Far Eastern Economic Review*, March 5, 1992, p. 50.

[118] The Real Property Gains Tax Act of 1975 provides for a tax to be imposed in respect of chargeable gain accruing from the disposal of any real property.

[119] See Doug Tsuruoka, "A Brake Gives Bumis a Break," *Far Eastern Economic Review*, March 21, 1991, pp. 44-45; and Tsuruoka, "Stake in the Cake," pp. 52-53.

[120] The FIC, which is comprised of high-ranking administrators from the Ministries of Trade and Industry, the Economic Planning Unit, and the Registrar of Companies, was originally set up in 1974. See Jesudason, *Ethnicity and the Economy*, p. 79. The conditions set out in the FIC rulings include minimum purchase value, housing types, terms of owner-occupancy, and resale period.

[121] It was reported that approvals of foreign purchases of Malaysian property were as low as 4 percent at the height of the FIC controversy in 1992. See *The Star*, September 9, 1993, p. 7.

property.[122] Nevertheless, in 1995 more stringent conditions were imposed when the NLC was again amended. This time, among other things, the amendments provided for state authorities to impose terms and conditions besides the imposition of a levy on foreign acquisition of landed properties (for a synopsis of the amendments to the National Land Code since 1985, see Appendix E). Subsequently, the federal government announced that a RM100,000 levy would be imposed on all property transactions involving foreigners.[123]

Alongside these changes, new financial mechanisms were instituted to support the domestic property market. In 1989, Property Trust Funds were established in the Kuala Lumpur Stock Exchange (KLSE) for the first time.[124] Property trusts are investment instruments to raise funds through the stock market for investment in the property sector.[125] As well as being a boost to the property market, these property trusts provide another avenue for "foreign money" into the Malaysian property sector.[126] In addition, these Property Trust Funds were given favorable tax treatment.[127] Interestingly, despite its hard-line stance on the foreign acquisition of landed properties in the country, the FIC agreed not to restrict the size of individual unit-holdings or the percentage level of aggregate unit-holdings by foreigners in these property trusts.[128] By 1993, the property sector represented 6.8

---

[122] See *The Star*, Business Section, March 12, 1993, p. 3; *The Star*, Business Section, September 9, 1993, p. 7.

[123] This levy came into effect on October 27, 1995.

[124] A person very much behind the effort to establish the Property Trust Funds was the former Finance Minister, Daim Zainuddin. He is noted for his background as a successful Malay businessman who succeeded through property deals. For details, see Jesudason, *Ethnicity and the Economy*, p. 107. The KLSE (first named as the Malaya Stock Exchange) was formed in 1963. The KLSE separated from the Stock Exchange of Singapore in 1973. For details on the KLSE, see Lin See-Yan, "Malaysian Financial Markets," in *Pacific-Basin Capital Markets Research*, Vol. III, ed. S. G. Rhee and R. P. Chang (New York: Elsevier Science Publishers, 1992), p. 67.

[125] According to the guidelines on Property Trust Funds issued by the Capital Issues Committee, at least 75 percent of funds in an unlisted trust or 80 percent in a listed trust must be invested in real property (Malaysian Securities Commission, "Guidelines on Property Trust Funds," dated October 24, 1991, p. 10). I would like to thank Ms. Seow Siew Mei, Assistant Manager of the Market Supervision Division of the Malaysian Securities Commission, for making these guidelines accessible.

[126] See Christopher Marchand, "Blocked Entrance: No Easy Ways to Buy into Malaysia's Property Boom," *Far Eastern Economic Review*, December 14, 1989, pp. 105-106. The first of such trusts, the Arab-Malaysia First Property Trust, set up by the Arab-Malaysian Bank, with Merrill Lynch Capital Markets, Swiss Bank Corporation Investment Banking, and SG Warburg Securities as its underwriters, offered seventy million units, of which half were taken by foreigners. See *New Straits Times*, July 25, 1989, Business and Finance Section, p. 13. In the launch of the second property trust, the First Malaysia Property Trust (FMPT), which was owned by the Bank of Commerce (70 percent equity) and Australian interests (30 percent), foreign institutional buyers were reported to have snapped up more than half of the 630,001 units offered. See *New Straits Times*, Business and Finance Section, October 18, 1989, p. 13. The foreign buyers were said to be from Hong Kong, Singapore, Britain, Japan, and North America. FMPT has invested in, among others, industrial parks in Penang and Johore Bahru.

[127] *New Straits Times*, March 7, 1989, Business and Finance Section, p. 13.

[128] Ibid.

percent of the Kuala Lumpur Stock Exchange's market capitalization, which stood at RM370 billion in total.[129]

The cap on foreign investments in the property sector changed again in 1997 with the rapid fall in value of the Ringgit Malaysia, which plunged the Malaysian bubble economy into an economic crisis.[130] Affected by the slowing economy and new currency controls, property developers lobbied for special concessions from the government to re-stimulate the property market. By May 1998, the RM100,000 levy on foreign property acquisition was lifted and FIC rulings on the foreign property acquisitions relaxed.[131] In addition, a nation-wide "house ownership campaign" was launched between December 12, 1998 and January 12, 1999 in a bid to bolster the property development sector. During this campaign period, controls on foreign property purchases were further liberalized with blanket approval from the FIC on purchases of properties worth more than RM250,000.[132] For details, see Appendix D.

The events described above indicate the degree to which the interests of the state and capital are embroiled in a struggle over the new material environment of Malaysian urban centers and the ad hoc and ambivalent nature of state policies on capital controls. Nonetheless, the state and capital are not the only players in the urban terrain. The relentless push to construct new icons of modernity can encroach on neighborhoods and uproot communities, creating conflicts over the urban terrain. This was precisely what happened in Kampung Serani in the city of Georgetown, Penang, and which gave rise to divergent claims about Portuguese-Eurasian heritage and identity as forms of contest over the redevelopment of the *kampung* site.

CONCLUSION

To recap, this chapter provides the historical, institutional, and theoretical contexts within which we can understand the competing meanings of nation, ethnicity, and class in modern Malaysian society. As demonstrated, the quest to be a fully industrialized nation has compelled a spate of economic liberalization measures, as well as another reimagining of the Malaysian nation at the national level. Policies concerning economic deregulation and new cultural subjectivities are in a constant state of flux as their implementation sets off debates and disputes, and as these policies and cultural visions are challenged and reworked by various groups inside and outside the state—all of which reflect the complex interrelations between economic and cultural dynamics in contemporary Malaysian society. These new conditions have special effects on the nature of the urban experience as various fractions of the state, capitalists, urban elites, communities, and ethnic groups strive to realize their contrasting cultural, class, and spatial imaginings of a modern urban Malaysia. These struggles give rise to a pervasive rhetoric concerning culture and ethnic identity, the highly contested urban arena, and a rapidly

---

[129] See *The Star*, October 18, 1993, p. 1.

[130] Ringgit Malaysia (RM) is the Malaysian currency.

[131] See *The Star*, May 1, 1998, p. 1; *The Star*, May 20, 1998, p. 2; and *The Star*, June 2, 1998, p. 13.

[132] Personal communication with Mr. Lim Hooi Siang, urban planner and conservation consultant based in Penang.

changing cityscape in which no simple convergence between various conceptions of modernity can be found. The next five chapters examine how the residents of the Kampung Serani conflict became caught up in this complex system of cultural and economic goals, and the degree to which new economic conditions and the cultural politics of ethnicity, class, and modernity in contemporary Malaysia determined the position of each of the players in the Kampung Serani conflict as they debated how to transform one segment of Penang's modern urban landscape.

CHAPTER FOUR

FROM *KAMPUNG* TO CONDOMINIUM

This chapter documents a fourteen-year long battle against eviction by a community of Portuguese Eurasians living in Kampung Serani, in the city of Georgetown, Penang. The conflict began when the landowner, the Roman Catholic Church, entered into a joint venture agreement with a private property developer to develop the *kampung* land into a luxurious condominium-cum-commercial project.

The purpose of this chapter is to introduce the details and chronology of this conflict over urban development. In doing so, I hope to achieve two things. First, this case provides a concrete example substantiating my argument that the urban arena has become the crucible for the complex articulation of power, cityscape changes, cultural identity processes, and modernity in Malaysia. Essentially this case illustrates how contests over the urban terrain can give rise to the reclamation of historical meanings and cultural identity. Second, the case study lays the foundation for the analyses in subsequent chapters of the connections between local level actions and the extra-local forces of economic, political, and cultural identity processes in contemporary Malaysia.

This chapter consists of two sections. The first section provides background information on the geography of the *kampung* and the players involved in the conflict as a basis from which to interpret the events that followed. In the second section, I present a chronology of events.

BACKGROUND INFORMATION

The Location: Pulau Tikus

Kampung Serani, before its complete destruction in 1994, was one of the few remaining *kampung* sites in the hub of the Pulau Tikus area, in the city of Georgetown, Penang. As far as official definition is concerned, Pulau Tikus is an area located within the Northeast administrative district and lies within the city limits of Georgetown. Hence, any reference to Pulau Tikus as an area is essentially a social definition and remains debatable (for details see Chapter Seven).

Pulau Tikus, when translated literally, means "Mouse Island." It is commonly believed to be named after a small island off the coast of the northern metropolitan area of Penang.[1] It has been a middle- and upper-middle-class residential town since the 1920s.[2] However, from the mid-1980s, it has become increasingly fashionable as a location for condominiums and modern commercial projects. Apart

---

[1] See Khoo Su Nin, *Streets of Georgetown, Penang: An Illustrated Guide to Penang's City Streets and Historic Attractions* (Penang: Janus Print & Resources, 1993), p. 55.

[2] Ibid.

from the increasing number of high-rise buildings, the vicinity has also long been occupied by a number of educational institutions. For example, there are three government-run schools, an international school, and a private college, all located within a few minutes walk from the *kampung* site.

The Land Plot

Kampung Serani stood on a rectangular piece of land, bordered by Burma Road, Leandros Lane, Kelawei Road, and College Lane (or Lorong Maktab). This 4.8 acre site is registered under two land lots in the Penang Land Office. These are Lots 354 and 355 within Section One of the North-east District of Penang Island.[3] Lot 354 is the bigger of the two lots, measuring 186,796 square feet. All the houses in Kampung Serani were located on this lot. The smaller Lot 355, measuring 4,228 square feet, is located alongside Burma Road. This lot was leased out by the Church to a coffin-making company. Title to the land is registered at the local Land Office under the name of the Titular Catholic Bishop of Penang.[4]

Buildings in the Kampung

When I returned to Kampung Serani for my fieldwork in March 1993, the *kampung* was an almost empty plot of land covered by high piles of red earth. The only structures left on the village site were three houses, the remains of a bulldozed house, and a shed (see Plates 4.1 and 4.2 in Appendices I and J).

Before the demolition of the *kampung* houses, there were thirteen houses (of which the Church owned three), two sheds, a coffin-making company, and a structure known as "Noah's Ark" (for a layout plan of the *kampung*, see Map 4.1 in Appendix M). Five of the houses stood along Burma Road, and another five lined Leandros Lane, the three other houses, two sheds, and Noah's Ark were located in the inner portion of the *kampung* site. Modern semi-detached housing, as well as apartment blocks facing Kelawei Road, mark the end of the village site. The *kampung* houses were an assortment of wooden houses with zinc roofs.

Of the structures in Kampung Serani, Noah's Ark was the largest, but also the most dilapidated. It was a timber structure with a masonry foundation, raised from

---

[3] All details regarding the Kampung Serani land plots are based on a search I conducted at the Penang Land Office on October 15, 1993.

[4] The title was registered by Deed Registration No. 1368 of November 26, 1889. The deed document notes an Original Tenure Grant No. 851 to the land lots, which indicates the existence of an older record of ownership. However, the Penang Land Office does hold the Original Tenure Grant.

A brief explanation of the history of land registration in Penang is necessary to understand its connection to the Deeds system. When the British East India Company occupied Penang after 1786, it instituted a system of issuing Grants of Title on the basis of a Deed system, starting in at least 1807. However, the titles issued in the Deed system were not uniform and incidents of tenure provided for were obscure in many instances. As such, in 1839 the Straits Land Act was passed, which provided (among other things) for a Land Office to issue titles. A series of enactments later provided a more stable deeds system. In July 1887, the Law of Property and Registration of Deeds Ordinances was implemented. Such was the position until the National Land Code 1965 was passed to provide a uniform system based on the Torrens Scheme for the whole of Peninsular Malaysia. See Judith E. Sihombing, *National Land Code: A Commentary* (Kuala Lumpur: Malayan Law Journal Pte. Ltd, 1981), p. 4.

the ground like a traditional Malay house. The building was named Noah's Ark because it was said to resemble a ship. I could find no written historical records regarding the Noah's Ark building. However, it is popularly believed that it was built over a hundred years ago by the then Pulau Tikus parish priest and that it served as the first "village school" in Pulau Tikus.[5] The administration of this school was handed over in 1906 to the Christian Brothers, who ran missionary schools in Penang at that time.[6] The school then became a branch of the St. Xavier's School set up under the Catholic mission. Since this was one of the earliest schools in Penang, many other Malaysians, apart from Eurasians in Pulau Tikus, had attended the Noah's Ark school. Some of these former students are now prominent members of the community. After Malaysia's independence, the missionary status of the Noah's Ark school led to its closure in 1961.

After Noah's Ark ceased to be used as a school, the Church rented the building to a private ballet academy. In 1980, when the ballet academy vacated the building, the parish priest allowed a Eurasian parishioner and his family to live there. This person eventually subdivided the building and sublet it without the Church's permission.

The Residents

There were about 150 residents living in Kampung Serani just before the first demolition of houses began in 1992. The *kampung* residents were ground tenants of the Church paying an annual ground rent of RM4 per house.

The residents in Kampung Serani were predominantly members of the Eurasian community. They are also referred to as the "Orang Serani," a local term referring to Eurasians.[7] Eurasians, as the term implies, are people born of unions between "Europeans" and "Asians." Apart from the Eurasians, there were a large number of Indian Catholic sub-tenants residing in the *kampung* and a Chinese Catholic family.

In spite of this multi-ethnic population, the Eurasian residents maintained that, until the 1950s, the Church only allowed Eurasians to reside in the village. The Eurasian residents strongly identified themselves as Portuguese Eurasians, although people of various other European origins could be found among their ancestors.[8] This is not surprising, as Kampung Serani is known as a pioneer

---

[5] See Anthony E. Sibert, "Preserve Noah's Ark," Typescript. A Catholic Brother who taught at the Noah's Ark school during the 1920s shared this opinion. Interview with Brother M. on August 3, 1993.

[6] Ibid.

[7] The term Serani is said to be derived from the Arabic word "Nazarene." See Chong Yoke Lin Linda, "The Portuguese-Eurasians (Serani of Penang)," in *Malaysian Ethnic Relations*, ed. S. Gardner (Penang: School of Social Sciences, Universiti Sains Malaysia, 1975), p. 120. See also Alan N. Baxter, *A Grammar of Kristang (Malacca Creole Portuguese)*, Pacific Linguistic Series B-95 (Canberra: Australian National University, Department of Linguistics, Research School of Pacific Affairs, 1988), p. 15. The term is also used in Singapore. See Myrna L. Blake, "Kampung Eurasians," Department of Sociology Working Papers No. 17 (Singapore: University of Singapore, 1973).

[8] Some of the original family names found among the kampung residents were: Gregory, Coombs, Peterson, Robless, Neuky, De'Souza, Holloway, Massang, De'Almeida, Andrews, Aeria, Rodrigues, Neuns, Scully, Boudville, George, Dawson, Fletcher, Gunther, Head, and Pinto.

settlement of the Portuguese-Eurasian community in Penang. The Kampung Serani Eurasian community is believed to have descended from a group of Portuguese-Eurasian migrants who arrived in Penang with some Portuguese priests in the early 1800s from the island of Phuket located in Thailand.[9]

The Kampung Serani Portuguese-Eurasian community was therefore closely associated with the Church in Pulau Tikus, and the residents commonly considered the land on which Kampung Serani stood to be part of their ancestral heritage.[10] During my fieldwork, the villagers claimed that the land was Endowment Land, that is religious charity land held in trust by the Church for the Portuguese-Eurasian community. While each had a different version of who had donated the land to the Church, they all agreed that the land was meant for the welfare of poor Portuguese Eurasians. This became one of the main contentions of the residents in this conflict, although no documentary proof of their claim was produced.

The Eurasians in Kampung Serani were seen by other Eurasians in Penang as the "poorer" section of their community.[11] This was because, since the 1960s, the more affluent residents had moved out of the village into middle-class housing estates in other parts of Penang Island.[12]

The Church

I shall briefly explain the administrative structures of the Church relevant to its decision to develop the *kampung* land. As mentioned earlier, the land on which Kampung Serani stood belongs to the Roman Catholic Church, and comes under the jurisdiction of the Roman Catholic Diocese of Penang.[13]

The parish of the Catholic Church of the Immaculate Conception, located at the edge of Kampung Serani towards the intersection of Burma Road and College Lane, is responsible for the administration of the village land. The parish priests here have long seen to matters of tenancy in the *kampung* as well as collecting

---

[9] See Chong Yoke Lin Linda, "The Portuguese-Eurasians (Serani of Penang)," p. 118; Fr. Manuel Teixeira, *The Portuguese Missions in Malacca and Singapore (1511-1958)*, Vol. II (Singapore and Lisboa: Agencia Geral Do, 1963), p. 327; James F. Augustine, *Bygone Eurasia: The Life Story of the Eurasians of Malaya* (Kuala Lumpur: Rajiv Printers, 1981), p. 10; and Rev. Felix George Lee, *The Catholic Church in Malaya* (Singapore: Eastern Universities Press, 1963), p. 46.

[10] Chong Yoke Lin Linda, "The Portuguese-Eurasians (Serani of Penang)," p. 129.

[11] The residents were largely of working-class background. Some examples of their occupations were: administrative personnel, telephone operator, schoolteacher, postal clerk, police inspector, hairdresser, land surveyor, factory production worker, manual laborer, mechanic, and hawker.

[12] According to a 1987 survey of about 58 percent of Penang's total Eurasian population, the largest number of Eurasians now live in the southern and western suburbs of the island (19.7 percent), followed by the northern suburb of Tanjung Bunga (16.7 percent), with the rest on the mainland. See Penang Eurasian Association, "Penang Eurasian Community Population Survey 1987," Research Paper, p. 2.

[13] The Roman Catholic Diocese of Penang covers the northern states of Perlis, Kedah, Perak, Penang, and Kelantan. Two other Roman Catholic Dioceses in West Malaysia are the Diocese of Kuala Lumpur and the Diocese for the states of Johor and Melaka. A Bishop heads each of these Dioceses. The Bishop is appointed by the Pope upon recommendations from the priests in each of the Dioceses.

ground rent from the residents.[14] The decision to develop the land was made by the then Bishop of Penang on the recommendation of the Financial Commission of the Roman Catholic Diocese of Penang.[15] The Financial Commission is one of the "advisory governments" to the Roman Catholic Diocese of Penang whose function is to advise or meet and discuss matters of finance with the Bishop.[16]

The decision on the development of Kampung Serani was primarily made by the Financial Commission. But this does not necessarily mean that there was a consensus on the matter among other members of the Church establishment. My interviews with a priest, a Catholic Brother, and a Church leader suggest that the Church authorities themselves were split in their opinions on how the Church had handled the conflict. While one person thought that it was a mistake on the part of the Church for not having imposed a condition on the developer to provide alternative housing for the residents, another individual disagreed, saying that the residents "had never bettered themselves but sat and waited at the expense of cheap ground rent from the Church." The third informant did not want to comment but instead pointed to the "dilapidated" condition of the "eye-sore" buildings in "the *lallang*-covered" *kampung* as causes for development.[17] Thus, while the Church decision was in one sense collective, its handling of the conflict was not uncontested within the Church itself.

This situation made it difficult to place the onus of the decision to develop the *kampung* land onto any particular person in the Church establishment. Nevertheless, as the chairperson of the Financial Commission was at this time a parish priest at the Church of the Immaculate Conception, the residents largely blamed him, and he has since been transferred to another parish. The antagonism towards this particular priest was exacerbated in the later stages of the conflict when, in the court proceedings instituted by the Bishop to evict the tenants, the priest was given the power to file affidavit evidence on the Bishop's behalf against the residents.

At this point, I should also note that the Kampung Serani case was not the first land development controversy involving the Church in the Pulau Tikus area. In 1982, the College General Catholic Seminary grounds, an 18.68 acre site located across Kelawei Road from Kampung Serani, was sold to a private developer. The sale and rezoning of the site sparked protests from Penangites.[18]

---

[14] The Church of the Immaculate Conception dates back to 1811, when it is said that the priest who led the Portuguese Eurasians to Kampung Serani first built a wooden church on the *kampung* site. See Teixeira, *The Portuguese Missions*, p. 327; Khoo Su Nin, *Streets of Georgetown*, p. 57. The present church was constructed in 1899. See ibid., p. 57.

[15] During the fourteen-year long Kampung Serani conflict, there was a change of Bishop.

[16] The Bishop appoints the members of the Financial Commission. Membership on the Financial Commission is comprised of priests and Church members who are generally "considered to be good in money matters." The other Commissions are the Justice and Peace Commission, the Pastoral Commission, and the Catechetical Commission. The Bishop is the de facto head of all these Commissions. (This information was obtained from my interview with A.A., a member of the Justice and Peace Commission, on September 11, 1993.)

[17] *Lallang* is the Malay word for weeds.

[18] The decision on the sale of the seminary grounds was made by all the Bishops in Malaysia (including the Dioceses in East Malaysia), as it was a regional seminary. For more details of this case, see Chapter Seven.

The Developer[19]

I shall call the property developer which entered into an joint-agreement with the Church to develop the Kampung Serani land Company Dreamland.

Company Dreamland was incorporated in 1979 by three Chinese businessmen, who own a major private company running supermarket-cum-department stores, pastry shops, and clothing outlets.[20] The original agreement entered into by the parties provided for Company Dreamland to clear the site and build shop-houses and terrace houses, and allocated a share of any profit on a 60:40 basis, with Company Dreamland entitled to 60 percent.[21] However, Company Dreamland ran into financial difficulties in the recession of the mid-1980s. In 1992, moves to develop the *kampung* site commenced after Company Dreamland was taken over by an Indonesian and domestic joint venture capital company, which I shall call Company Highview. Following the take-over, the development plans for the village site were redefined into a commercial center and a condominium project.

Company Highview bought into company Dreamland in 1991 by taking up half of the company's share equity.[22] In this joint venture, Company Highview became the active partner in pursuing the Kampung Serani development project, and all subsequent negotiations on the Kampung Serani conflict were undertaken by Company Highview. Company Highview itself has been very active in Penang, with three condominium projects in the Pulau Tikus area alone and a further three (two condominiums and a commercial project) on Penang Island.

The Mediator

Sometime in 1984, the Penang Eurasian Association (PEA) became a mediator on behalf of the *kampung* residents in their negotiations with the Church and the developer over terms of compensation for vacating the village.

Lead by elite Eurasians, the PEA has increasingly sought to legitimize its position as the guardian of Eurasian culture and identity, particularly since the mid-1980s. A significant factor behind this trend is attributed to a national government policy which requires official intercession by the PEA on behalf of the Eurasian community for Eurasians to benefit from a privileged government investment scheme.

In 1984, the Malaysian government opened the Amanah Saham Nasional (ASN), a national unit trust scheme, to Eurasians of Portuguese descent who are commonly referred to as Portuguese Eurasians.[23] This national investment scheme is

---

[19] All details on the developers involved in the conflict are based on a search I conducted at the Registrar of Companies, Penang, on January 29, 1993, unless stated otherwise.

[20] In 1984, this private company bought into a publicly listed company trading in pharmaceuticals and medical supplies and in 1985 become a major shareholder (*The Star*, July 27, 1993, Business Section, p. 4). A member of the royal family from the state of Negeri Sembilan was the Chairman of this publicly listed pharmaceutical company in 1993.

[21] This is from the Minutes of the Dialogue between the Kampung Serani Residents and the Bishop, dated January 10, 1980.

[22] Company Highview itself was incorporated as a property development company in 1984 with 51 percent domestic and 49 percent Sino-Indonesian capital. By 1992, the capital ratio had shifted to 52 percent Malaysian and 48 percent Sino-Indonesian.

[23] The ASN, launched on April 1, 1981, was established under the New Economic Policy to promote active distribution of corporate wealth among individuals within the *bumiputera*

strictly reserved for *bumiputeras* (Malays and other indigenous groups). As such the eligibility of the Portuguese Eurasians may at first seem "puzzling" as they have yet to be officially recognized as *bumiputeras*.[24] However, the "eligibility" of the Portuguese Eurasians for privileges generally reserved for Malays and other indigenous groups can be explained. As I discuss in Chapter Six, it is a repercussion of current identity politics, where certain groups have successfully laid claims to indigenousness on the basis of their historical presence in Malaysia. The Portuguese-Eurasian community is one of these groups, as their history in Malaysia dates back to the sixteenth century in Melaka.

In order to qualify for the ASN, Portuguese Eurasians must be able to prove their Portuguese descent. The initial requirement is documentary evidence in the form of a birth certificate stating that the person's ethnicity is "Eurasian." Then come the various discretionary processes overseen by the Eurasian Associations in the different states. In Penang, this function is performed by the PEA. The other means of verification of Portuguese descent is through family names and adherence to the Roman Catholic faith, the legitimacy of which must ultimately be vetted by the Regidor (the community leader of the Portuguese settlement) in Melaka. The PEA is the channel for processing these applications in the state of Penang. All applications in the state must be first vetted by the PEA executive committee. The applications are then sent to the Regidor in Melaka.

Since the introduction of this national policy, the Portuguese-Eurasian community in Malaysia has been actively lobbying for official recognition of their *bumiputera* status. Although their discourse singles out Portuguese descent, its main preoccupation is reclaiming a Malayness as part of their heritage. These Portuguese-Eurasians claim that their culture is closer to Malay culture than to that of the Portuguese. In fact, they have coined the term "Luso-Malay" to refer to themselves, which reflects an overt identification with the Malays.

In keeping with the terms of this national debate, the PEA leaders have been actively engaged in constructing a homogeneous Eurasian history and culture focused on this Portuguese-Eurasian identity, in spite of the heterogeneous nature of the Penang Eurasian community. We will see how the PEA's engagement in this construction of a Portuguese-Eurasian identity not only determined positions in the Kampung Serani negotiation process, but also finally won the PEA a "heritage house," a gift from the developer to showcase Portuguese-Eurasian history and culture in Penang.

---

community. See Malaysia, *Malaysia Year Book 1990-91* (Kuala Lumpur: Berita Publishing Sdn. Bhd, 1990), p. 290. Another sister scheme is the Amanah Saham Bumiputera (ASB). Both unit trusts are run by the Permodalan Nasional Berhad (the National Equity Corporation). In 1993, the ASN declared 12.2 percent dividends while the ASB paid 9 percent dividends and 4.5 percent bonus—the highest rates of return in the histories of the two schemes (*New Straits Times*, November 30, 1993, p. 1). There is an imposition of a RM50,000 ceiling for individual investments in these funds to constrain wealth concentration.

[24] Eurasians are categorized as a non-indigenous population under the grouping of "Others" in the Malaysian Population Census. See Malaysia, *Malaysia Year Book 1992-93* (Kuala Lumpur: Berita Publishing Sdn. Bhd, 1992), p. 74.

CHRONOLOGY OF A CONFLICT: TOWARDS A RECONSTRUCTION OF EVENTS

What follows is a reconstruction of the series of events that took place in the Kampung Serani conflict between 1980 and 1994. This reconstruction is based largely on data gathered from my conversations and interviews with all parties involved in the conflict—the *kampung* residents, the PEA, the Church authorities, and the developer. My reconstruction cannot be an entirely objective representation of the facts, but is, rather, a narration of events as perceived, most significantly, by the *kampung* residents who were the most directly affected in this conflict. It is their recollection of the sequence of events that I have relied upon. An outline of the sequence of events is provided in Chart 4.1 in Appendix F.

I have endeavored to present the details in chronological order, as timing is important to this narration in two major ways. First, it will indicate the significant points at which the historical and cultural arguments first emerged and then shifted over time as a result of their contestation, negotiation, and reconstruction. Second, as will also become evident in the later chapters, the course of events in the Kampung Serani conflict correlates with Malaysia's property cycles.

There are several instances when I skip ahead in time in order to put forth an argument or to signal the interrelationship between events. I have also included some relevant circumstantial accounts to provide better insight. We must also bear in mind that the resulting narrative is essentially a montage of often disparate and overlapping events, and is thus undoubtedly a neater account than the actual circumstances.

Lastly, as it is inevitable that this reconstruction will be considered controversial and sensitive by many of those involved, I have tried as far as possible to base my narration on written documents such as reports, letters, records of meetings, circulars, pamphlets, newspaper articles, and so on, from which the veracity of these events can be confirmed. These documents were largely provided by the *kampung* residents. I have also specifically referred to two PEA documents which were specifically prepared by the Association to clarify its involvement in the Kampung Serani conflict. These documents are: "The Penang Eurasian Association and the Kampung Serani Issue Report" (PEA Report 1992), and the PEA's "Annual General Meeting Report, 1993."[25] Needless to say, the interpretation of these events is mine alone.

1980—Setting the Scene

Towards the end of 1979, Kampung Serani was swarming with rumors that the Church had signed a deal with a property developer to develop the area. This rumor was confirmed when the residents received eviction notices from the Bishop's lawyers in January 1980.[26]

---

[25] Penang Eurasian Association, "The Penang Eurasian Association and the Kampung Serani Issue Report," Typescript, dated June 20, 1992; and Penang Eurasian Association, "Annual General Meeting Report, 1993," Typescript.

[26] Lawyers representing the Bishop issued the eviction notices dated January 1, 1980. These notices gave the residents until March 30, 1980 to deliver vacant possession of their premises. There was no mention of any terms of compensation.

Upon receiving the eviction notices, the residents held a meeting at which time they set up a Residents' Association to represent their interests.[27] They decided to seek an audience with the Bishop to discuss the matter.[28] This was to be the first and only meeting between the Bishop and the Residents' Association throughout the fourteen-year conflict. At the dialogue, the residents handed a letter of appeal against the eviction notices to the Bishop. As it marks the initial tone of the residents' appeal demands, I reproduce the major part of this letter below:

> We kindly request you, my Lord to kindly inform us of what compensation is accorded to us, chiefly alternate accommodation. We ask you to consider the plight we are in. We are unable to find new lodgings and accommodation, together with the fact that the majority of us have lived here for a long time and that a few are advanced in age. The present trend of events have caused us very much worry and acute anxiety.[29]

The dialogue centered on the residents' request for alternate accommodation in the form of low-cost flats, either on the *kampung* site or on other land belonging to the Church. At this initial negotiation attempt, the residents reminded the Church of its long history in Kampung Serani, and asserted their status as descendants of the pioneer group of Portuguese Eurasians who arrived in Penang in the 1800s.

When the Church made no concrete promises during the dialogue, the residents decided to take other measures.

Early Itinerary—The Search for Political Patronage

The residents decided to contact two Penang state-level politicians to press their case. One was the State Assemblyman representing the constituency in which Pulau Tikus is located and the other was a State Executive Councilor who was the head of the State Housing Committee.

At the meeting, the two politicians advised the residents to seek details of the development plan by writing to the various relevant state authorities as well as to the Church.[30] The Residents' Association acted on this advice. The Association's letter to the Bishop's lawyers prompted this reply:

> Please be informed that under the terms of the Joint Venture Agreement entered into by our client and the Developers, the responsibility of paying compensation, if any, is that of the Developers. In view of this we would advise you to deal directly with the Developers in future as regards the matter raised by you in your aforesaid letter.[31]

---

[27] From Minutes of Residents' Association meeting, dated January 9, 1980.

[28] Details of this dialogue are based on the minutes taken by the Residents' Association of the dialogue with the Bishop, dated January 10, 1980.

[29] Letter dated January 10, 1980.

[30] This meeting was held on January 20, 1980 at a coffee shop in Pulau Tikus. Details of this meeting are based on the minutes of this meeting taken by the Residents' Association, dated January 20, 1980.

[31] Letter dated March 12, 1980.

Soon after, in April 1980, the residents received a letter from Company Dreamland's lawyers requesting a meeting.[32] The residents rejected the offer.[33] At this point, they did not want to deal with the developer, as they believed the Church would be more compassionate toward their plight. Company Dreamland was not deterred and sent one of its "agents" to negotiate terms of compensation with individual residents.[34] No one accepted the developer's offer at this stage. The residents had not yet given up their fight.

History and Heritage

The residents realized that an effective way to make the Church consider their demands seriously was to get public sympathy on their side. They turned to the media to highlight their struggle. Here, they focused on the history and the Eurasian heritage of Kampung Serani to garner media attention.

As a result of their efforts, the first press coverage was an article on Noah's Ark in *The New Straits Times* on October 6, 1980.[35] The Residents' Association also contacted the newspaper for which I then worked, the *National Echo*, which led to my article in that newspaper on November 3, 1984.[36]

If we consider the residents' discourse at this stage of the conflict, we will note the subsequent re-workings of this discourse by the PEA at the height of the conflict in 1992. The earliest argument in the residents' repertoire concerned the historical and cultural significance of Noah's Ark. In their argument for its preservation, they focused on the fact that the building was the first school in Pulau Tikus. Noah's Ark, they argued, represented a piece of Penang's history. Many older Penangites, who were not Eurasian, had also received their early education there, and felt proud of the achievements of Noah's Ark.

In conjunction with their arguments about the value of the Noah's Ark building, the residents also asserted the historical significance of Kampung Serani itself. In this, their focus was on the historical link between the Church and the Eurasian community in Kampung Serani. They highlighted their ancestors' role in, and contributions to, the establishment and growth of the Church. Invoking this heritage, the residents contended that the Church could not ignore their request for alternative accommodation.

---

[32] Letter from the law firm representing Company Dreamland, dated April 18, 1980.

[33] Letter from Residents' Association to law firm representing Company Dreamland, dated April 24, 1980.

[34] This information is based on notes compiled by the Secretary of the Residents' Association titled, "Our general impressions regarding meeting with Datuk K.G.K.," (n.d.). In Malaysia, it is common for the developer to engage "agents" who act as its intermediaries to cajole and intimidate residents living on a proposed development site to accept the terms of compensation offered by the developer and vacate their premises. The "agents" usually earn commission from the value of each successful transaction.

[35] This article in the "Sri Tanjung Column," was captioned "Campaign to save 'Noah's Ark'." The article provoked two responses to the editor of the newspaper calling for the preservation of Noah's Ark, which were published in *The Star*, October 13, 1980 and *The Star*, November 10, 1980.

[36] The article was in two parts, captioned "Residents in the dark over rezoning move" and "Tracing roots of the Eurasian community." *National Echo*, November 3, 1984, pp. 28-30.

Why did the residents put Noah's Ark at the forefront of their arguments, so that its fate became so eminent that it rendered insignificant their other concerns? In my opinion, this was initially a matter of strategy. Considering their action within a wider Malaysian context, we must remember that Kampung Serani was one of many villages in the country facing the threat of redevelopment. In this context, the following hypotheses may explain their choice of action. First, the residents would have realized that portraying their case as one that figured just another *kampung* resisting redevelopment would not be an effective way to gain the public attention they wanted. Second, they would have known that if they portrayed their struggle as one pitting a community of Catholic Eurasians against the Church, the conflict could easily be seen as an internal religious squabble and deemed too sensitive an issue to attract public involvement. Third, they would have realized that, by portraying their struggle as one that sought to preserve Noah's Ark—a relic of some historical significance not only to the *kampung* community but also to the wider public—they could not only attract attention to their plight, but also act to validate their historical and cultural assertions in relation to Kampung Serani itself. The residents' attempt to represent themselves as a culturally unique group was in line with the trend of a heightened rhetoric of culture and identity at both the state and wider levels of Malaysian society.

The residents' strategy was to use Noah's Ark as a dominant symbol in their discourse on Eurasian cultural identity to ensure that the articulation of the historical and cultural heritage of Kampung Serani, and thus their plight, would be heard.

Bearing this in mind, let us consider the other strategies employed by the residents.

Other Strategies

While the "impasse" in negotiations remained, the Penang City Council issued a notification on August 20, 1983 that it was going to re-zone the Kampung Serani land. The land was to be re-zoned from its original "residential" to a "semi-residential and commercial" zoning. This notification served as clear warning to the residents that fast action was needed.

At this point, the residents decided to seek the assistance of the Consumers' Association of Penang (CAP), a local consumer activist group, which was also known to take up the causes of ground tenants facing eviction.[37] CAP advised the *kampung* residents to send memoranda of objection to the re-zoning of the two plots of land to the City Council.[38] The residents' contact with CAP then faded, only to be reestablished in 1992, when the residents needed legal assistance against the court proceedings to evict them. One of the reasons for the lapsed contact with CAP

---

[37] In the early 1980s, the CAP represented ground tenants in a tragic case of eviction which resulted in the death of a woman ground tenant in the Thean Teik Estate development project in Penang. See Chan Chee Khoon, Chin Wey Tze, and Loh Kok Wah, *Thean Teik and the Other Side of Development* (Penang: Aliran, 1983).

[38] The residents' protest letter against the rezoning was dated October 29, 1984. Copies of the letter were also sent to the Prime Minister's Department, the Penang Chief Minister's Office, the Titular Roman Catholic Bishop of Penang, and the Ministry of Land and Mines. CAP also sent a protest letter against the rezoning to the City Council. By November 1984, the rezoning was still not approved. I have no records of when the rezoning was actually approved.

was that the residents decided to approach another would-be patron whom they thought would be more effective in mediating on their behalf in the dispute with the Church. This patron was the Penang Eurasian Association.

Enter the Elite

It was at a Residents' Association meeting on February 12, 1984 that the decision was made to request the members of the executive committee of the PEA to assist in their negotiations for compensation with the Church.[39] The decision was made because the residents felt that the PEA leaders had better access to the Church authorities, as many of them were also Church leaders. The PEA leaders agreed to the residents' request. At around the same time, the residents of the first three houses in Kampung Serani settled for cash compensation with Company Dreamland.[40]

Soon after this, the effects of the mid-1980s economic recession began to be felt. Company Dreamland encountered financial difficulties and as a consequence its development plans for Kampung Serani lapsed. The activities of the Residents' Association also wound down. There was a slight flurry of activity in 1987 when Company Dreamland sent out fresh eviction notices to the residents, after which the residents revived the Residents' Association and elected a new group of committee members. Things again came to a halt after this, although the tranquillity was short lived.

A Whirlwind Affair—the 1990s

With the national property boom generated by the flourishing Malaysian economy, the Kampung Serani development plan was re-instated in 1990. By early 1991, rumors once again pervaded Kampung Serani, this time about Company Dreamland's joint venture with another property developer, Company Highview.

I should make it clear that although the name of Company Dreamland did not change after the joint deal, I have chosen not to retain the name Dreamland but use the name Company Highview after this merger to indicate the entry of a new player in the dispute.

The change of ownership was seen as an ominous sign by the residents, as they knew that Company Highview was an active developer in the Pulau Tikus area. True to its reputation, Company Highview pushed things along, and in early 1992 sent out fresh eviction notices to the residents.[41]

As in the past, the eviction notices were issued in the name of the Bishop. However, this time, the notices were sent by the legal firm representing Company Highview, and not by the Bishop's own lawyers. This change marked the

---

[39] Report of the Residents' Association meeting, dated February 12, 1984, entitled, "Summary of events happened [sic] to Kampung Serani from Feb. '84 to 1987."

[40] One household settled for compensation of RM40,000, as the owner was migrating to Australia. The other two houses belonged to a Catholic priest, who did not live in the *kampung*, and were rented out. This is based on information from an undated compilation titled "List of Residents and Compensation Details" by the second elected Secretary of the Residents' Association.

[41] These eviction notices were issued between February 1992 and July 1992.

integration of the Church and the developer as one party. Their integration was further cemented in 1993 and 1994 when the Bishop, as the landowner, instituted court action on behalf of the developer to evict the residents, in which he was represented by Company Highview's lawyers. In these circumstances of intertwining interests, it became increasingly difficult to distinguish the Church as a separate entity from the developer. As we shall see in the next chapter, this was to have deep repercussions on the Church's relations with the residents as the conflict intensified.

For the rest of this section, I shall elaborate on the intensive series of mediations that took place when things heated up, beginning in 1991.

Of Mediator and Competitor

In order to have a better understanding of the series of mediations that followed the 1992 eviction notices, we need to bear in mind that at this point in time, the Pulau Tikus area was engulfed by development activities (see Chapter Seven). This environment was important in prompting the PEA to become actively involved as a mediator in the Kampung Serani conflict.

Some time early in 1991, a PEA leader was contacted by another property development company active in the Pulau Tikus area which expressed its interest in developing the village site.[42] I shall call this developer Company Golden-Heights. (Company Golden-Heights is closely connected to another major developer in the Pulau Tikus area, which I shall call Company Golden-Point.)[43] Company Golden-Heights stated its readiness to offer the PEA a *"permanent structure"* in recognition of the "Eurasian heritage" in Kampung Serani.[44]

Why did Company Golden-Heights choose to approach the PEA, and not the *kampung* residents, when they could after all have contacted the Residents' Association? It seems reasonable to assume that Company Golden-Heights' move was prompted by the socially recognized role of the PEA as the guardian of Eurasian culture and identity in Penang, a role it has held increasingly since the mid-1980s.[45] I will further elaborate on this matter in Chapter Six.

On receiving this offer from Company Golden-Heights, the PEA leaders met with the Bishop to persuade the Church to consider it. The initial reaction of the PEA leaders was to meet with the Bishop and not with the residents. At this

---

[42] All details of the involvement of the PEA from this point on, unless indicated otherwise, are based on the "PEA Report 1992" prepared by the PEA.

[43] Among Company Golden-Heights' projects in Pulau Tikus are a new commercial project and an apartment project located immediately opposite the Church of the Immaculate Conception. For more information on its joint-venture projects with Company Golden-Point, see Chapters Seven and Eight.

[44] "PEA Report 1992," p. 1 (my emphasis). In 1980 when the conflict first began, another developer had vied for the right to develop Kampung Serani. This company had written to the Church and the *kampung* residents stating its offer of thirty flats as compensation for the residents. The Church did not respond to this offer. (This information is based on a letter from lawyers representing this developer to the Residents' Association, dated March 27, 1980.)

[45] The *kampung* residents pointed out that this contact was also facilitated by the friendship between a Company Golden-Heights employee and a PEA leader. The employee was a Eurasian male who graduated from the School of Housing, Building and Planning, at the University Science Malaysia, in Penang.

meeting with the Bishop, the Association leaders appropriated the historical and cultural arguments in support of Kampung Serani to call on the Church to consider Company Golden-Heights' new offer. The community leaders justified their involvement as being for "the needs of the Eurasian community."[46]

By this time, Company Highview had bought into Company Dreamland. During negotiations between Company Golden-Heights, the PEA, and the Church, Company Highview was also moving swiftly regarding the development of Kampung Serani. Company Highview had sent its "agents" to negotiate with the *kampung* residents, targeting the sub-tenants first. They also used local "Pulau Tikus thugs" to approach the sub-tenants.[47] No residents accepted their overtures at this stage, but these incidents created distress and unrest among them. As the agitation among the *kampung* residents heightened, the PEA's role as mediator intensified in equal measure to its ever louder claims that it represented and safeguarded Eurasian heritage in Penang.

PEA's Reworking of Discourse and Demands for a Heritage House

With tension mounting in the *kampung*, the PEA leaders requested a meeting with the Bishop, again to bring to his notice the "explosive nature of the situation."[48] The PEA leaders used the offer by Company Golden-Heights to pressure the Church and Company Highview. Here, the community elite requested that the "the Bishop write to developer [Company Highview], suggesting that the needs of the PEA are considered with a permanent structure [my emphasis] and the residents adequately compensated."[49]

Subsequently, the Association leaders organized a meeting with the *kampung* residents to inform them of Company Golden-Heights' offer. The residents' recollection of this meeting was that the PEA told them that Company Golden-Heights was ready to negotiate better terms of compensation for the residents and that it had offered to build a "clubhouse" for the Association.

The residents recounted how the executives of the Association talked of the possibilities of the "clubhouse" as somewhat similar to the Portuguese Square in Melaka—a tourist attraction and a center of Portuguese-Eurasian culture (for details see Chapter Six).

Since its establishment, the PEA had never had premises of its own, but had been operating from the homes of its executive committee members. In 1991, it started a community center called Kaza Eurasian in a rented building.[50]

The *kampung* residents were not opposed, at this stage, to the developer's offer of a PEA "clubhouse" on the *kampung* site as part of any solution to the conflict. After all, most of the villagers were members of the PEA and had benefited as subscribers to the ASN unit trust investment schemes. In fact, many of them recalled that when they first heard of the offer, their hopes were actually raised. They

---

[46] "PEA Report 1992," p. 2.

[47] Information from the remaining Kampung Serani residents. See Chapter Five.

[48] "PEA Report 1992," p. 3.

[49] Ibid.

[50] In late 1993, the center moved to larger premises in a rented government bungalow. The opening ceremony of the Kaza Eurasian center was held on September 27, 1993. It was attended by the Chief Minister of Penang (see *The Star*, September 27, 1993, p. 10).

believed that if Company Golden-Heights was willing to offer a "clubhouse" to the PEA, they had a better chance of receiving more favorable terms of compensation for themselves.

I want to draw particular attention to the language of "clubhouse" used at this stage of the negotiation process. As the PEA continued its demands for a compensatory building, its use of the term "clubhouse" eventually gave way to the term "heritage house." This change in appellation of the proposed compensatory building represents, in my view, an attempt to align the building to the wider interests of the larger Eurasian community. As a "clubhouse," it could be interpreted as merely serving the interests of the PEA.[51]

Throughout my fieldwork, I found that the residents persistently referred to the compensatory building offered to the PEA as the "clubhouse." They refused to recognize the term "heritage house" even after an agreement on the matter was eventually signed between the Church, Company Highview and the PEA.[52] According to the residents, "clubhouse" was the term used by the PEA leaders during their first meeting to discuss the offer from Company Golden-Heights. The residents argued that the compensatory building was entirely for the self-interest of the Association and could never be a "heritage house," as it could not replace the Noah's Ark building, which was eventually demolished.

In fact, an examination of the "PEA Report 1992" indicates that the PEA leaders were aware of the sensitivities involved in the term "clubhouse." This is reflected by the fact that the "PEA Report 1992" documents events during this meeting without any mention of the term "clubhouse." The report instead used more neutral language to describe the building offered by Company Golden-Heights—"a permanent structure." Towards the end of the report, in relation to a stage when more concrete negotiations had taken place, the term "heritage house" was used. In the next two chapters, I will explore this controversy further.

From this point on, there was an escalation of the conflict. It was evident that Company Highview was determined to clear the *kampung* land of all the buildings on it. By this time, a few of the sub-tenants had already settled for cash compensation and had moved out of the village. For the rest, things would become unpleasant.

The first hostile incident occurred on March 12, 1992, when a resident's house was partially bulldozed by Company Highview before any agreement over compensation with the house-owner. This owner was a sixty-six year old female living on her own.[53] Although the house remained standing after the initial bulldozing, Company Highview successfully demolished it on its second attempt.[54]

In a more prosperous community, the act of bulldozing before any compensation agreement was reached could have led to court action, as the residents were not illegal "squatters" but ground tenants (as the courts would later rule). To remove

---

[51] In Malaysia, a "clubhouse" is generally associated with recreational pursuits. There was a boom in "clubbing"—the rush to join "clubs" as a sign of social prestige in Penang with the increased affluence resulting from the booming economy in the 1990s. For details of contemporary urban changes in Penang, see Chapter Seven.

[52] See *The Star*, September 17, 1994, p. 20.

[53] For details see the case of Mary Carrier in Chapter Five.

[54] The *kampung* residents propped up what they could of the remains of the house in an effort to maintain a structure on the site in order to make a statement that the developer had "illegally" bulldozed the house.

ground tenants, a landowner must obtain an order of the Court, and cannot legally resort to "self-help." Even if the residents were indeed "squatters," this course of self-help by the developer without the aid of the courts would not have been encouraged by common law.[55] Nevertheless, Company Highview got away with this legally and morally questionable act.

During this period, tension was running high among the residents and Company Highview had effectively played on this sentiment by giving an example of its determination to evict the residents. It was obvious that Company Highview had carefully chosen its target—a lone, aged, and female resident, from whom resistance to the developer's act was least likely.

Concurrent to these events, the PEA leaders stepped up their level of involvement and arguments by initiating a campaign to save the Noah's Ark building. During this period one PEA leader—an academic by profession—wrote an article on the historical significance of Noah's Ark as the first school in Pulau Tikus.[56]

The article demonstrates two things: firstly, the differences between this current discourse and the residents' arguments in the 1980s; secondly, the PEA's engagement with wider constructions of Portuguese-Eurasian identity in contemporary Malaysia.

Essentially, the author states that there is a need to preserve the Noah's Ark building due to its contribution to modern Malaysian education and its monumental value to the Portuguese-Eurasian community in Pulau Tikus.

As we can see, Noah's Ark was prominent in this discourse, as in the residents' earlier arguments. The striking difference was that, this time, while positing the significance of the Noah's Ark school, the author called for a recognition of the Eurasian community's contribution to modern education in Malaysia through the Catholic missionary schools. This contrasts with the residents' earlier arguments in which, along with the Noah's Ark building, the history and cultural significance of Kampung Serani was emphasized.

The author was therefore pursuing another agenda: the identification of a distinct Eurasian contribution to the nation.

In order to understand the basis of the PEA's argument, we need to know the background of the connection between the Catholic missionary schools and the Eurasian community in Malaysia. The Noah's Ark school was first set up by Catholic priests in Pulau Tikus parish and taken over by the Christian Brothers Catholic Mission. The Catholic missions, in particular the Christian Brothers and the De La Salle Brothers, played a significant role in laying the foundations of

---

[55] The legal position of squatters and tenants is stipulated in Order 113 of the English Rules of the Supreme Court 1965 (the equivalent of Order 89 in the Malaysian Rules of the High Court, 1980). If one is found to be a squatter, the owner is not obliged to go to the courts to obtain possession. Although the law permits an owner to obtain a remedy by his or her own act, it does not encourage such a course. I quote a High Court judgement in one of the Bishop's lawsuits against the residents to demonstrate this legal principle; "In a civilised society, the courts should themselves provide a remedy which is speedy and effective; and thus make self-help unnecessary. The courts of common law have done this for centuries. The owner is entitled to go to the court and obtain an order that the owner 'do recover' the land, and to issue a writ of possession immediately." See Anne Khoo, "Titular Roman Catholic Bishop of Penang V. Stephen Ramachandran: High Court (Penang)—Originating Summons No. 24-805-92." *Malayan Law Journal* 3 (1994): 9-10.

[56] See Sibert, "Preserve 'Noah's Ark'."

modern education in Malaysia through the missionary schools they set up all over the country. Eurasians formed a majority of the students in these early missionary schools, and eventually Eurasians also predominated among the earliest school teachers in Malaysia.[57] This is the foundation for Eurasian claims demanding recognition for their contribution to modern Malaysian education.

A second new element in this article on Noah's Ark is the emphasis on the language used in the early days of the Noah's Ark school. The medium of instruction was Malay.[58] Given that in the early days of the Noah's Ark school, the majority of the students were said to be Eurasians,[59] the author is clearly arguing for a construction of Eurasians as Malay-speaking. In the case of the Noah's Ark school, the majority of Eurasian students were Portuguese Eurasians from Kampung Serani and its vicinity, and thus there is a particularly strong association between the Malay language and Portuguese-Eurasian identity. This has been noted elsewhere. For example, Chong Yoke Lin Linda noted that the older generation of Eurasians in Kampung Serani spoke Malay, along with some Portuguese and Siamese.[60] The essential difference between the PEA and the residents' line of argument was the PEA's emphasis on the Eurasian contribution to the nation (through education) and the basic Malayness of Eurasians (as demonstrated by their use of the Malay language).

However, this emphasis by the PEA is essentially politically motivated and, I maintain, in line with their current reclamation of a "Malayness" or indigeneity in their construction of a new Portuguese-Eurasian identity (see Chapter Six). Furthermore, this interest in claiming indigeneity is reflected in another PEA argument during this stage of the conflict, which is that the ancestry of the Eurasian community in Kampung Serani could be traced to the earliest Portuguese-Eurasian community in Melaka.[61] According to this argument, the Portuguese Eurasians who arrived in Pulau Tikus in the 1800s were descended from a group of Portuguese Eurasians who fled Dutch persecution in Melaka. This group, it was said, first settled in the Celebes and then moved to Phuket before they finally came to Pulau Tikus.

I now discuss the strategies used by the PEA to disseminate their reworked discourse.

Public Protest

After the first bulldozing incident, the PEA leaders met again with the Bishop. At this meeting, Noah's Ark became the main focus of discussion, with the PEA leaders focusing on the need for the preservation of Noah's Ark as a "symbol of

---

[57] See Augustine, *Bygone Eurasia*, p. 18; Rev. Anthony MacNamara, "The History of St. Xavier's 1852-1992," in *Xaverian* (the magazine of St. Xavier's Institution), Penang, 1992, pp. i-xxv; Lee, *The Catholic Church in Malaya*, pp. 43-44; and Bernard Sta Maria, *My People, My Country* (Malacca: The Malacca Portuguese Development Centre, 1982), p. 114.

[58] See Sibert, "Preserve 'Noah's Ark'."

[59] Ibid.

[60] Chong Yoke Lin Linda, "The Portuguese-Eurasian (Serani of Penang)," p. 123.

[61] This is from the speeches delivered by four PEA leaders during the protest gathering outside Noah's Ark on March 15, 1992 (see "PEA Report 1992," Appendix).

the Eurasian heritage in Kampung Serani and Pulau Tikus."[62] Nonetheless, the leaders received a non-committal response from the Bishop. Realizing that they were getting nowhere, the leaders decided that the best approach was to seek "public support through the media."[63]

Thereafter, the leaders met with a senior reporter of a local English-language newspaper to seek coverage of the Noah's Ark building. It is no coincidence that this reporter was a relative of one of the PEA leaders.[64]

At this meeting, the idea of staging a protest gathering in front of Noah's Ark was discussed and agreed upon as the best strategy to gain immediate press coverage. The necessary arrangements were made, and *kampung* residents were informed and asked to participate. The residents enthusiastically participated, believing that the demonstration would help their cause. The PEA also contacted the various local newspapers. The day before the protest, the newspaper originally contacted by the Association publicized the impending protest.[65]

On March 15, 1992, a "Coffee Morning-cum-Protest Gathering" was held on the grounds of the Noah's Ark building, attended mainly by Kampung Serani residents, but also by members of the press, concerned individuals, and members of the Penang Heritage Trust movement, a conservationist group in Penang. During this protest, the article written by the PEA leader on the historical significance of the Noah's Ark building was circulated to the press and its arguments were reproduced in the public speeches delivered by the PEA leaders. This protest succeeded in precipitating seven articles in the press the following day.[66]

These reports sparked several responses from the public, including some prominent public figures. For instance, on March 15, 1992, a famous Malay educator, who had received his early education at the Noah's Ark school, wrote to express sympathy with the PEA's calls for the preservation of Noah's Ark.[67] The Secretary of the Penang Heritage Trust movement also responded, echoing the earlier plea to preserve Noah's Ark.[68]

The publicity and the public response all acted to consolidate the PEA's legitimacy as the sole representative of the *kampung* residents. Nonetheless, the legitimacy of the PEA still depended on its recognition by the developer, Company Highview.

---

[62] "PEA Report 1992," p. 4.

[63] Ibid.

[64] Information gathered from the *kampung* residents.

[65] See *The Star*, March 14, 1992, p. 8.

[66] Among these are: "Turn Noah's Ark into heritage house: Eurasian community (PEA)," *The Star*, March 16, 1992 and "PEA queries ownership of Kg Serani land," *New Straits Times*, March 16, 1992. The others were found in the vernacular press.

[67] This article appeared in Datuk Mohamed Sopiee's weekly column with the caption, "Preserve Ark as Eurasian heritage house." As this article appeared on the day of the "protest gathering" itself, it was obviously sparked off by the previous day's news item in *The Star*, March 14, 1992.

[68] This letter-to-the-editor is captioned "'Noah' way to treat community," *The Star*, March 29, 1992.

Issues of Representation: Legitimacy and Identity

The public attention sparked by the protest gathering inevitably led Company Highview to contact the PEA leaders for a meeting. At this meeting, the PEA leaders reported that they "spoke at length on the history of Kampung Serani, Noah's Ark, and the Eurasian Cultural Heritage."[69] Company Highview was said to have expressed sympathy with the PEA's cause, but indicated that the ultimate decision on the matter lay with the Church.

I have mentioned before that the PEA leaders were also leaders in the Catholic Church. Among these, one was the chairperson of the Justice and Peace Commission of the Catholic Church of the Diocese of Penang.[70] This Commission was established based on the idea that "good Christians" must also include justice and peace as essential components of their faith.[71] In fulfilling its role, the Commission has often looked beyond Church issues and at times taken stands on local and international issues, such as the development of Penang Hill and the Gulf War between the United States of America and Iraq.[72] Therefore, the Kampung Serani conflict was an issue well within the concern of the Commission. Not surprisingly, after the meeting with Company Highview, the issue of Kampung Serani was placed on the agenda of one of the Commission's meetings.[73]

It is obvious that this move by the PEA leaders was an attempt to pressure the Bishop into making a commitment to support the PEA's request for a "heritage house." As it turned out, the Bishop was "unable to attend this meeting."[74] However, the PEA leaders did not give up, and a special meeting was arranged a few days later. I quote the reported result of this meeting:

The outcome of this meeting was that the Bishop would call a meeting of the three parties, i.e., the church, developer, and Association.[75]

This is an indication that neither the Church nor the PEA leadership considered that the *kampung* residents who lived on the site were concerned parties in the conflict, or at least not in the negotiation process.

Consequently, the PEA leaders set out to list the Association's priority of demands in order to negotiate with the developer. I reproduce this list of priorities:

---

[69] "PEA Report 1992," p. 5.

[70] This Commission was established in 1985 and has fifteen committee positions, appointed by the Bishop. (This is based on information from an interview with A. A., a member of this Commission, on September 11, 1993.)

[71] This shift to include matters of human dignity has emerged since the 1960s in the theological development of the Catholic Church in Asia. It reflects a time when the Catholic Church in Asia was undergoing a "reflection" process, resulting in a coming together of justice and peace issues with their "faith." Interview with A. A. on September 11, 1993.

[72] I refer to the controversy in 1990 over a proposed plan to build a RM400 million international resort on Penang Hill. Public protests in the "Save the Penang Hill Campaign" successfully led to the rejection of the plan.

[73] "PEA Report 1992," p. 6.

[74] Ibid., p. 5.

[75] Ibid., p. 6.

- Noah's Ark would be rebuilt on its present site. It would be called Heritage House of the Malaysian Eurasians, preserving the best of our past and present for all—Malaysian and visitors alike—to understand and appreciate. Attached to the Ark would be low-cost flats which could be sold or rented to the residents or other Catholics. Both these demands could in some way fulfil the historical association of the community with the land.
- Noah's Ark would be rebuilt, at a different location in *Kampung Serani* but with the same facilities as the above.
- Noah's Ark would be rebuilt at a different location, but with accommodation provided within the building.
- Noah's Ark would be rebuilt at a different location, but without accommodation. [76]

It is evident that the PEA gave a higher priority to the reconstruction of the Noah's Ark building than to accommodation for the residents. The list also indicates that contrary to the notion of preserving the Ark as the material symbol of Eurasian heritage, the PEA was willing to concede that the existing Noah's Ark building would be demolished and replaced by a new one. Having worked out their demands, the PEA proceeded to solicit the residents' list of demands.

To this end, the PEA met with the first Secretary of the Residents' Association, whom the residents had regarded since the beginning of the conflict as the *kampung* spokesperson. This meeting is notable, for it marked the beginning of a rift between the PEA and the *kampung* residents over identity politics, and in particular over the symbols of a specifically Portuguese-Eurasian identity.

According to the *kampung* spokesperson, the meeting became strained. According to him, the main cause of the tension was that the *kampung* residents insisted on compensation in the form of alternative accommodation, either on the village site or elsewhere.[77] Once this note of discord had set in, the *kampung* "spokesperson" recounted that his role as the residents' representative became an issue of contention in the meeting.

An ethnic Indian very much assimilated into the Eurasian way of life, Paul Gunasekaran (a pseudonym),[78] the spokesperson, was a moving force in the articulation of a Portuguese-Eurasian cultural heritage in Kampung Serani from the beginning. Moreover, his role as spokesperson for the *kampung* residents has never been challenged from within.

Nonetheless, Paul recounted how at the meeting with the PEA leaders, the latter challenged his right to speak on behalf of the *kampung* residents, since he was not a Eurasian person.[79] Thus began the strained relationship between Paul and the PEA leaders that ultimately resulted in complete estrangement. This discord also meant that a group of residents, some of whom were committee members of the

---

[76] Ibid., p. 7. Emphasis in original.

[77] Ibid., p. 7.

[78] For details, see the case of Paul Gunasekaran in Chapter Five.

[79] I have reproduced this allegation because it was a repetition of another incident that was witnessed by other *kampung* residents. I had the first incident and the contents of the allegations confirmed by the residents. For details of this issue over representation, see the case of Paul Gunasekaran in Chapter Five.

Residents' Association, stood by their *kampung* spokesperson and also distanced themselves from the PEA.

The Developer Meant Business

As negotiations were taking place, Company Highview had its own agenda. It had been negotiating with the sub-tenants, and at this point the families living in the Noah's Ark building agreed to cash compensation and moved out.[80] Sensing victory, the developer stepped up its offensive.

On the morning of March 26, 1992, when most of the men in the *kampung* were at work, Company Highview sent in the bulldozer again to the house that was partially bulldozed before. Faced with the threat of further demolition, the residents decided to apply for a court injunction to stop the developer on the very day of the demolition.

Remarkably, at this time we find that the competing developer, Company Golden-Heights, was exceptionally swift in coming on to the scene. Company Golden-Heights took advantage of the situation and offered to "assist" the residents in their legal action against Company Highview. Company Golden-Heights not only recommended a lawyer to handle the case for the residents but also paid for the legal costs incurred in the court injunction application.

The court responded efficiently to the injunction application. Two days after the application was made, on March 28, 1992, the Penang High Court granted the residents' application for an injunction to restrain the Bishop and Company Highview or their agents from entering the *kampung* land. The residents also secured an order stopping the demolition of ten other houses.

With the imposition of the court injunction, Company Highview began to negotiate with the PEA leaders.

The "Heritage House"—A Vision Come True

Company Highview called another meeting with the PEA leaders indicating the seriousness of its intentions. With this meeting approaching, the PEA leaders arranged to meet with the residents. This meeting was a watershed, marking a break in the PEA's role as mediator and representative of the residents in the negotiation process. From this point on, the PEA would proceed to negotiate its own demands.

Before we go on to consider proceedings at this meeting, we must remember that by this time a group of residents had already disputed the PEA's representative role. Therefore, it is not surprising that not all of the *kampung* residents turned up at the meeting called by the PEA. Hence, the PEA leaders must have been well aware of the hostile undercurrents.

At this meeting, the PEA leaders declared that because they "did not get the mandate to speak for the residents" and "in view of the [court] injunction," their negotiation from this point on "would center on the Association's demands only."[81]

On this basis, the PEA leaders met with Company Highview. At this meeting, Company Highview announced its decision to provide a Heritage House for

---

[80] The compensation payments were said to be in the range of RM2,000 to RM25,000.

[81] "PEA Report 1992," pp. 8, 9.

Malaysian Eurasians to replace Noah's Ark. According to the "PEA Report, 1992," the developer was "convinced ... of the need to maintain the Eurasian heritage at the land."[82] Nonetheless, the ultimate decision was still dependent on the Bishop's approval granting the land site.

Following this agreement between Company Highview and the PEA, several other similar meetings took place to study the details of the development plan for the "heritage house." At one of these, the PEA leaders did attempt to speak on behalf of the *kampung* residents, proposing the construction of a high-rise building as the "heritage house" with low-cost flats to accommodate the residents.[83] Company Highview did not agree to this proposal.

Meanwhile, rumors of the Company Highview/PEA agreement on a "heritage house" had spread to the *kampung* residents, as well as the Penang Eurasian community in general. There were diverse views on the matter. The residents, not surprisingly, perceived this development as a "betrayal" by the PEA. They felt that the PEA leaders, none of whom had ever lived in the *kampung*, had no right to gain from the conflict, arguing that the offer of the "heritage house" was at their expense, and pointing out that a block of low-cost flats could easily have housed all of them.

Meanwhile, the residents were left to fight on their own. With a sense of despondency, many residents sold out during this period. The residents' predicament was aggravated when on July 10, 1992 the court lifted the injunction imposed on Company Highview following an *ex parte* appeal. Soon afterwards the Noah's Ark building was demolished. The residents mockingly recounted how after all the hullabaloo in front of the Noah's Ark building to protest for its preservation, its destruction took place without the slightest commotion. The residents described how the Noah's Ark building was "gently taken down," plank by plank, and not bulldozed like the other *kampung* houses which had been demolished.

By this time only three houses, a shed, and the remains of the first bulldozed house were left standing. Only nine families, all of whom I contacted during my fieldwork, remained. These residents were steadfast in refusing to accept the developer's offer of cash compensation. As a result, court suits for their eviction were filed against them by the Bishop on behalf of Company Highview.

Before I go on to discuss the lawsuits, I want here to document the final arbitration process which led to the completion of the "heritage house" offer to the PEA.

The continuing controversy over the "heritage house" led to some hesitation on the part of the Church authorities to make a clear commitment to offer the land site. By late 1993, the Bishop was still procrastinating over the signing of a memorandum of understanding between the three parties for the "heritage house" site. I believe that this was largely due to the fact that the residents' court cases were still pending. In such an environment, signing the accord would have created further uproar.

But the PEA leaders were impatient. They again sought to use the media to exert pressure on the Bishop. For instance, on September 4, 1993, an article appeared in *The Star*. Entitled "Developer offers to build Heritage House," the

---

[82] Ibid., p. 9.
[83] Ibid., p. 10.

article was essentially a press statement by the PEA pointing out that the agreement by the developer to allocate a site on the Kampung Serani land for the building of the Eurasian Heritage House was still awaiting Church approval. This was followed by another article in *The Star* on October 10, 1993, with the headline "Eurasians seek land from church for heritage house." The PEA's persistence worked.

Some time after my fieldwork, I received newspaper clippings from Penang, dated October 15, 1994, reporting that a memorandum of understanding had been signed between the PEA and the Roman Catholic Bishop, which allowed the Church to execute a ninety-year lease in the PEA's favor for a 929 square foot site at Kampung Serani.[84] It was said that the Heritage House would be completed in a year's time, at an estimated cost of RM350,000 and would have a built-up area of 456 square meters. In addition, it was confirmed that the PEA's plans for the "heritage house" would include the establishment of a museum and a center for cultural activities for the Eurasian community.[85] For a visual presentation of the new development on Kampung Serani and the heritage house, see Plates 4.3 and 4.4 in Appendices K and L.

The Lawsuits

In late 1992, the Bishop proceeded to institute court proceedings against the remaining residents after fresh eviction notices were issued.

When the residents received their summonses, their immediate reaction was to re-approach CAP (which they had first contacted in the early 1980s) for assistance. CAP's legal counsel eventually acted as the defense lawyers for two of the *kampung* families.[86] The other families were referred to other lawyers.[87]

The claims made by the Bishop against the *kampung* residents were primarily under Order 89 of the Rules of the High Court 1980, for possession of his premises on the ground that the occupiers were in occupation without his license or consent.[88] In other words, the Church and developer were alleging that the residents were illegal squatters.

This allegation deeply angered the residents, given their long association with the Church. By this time, hostilities became so intense that the residents were convinced that the legal system would provide them more justice than anything they could expect from the Church or Company Highview.

While it is beyond my expertise to analyze the technical aspects of these court proceedings, I will endeavor to discuss the significance of the relevant legal

---

[84] This news appeared in *The Star* newspaper twice, first on October 15, 1994, p. 17 and then again on October 17, 1994, p. 20.

[85] *The Star*, October 15, 1994, p. 17 and *The Star*, October 17, 1994, p. 20.

[86] One of these families later terminated this relationship and engaged the services of a private law firm.

[87] They were referred to a Penang lawyer who has built a reputation by defending the ground tenants in the controversial Thean Teik estate development conflict.

[88] One exception was a proceeding instituted under the Subordinate Courts Rules Order 26A, which was primarily an application on the ground that the resident had no claim on the premises on which he was living (for details, see the case of Anthony D'Mello in Chapter Five).

principles to the position of the *kampung* residents as ground tenants facing eviction.

I have chosen to discuss the case on which the court initially ruled on February 7, 1994, to dismiss the above-mentioned application by the Bishop with costs, as it set the precedent for the other cases. Subsequent to this judgement, the court similarly dismissed four other cases involving sub-tenant families on February 9, 1994.[89]

Incidentally, this particular case was against the *kampung* "spokesperson." Much to the benefit of my examination of this case, I discovered after my fieldwork that it was reported in the *Malayan Law Journal*.[90] Without going into the particularities involved in this case, its pertinence to our discussion lies in the fact that the court found this resident not to be a squatter but rather to be a lawful tenant holding over after the termination of the tenancy.[91]

Let us be clear on how the court defined a squatter:

> He is one who, without any colour [sic] of right, enters on an unoccupied house or land, intending to stay there as long as he can. [92]

In the case of a person found to be a squatter, Order 89 would have applied as it is "confined to squatters simpliciter, i.e. those whose initial entry itself upon the land is unlawful and whose continued occupation of the land remains unlawful."[93]

Having determined that this *kampung* resident was a lawful tenant, what does the law have to say about the manner in which the owner/developer can take possession of the land in such a situation?

We find the answers in the court's deliberations:

> Even after the tenancy is determined, he [tenant] still has possession. If he remains in possession and in occupation, there is high authority for saying that the owner is not entitled to take the law into his own hands and remove the tenant by force. He should go to the court and get an order for possession. Otherwise he is guilty of a criminal offence contrary to the statute of forcible entry . . . . He may not be liable to a civil action for damages . . . . But nevertheless, his conduct is unlawful and should not be countenanced by the law.[94]

While this statement in the court's judgement clearly indicates that the developer must use legal means to gain possession, the *kampung* residents were further ensured of this protection under Section 32 of the Rent Control Act 1965 which stipulates that "where a tenancy has come to an end but the occupier continues to reside in the premises, it is not lawful for the owner to recover

---

[89] The other court hearings continued on after my fieldwork ended and some were eventually settled out of court.

[90] Anne Khoo, "Titular Roman Catholic Bishop of Penang," *Malayan Law Journal* 3 (1994): 4-14.

[91] Ibid., pp. 5, 13. For further details, see the case of Paul Gunasekaran in Chapter Five.

[92] Ibid.

[93] Ibid., p. 9.

[94] Ibid., p. 11.

possession otherwise than by the proceedings in the court."[95] The Rent Control Act 1965 applied to all buildings built in Malaysia before February 1, 1948. This meant that tenancy of the Kampung Serani houses, all of which were built prior to this date, would come under the jurisdiction of the Rent Control Act.[96]

Having clarified the court's ruling, I should also say that the court's dismissal of the case did not prevent the Bishop and the developer from commencing proceedings for possession by writ in the usual way.[97] The law therefore provides no ultimate protection from eviction, but rather acts to ensure that the owner/developer's action of taking possession is carried out in a lawful and civil manner.

This still leaves us with the inevitable question of compensation. What does the law provide as regards to compensation in the event of the eviction of lawful tenants? For this, we must look at the principle of *tenancy couple with equity* under English Common Law. A precedent for this principle was set in the Malaysian Federal Court (now known as the Supreme Court) decision in the case of Mok Deng Chee vs. Yap See Hoy in 1982.[98] This principle of equity presupposes that the tenant cannot be asked to leave by mere notice to quit. There must be some compensation given. The problem remains that there is no minimum specification or instrument to help determine the level of compensation. Therefore, it is common to find that in cases of eviction, the level of compensation is often determined by agreement between the parties involved—usually the landlord/developer and the tenant.

In the light of the existing legal framework, it was inevitable that the remaining *kampung* residents had little choice but to reach an agreement on the terms of compensation with the developer and vacate their premises. It is these final negotiations in Kampung Serani to which we shall now turn.

The Dissipation

While we have seen that the majority of the remaining *kampung* residents were found by the court to be lawful tenants, there were two sub-tenant families in Kampung Serani found by the court to be squatters.

The court's decision on one of these cases was in fact delivered as early as July 5, 1993.[99] This was the case against the owner of the remaining shed in the *kampung*.[100] The shed owner appealed against the court's decision but lost his appeal on July 29, 1993. Consequently, on the morning of August 5, 1993, Company Highview sent in a bulldozer to demolish the shed.

Encouraged by this early victory, Company Highview was initially confident that it could get rid of the residents by way of the courts. This confidence was reflected in the fact that the developer stopped further attempts at negotiation for most of 1993. In addition, Company Highview made several moves marking its

---

[95] Ibid.

[96] This Act was repealed in January 2000.

[97] Ibid., p. 14.

[98] Interview with lawyer, Y. J. K. on September 2, 1994.

[99] Court judgement on the other case was delivered some time in early 1994.

[100] For details, see the case of the Rath family in Chapter Five.

determination to start construction work as early as possible. First, it started piling works on October 26, 1993 after procuring a test piling permit from the Penang City Council.[101] Some time later in the same year, it began advertising for the sale of the commercial units of its development project.[102]

It was only after the court's rulings in February 1994 to dismiss the Bishop's applications that Company Highview began to change its approach. Initially, however, the developer still seemed determined to pursue its legal action when it filed appeals in the Supreme Court against these High Court decisions.

But in May 1994, the developer started contacting the residents individually to negotiate terms of compensation.[103] This time, the negotiations were conducted personally by Company Highview's Managing Director. The developer indicated to these residents that it wanted to reach a compromise.

Meanwhile the remaining residents were also advised by their lawyers to reach a settlement with the developer. By this time, the developer had started its first phase of the project and the residents were living amidst deafening conditions. As a result of these negotiations, the residents gradually reached settlements with the developer and, one by one, they began to leave Kampung Serani. The first settlements were struck in the middle of 1994, and by the end of October 1994 the last of the remaining houses was brought down.

Kampung Serani then ceased to exist.

Not surprisingly, the levels of compensation varied greatly from resident to resident, as each deal was negotiated individually. The compensation amounts ranged from around RM8,000 for a sub-tenant family, to between RM60,000 and RM130,000 for house owners. The residents have found alternative housing all over Penang and some have even moved to the mainland. A majority of them are still tenants.

Hence, after a fourteen-year long struggle, 1994 marked the complete deracination of the Kampung Serani residents from their over a century-old ancestral home.

CONCLUSION

In concluding this chapter, I wish to highlight some of the most important points raised in this case study and the questions arising from them.

This chapter detailed how the redevelopment of Kampung Serani into a modern condominium-cum-commercial project essentially embroiled the landowner (the Church), the developer, and community groups (the residents and the PEA) in a complex struggle over urban space.

---

[101] The beginning of this piling work caused the residents much distress, as their court suits were still pending. In order to confirm whether the developer had already procured a building permit to start construction work, I made an inquiry at the Penang City Council. I was told that the developer had not procured a building permit at this point, but had been given a test piling permission, which unfortunately did not have a stipulated time period on it. (These details are based on information given to me by a Mr. Song, a Penang City Council Building Inspector, in my telephone enquiry made on October 27, 1993.)

[102] See *The Star*, Section Two, December 15, 1993, p. 55.

[103] The details of the negotiation process that follows are based on my correspondence with Paul Gunasekaran, dated March 16, 1994; April 7, 1994; July 1, 1994; and October 24, 1994, after I left the field. I revisited the field site for two weeks in August 1994.

We have seen how the historical circumstances of Kampung Serani, as a "nucleus" for the Portuguese Eurasians, gave rise to the residents' reclamation of this cultural heritage as a form of dissent in the face of the *kampung*'s threatened destruction. However, this "cultural heritage and identity" was also appropriated and reworked by the more powerful PEA for its own interests. In addition, the PEA's reworked discourse and its vision of a "heritage house" were conspicuously influenced by the Association's interests in the larger construction of a Portuguese-Eurasian identity in Malaysia. Yet, in the ensuing conflict, the residents finally lost out and were evicted, while the PEA won a "heritage house" from the developer and the Church.

We have also noted that the course of events in the fourteen-year long conflict correlated with property cycles in Malaysia. The year 1980, in which the development plans for Kampung Serani began, and the year 1990, when the project was reinstated, marked the beginnings of two property booms in Malaysia.[104] The hiatus in activities during the mid 1980s can be explained by the collapse of the property market in Malaysia.[105]

Several questions arise from the foregoing and will be addressed in the ensuing chapters. Firstly, we need to ask why the PEA's discourse gained prominence over the residents' articulations and won the Association a "heritage house" in the conflict. As we have seen, the discourses on Portuguese-Eurasian identity in the conflict were based on the arbitrary and contingent appropriation of local and wider historical factors. This inevitably leads us to the questions of what was at stake in articulating these differences. What processes were involved in the construction of competing discourses of Portuguese-Eurasian identity? Why was the PEA interested in possessing a "heritage house" on the *kampung* site? How did the residents respond to the PEA's cultural representations?

Secondly, the conflict also raises the question of why the Church, a non-commercial establishment, entered into a joint venture with a private developer.

Thirdly, why did Company Highview give in to the PEA's demands for a "heritage house" but not to the residents' requests for low-cost housing, and why was its competitor, Company Golden-Heights, so interested in the *kampung* site that it offered a "clubhouse" to solicit support from the PEA and the residents?

In the ensuing four chapters I will attempt to explore these and other questions.

---

[104] These were the property booms of 1981-1983 and the present one which started in 1989. See Aloysius B. Marbeck, "Investing in Residential Property," *Property Malaysia* (June-July 1993), p. 62.

[105] Malaysia experienced a severe economic depression from 1984 to 1989. For an account of the depression, see Khoo Kay Jin, "The Grand Vision," p. 51; and Linda Y. C. Lim and Pang Eng Fong, *Foreign Direct Investment and Industrialization in Malaysia, Singapore, Taiwan and Thailand* (Paris: Development Center of the Organisation for Economic Cooperation and Development, 1991), pp. 22, 40. Property developers were one of the worst hit during this recession (see Marbeck, "Investing in Residential Property," p. 62).

CHAPTER FIVE

KAMPUNG SERANI RESIDENTS' BATTLE IN VAIN

This chapter presents the ethnographic narratives of the nine families who still lived in Kampung Serani when my fieldwork began. It represents an attempt to understand the significance of the conflict by exploring how the residents perceived, experienced, and responded to changing circumstances as they fought to stay on in Kampung Serani.

I will introduce the protagonists in each of these families, their biographies, and their association with Kampung Serani so that we will be in a better position to understand what the village meant to them, their particular predicaments, and their responses to the conflict. In particular, I will focus on how the residents reclaimed and reconstructed their personal, cultural, and historical relationships to Kampung Serani in response to the changing circumstances of the conflict.

In presenting the residents' experiences and narratives, I wish to demonstrate that voices, other than those of the PEA, were developing local discourses on Portuguese-Eurasian heritage and identity. I will show how the residents were, to an extent, empowered by their lived experiences and deep attachment to Kampung Serani as they struggled to protect themselves, their families, and their community from the sinister forces of eviction and power politics in the conflict. In particular, the residents of Kampung Serani articulated a competing discourse throughout the conflict, a discourse shaped by their "multiple *habitus*," so to speak, that is, their individual sensibilities, particular associations with the village, imminent politics, and collective agenda. In examining these narratives, this chapter reaffirms this book's argument regarding the primacy of local, preceding, or existing social and cultural forces in mediating social action and the production or interpretation of cultural meanings.

I will not use the real names of the respondents but will adopt pseudonyms in line with their ethnicity. The premises occupied by the residents will be identified according to their postal addresses (see Plates 4.1 and 4.2 in Appendix I and J for a view of these houses).

Five of the nine families I discuss considered themselves Eurasian. The remaining four families were non-Eurasians (one Chinese and three Indian). All nine families were Roman Catholic.

The "Eurasian" families were the Gunasekarans, the D'Mellos, the Lings, the Pestanas, and the Carriers. The Gunasekaran family lived in the house at 356A Leandros Lane. The D'Mello, Ling, and Pestana families lived next door at 356C Leandros Lane. Carrier was the owner of the bulldozed house at 350 Leandros Lane. Three of these Eurasian families—Gunasekaran, D'Mello, and Pestana—claimed consanguinity through matrilineal kinship traced to a man called J. Pasqual, who was a teacher at the Noah's Ark school. (The family tree of these three families is illustrated in Chart 5.1 in Appendix G.)

Among the non-Eurasians, the Yeap family lived in the house at 350B Leandros Lane. The three Indian families—the Dashans, the Raths, and the Yagambarams—were all tenants. The Dashan family was a tenant of the Gunasekaran household, while the Rath and the Yagambaram families were tenants of the Yeaps. The Rath family also owned the shed still standing when I began my fieldwork. (For the location of these remaining premises in Kampung Serani, see Map 4.1 in Appendix M.)

All interviews, except in the case of the Yeap family, were conducted in English—the mother tongue of the Eurasian residents and lingua franca of the *kampung*. The quotations in this chapter are reproductions of our conversations that were largely recorded on audio cassettes. The Chinese family spoke Hokkien and the translations are mine.[1] Despite the PEA's emphasis that Penang Eurasians once spoke Malay, I found that none of the Eurasian families spoke Malay at home, with each other, or with me, although like many other Malaysians, they were conversant in the national language.

THE MAKING AND UNMAKING OF A PORTUGUESE EURASIAN[2]

Standing at 356A Leandros Lane was a well-maintained double-story wooden house, painted white and with a red zinc roof. Here lived the family of Paul Gunasekaran, a retired schoolteacher, and his wife, Pauline D'Aranjo. They had six children—three boys and three girls. The two youngest children, twin girls, were adopted at the age of seven.

Paul was the *kampung* spokesperson mentioned in the previous chapter and served as the first Secretary of the Residents' Association. Paul was known to be the prime mover behind the use of Portuguese-Eurasian historical and cultural heritage in defense of Kampung Serani. When the conflict started, Paul not only took the initiative to look up materials available at the local public library on the Eurasian community in the Pulau Tikus area, but was also the first person to point out the historical significance of Noah's Ark, in a speech delivered to the Penang Reflection Group meeting of Church leaders in the early days of the conflict.[3] When the Residents' Association turned to the media to gain public support, it was Paul who briefed the press on the background of Noah's Ark and Kampung Serani.

It was at one such briefing that I, a cadet reporter working on the Kampung Serani story, first met Paul in 1984. During this first encounter, I found Paul to be warm, gregarious, articulate, and very much a raconteur. There was a distinct

---

[1] Hokkien, one dialect of Chinese, is also my mother-tongue.

[2] Information and the quotations herein are based on my recorded interviews with Paul Gunasekaran on March 7, 1993, March 14, 1993, March 28, 1993, September 5, 1993 and October 19, 1993. Additional reference sources will be specified individually. The information here has been read and verified by Paul himself.

[3] This meeting was held on November 5, 1980. The Penang Reflection Group is a group which meets monthly and is comprised of Church leaders, priests, and the Bishop. On this occasion, Paul was invited to speak on behalf of the *kampung* residents through the mediation of a sympathetic faction within the Church establishment which sought to give the *kampung* residents a chance to present their views. A written version of Paul's speech, entitled "Kampung Serani," dated November 5, 1980, was made available to me.

genuineness and passionate idealism about Paul that left a strong impression on me. This impression increased as I got to know him better during my fieldwork.

When the house of his neighbor, Mary Carrier, was bulldozed by the developer, Paul took her in to live with his family for over a year. Paul's compassionate nature was, I believe, in part derived from his childhood involvement with Christian missionaries. Paul lived in an orphanage run by Anglican missionaries from the age of eight. In 1951, at the age of twelve, Paul was taken to live at the Catholic orphanage in Pulau Tikus. The orphanage was located in the vicinity of Kampung Serani, just opposite the Church of the Immaculate Conception across Burma Road.[4]

It was here that Paul, an Anglican, converted to Catholicism. Paul's stay at the orphanage eventually led to his forging links with the Kampung Serani community and to his gradual assimilation into a Eurasian way of life.

Paul was born on June 25, 1939, the second of four siblings. His parents were migrants from South India who had settled in Seberang Perai, where Paul's father found work as a railway fireman.[5] Originally, Paul was a Hindu. His connection with the Anglican orphanage which eventually brought him to Kampung Serani was brought about by a series of tragic events during the Japanese occupation of Malaya.[6] These events began when Paul's father was taken by the Japanese to work on the infamous "Burma Death Railway." While many forced laborers did not survive the ordeal, Paul's father did. However, he returned home in 1946 only to find that his "best friend" whom he had entrusted to take care of his family had developed a relationship with his wife. This difficult situation turned tragic when this "best friend" poisoned Paul's father.[7]

Two years later, Paul's mother remarried, but Paul and his brother could not get along with their stepfather. It was at this point that Paul and his brother were sent to the nearby orphanage, run by Anglican missionaries. At the orphanage, Paul became an Anglican. It was also here that a priest by the name of Reverend Scott came to play a prominent role in Paul's life.

Paul recounted how Reverend Scott took a special interest in him and his brother. When Reverend Scott was sent back to England two years after Paul had entered the orphanage, the priest took Paul and his brother back to their mother before he departed.[8] On her children's return, Paul's mother left her husband and moved together with the children to a rubber estate where she found work. Reverend Scott, however, reappeared in Paul's life a year later. Upon the priest's return to Malaya, he tracked Paul and his brother down, and came to the rubber estate to take them back to the orphanage. This touched Paul deeply, as he strongly believed that he would have had been destined otherwise to be a rubber

---

[4] The building still stands today and is used as a private school. The law firm that represented Company Highview and acted as the Bishop's legal representative in the lawsuits against the residents set up office space in this building during 1993.

[5] Seberang Perai is located in the mainland portion of Penang state.

[6] The Japanese invasion of Malaya began in 1941 and Japanese occupation lasted until 1945.

[7] Paul's father died after he was offered a drink that had been mixed with glass-powder. This is a local folk-method of murder known in Malay as *santau*. The cause of death from *santau* is usually from internal hemorrhage. According to Paul, his father's murderer committed suicide at the police lock-up.

[8] Paul explained that Reverend Scott got into trouble because he had converted two Malay boys to the Anglican faith, and, as a result, had to be sent back to England.

estate worker. The influence of Reverend Scott on Paul's life was evident when Paul explained that his decision to adopt twins in 1978 was inspired by the memory of the priest.[9]

Shortly after Reverend Scott took Paul and his brother back, the Anglican orphanage closed down and Paul was transferred to the Pulau Tikus Catholic orphanage-cum-school where he began his primary education at the Noah's Ark school.[10] Paul lived in the orphanage until his third year of secondary school, when a Chinese Christian family living nearby Kampung Serani took him in.[11]

After finishing his secondary education, Paul got into a Teachers' Training College and became a qualified teacher in 1962. Again his destiny remained linked to Pulau Tikus.[12] He began his teaching career at St. Xavier's primary school, located just opposite Kampung Serani along Burma Road. Paul remained as a teacher at this school for thirteen years.[13]

Since the age of twelve, Paul's life has essentially revolved around the vicinity of Kampung Serani. Over the years, Paul has become familiar with the families living in Kampung Serani, and, in fact, grew up with many of his current neighbors. When I met Paul in 1993, he was often nostalgic about the past. Paul recounted how his favorite past-time during his younger years was to "roam from one Eurasian house to the next" which, in the process, he said, led him to meet and eventually "fall in love" with Pauline.

At this time, Pauline was living in College Square, just opposite the Church of Immaculate Conception and across College Lane. But she also spent much of her time in Kampung Serani, where she had relatives.[14]

In 1963, Paul and Pauline were married in the Church of the Immaculate Conception. After the marriage, they initially rented a house in Fettes Park, a residential area about ten minutes drive from Kampung Serani. However, in 1973 Paul and Pauline took up residence in Kampung Serani when they were invited by Pauline's uncle, I. Rajan (himself an Indian who was married to one of J. Pasqual's daughters), to live with him in the house at 356A Leandros Lane.

---

[9] The twins were students at the school where Paul was teaching. Originally, Paul was approached to adopt only one of the twins. However, Paul believed that the twins should not be separated and so instead adopted both of them. According to Paul, the twins were separated at birth and "given" to their respective relatives because of a superstition among the local Indian community that, because the twins were the eighth-born, they would bring bad luck to their family. Remarkably, Paul did not convert the twins to Catholicism and they retained their original Hindu faith.

[10] Paul explained that the closure of the orphanage was because Reverend Scott was transferred to Sarawak. Prior to his transfer he had arranged for the boys at the Anglican orphanage to be sent to the Catholic orphanage in Pulau Tikus.

[11] This house is located next to the College General Catholic Seminary.

[12] Paul's elder brother, who was in the Pulau Tikus orphanage with Paul, lived with a Chinese Catholic family in the Pulau Tikus vicinity. Paul's brother worked for Malaysian Airlines and migrated to Australia after his retirement.

[13] As mentioned in Chapter Four, the St. Xavier's primary school had replaced the Noah's Ark school.

[14] The D'Mello and Pestana families in Kampung Serani were Pauline's maternal cousins. These families were descendants of Lena Pasqual, the second daughter of J. Pasqual, the schoolteacher at Noah's Ark. Pauline was a descendant of Rose, the eldest daughter of J. Pasqual.

For Paul, his marriage to Pauline and his residence in Kampung Serani completed his assimilation into a Eurasian way of life. In retrospect, Paul explained how he felt about his identity:

Because of my background, I lost my Hindu religion, tradition, custom, and way of life as an Indian. So, when I married Pauline, I did not know how to build a home. My wife has the ability to do it. So the children all grew up in her way of life, in the Catholic Eurasian way of life. My children, my wife and I identify ourselves so much within the Eurasian community. Every time there is a Eurasian death, marriage, burial, sickness, whatever, we identify ourselves with them. My own children would joke about the idea of us going to the functions held by the Indian Association of Penang. They laughed because they could not speak a word of Tamil [with the exception of the twins]. They feel so Eurasian. Throughout the years it has been like this. I have been a member of this community for more than thirty years and will always feel that I am part of it.

Paul said he felt no qualms whatsoever over his right to advocate the significance of Kampung Serani's Eurasian cultural heritage when the conflict began. It was perhaps inevitable that with Paul's articulate nature and his readiness to speak up, he ended up being recognized by the *kampung* residents as their spokesperson in the process.

When I talked to Paul in 1993, after his role as spokesperson had been disputed, he defended himself in the following way:

I have had the opportunity to mix with Eurasians since an early age, that was why in 1980 I could stand up and fight for the people here. Could I have possibly stood up and fought for a cause to which I knew next to naught? That was why I had to do my homework and know the facts. That was why we often went to the library to find as much information as possible.[15]

Indeed, Paul's prominence in the residents' fight made him a controversial figure. In my interviews with other residents and Church authorities, I found that Paul was either singled out as the "ring leader" or "trouble-maker," and there were various speculations over his real intentions in the conflict. In one instance, Paul was referred to as an opportunist who "wants a bite of the cake."

However, as it turned out, Paul was the least compensated among the final three house owners when, in the end, they each negotiated individually with the developer.[16] In hindsight, there were indeed several opportunities when Paul could have sought advantage from the developer if he had wanted to. In fact, Paul

[15] Paul was accompanied by F. Gregory, an old timer in the *kampung* who passed away in 1985, during his literature search at the Penang State Library.

[16] Paul received RM80,000 while the other two house owners received RM110,000 and RM130,000. Letter from Paul, dated May 13, 1994, and letter from Matthew Yeap, dated October 2, 1994.

had been approached several times by the developer, but he had stood firm.[17] He explained why:

> I stood my ground. I was the man who looked up all the historical documents. I even went to the Bishop's house to make a passionate plea on behalf of Noah's Ark and the residents but to no avail. Rather I was scorned. When one grows older, one becomes more sentimental, one wants to hold onto some things, especially things that would be destroyed because of men's greed. The desire to hold on to such things becomes practically an obsession.

When I spoke to Paul, he was determined to be philosophical rather than bitter over the doubts raised against his character. He likened it to throwing mud on a wall: "not all will stick, neither will all fall off." He consoled himself that, "When you fight the establishment, it doesn't mean you are bad."

The one controversy in the conflict that Paul had found hard to come to terms with, however, was the issue over his "Eurasian-ness." Paul was deeply hurt by two incidents in which his role as the *kampung* spokesperson was disputed because he was considered to be a non-Eurasian.

Below is a description, as Paul remembered it, of the first of these allegations that occurred in late 1991:

> He [a PEA leader] came to my house for a talk as the Bishop was going to meet them. He then commented, "Any statements we make in the press, it is very important that a Ling, a Rath, or a [Gunasekaran] cannot speak. Anything that has got to do with Kampung Serani and Noah's Ark must come from a Eurasian mouth." I cried. My wife was present which was very painful for her to hear it. My brother-in-law and my two neighbors were there as well.

As already mentioned in the previous chapter, the second incident took place during the meeting with several of the PEA leaders. Paul recounted bitterly:

> This next incident, I will repeat it to you even if you ask me to do it a hundred times. . . . Before going, they said, "Paul, can we tell you something." I said, "go on." And I quote the exact way it was put. They said, "Paul Gunasekaran, we the Penang Eurasians are extremely proud of what you have done all these years. We are deeply indebted to you. And we don't deny that you have worked extremely hard. But today, times have changed. Situations have changed, Paul. Any press statements made regarding the Eurasians, must come from a Eurasian. Therefore Paul, can we ask you that should any statements be made, that it be made by a Eurasian. You can't do it because you are not a Eurasian."

These two episodes indicate that Paul's "Indian race" had been used as the ground to dispute his Eurasian identity. The disputation of Paul's Eurasian identity was, I suggest, caused by the PEA's engagement in the current constructions of Portuguese-Eurasian identity that enabled it to use racial grounds to discredit

---

[17] In 1980, Company Dreamland offered Paul RM50,000 as compensation, which he refused. In late 1992, when the lawsuits were initiated against Paul, Company Highview offered him RM40,000, which he also refused.

Paul's role as the residents' representative. This issue will become clearer in the next chapter where I show how the current constructions of Portuguese-Eurasian identity are shaped by rhetorical explanations of racial and cultural characteristics of Portuguese-Eurasian identity derived from the community's historical experience in Melaka.

Paul, however, felt much agony over these comments. After all, he had lived most of his life as a member of the Eurasian community in Kampung Serani. The PEA's comments not only dispirited Paul in his fight for Kampung Serani, but also set off an internal struggle within Paul to come to terms with the doubts raised over his identity. Throughout my fieldwork, I found that Paul oscillated between two extremes when he tried to reconcile his Eurasian identity. He would either succumb to the claims that he could not be considered a Eurasian as he was born an Indian, or he would instead negate the PEA's allegations by pointing to the incongruities he found in them. I quote an exclamation made by Paul during one of his moments of resignation:

Basically I have never considered myself a Eurasian. I am not a Eurasian, ethnically, I am Indian. My mother and father are both Indians. Full blooded Indians.

At other, more rational, moments, Paul would conclude differently:

There are other Indians in the PEA. Why ostracize me? Is it a personal vendetta?

During instances like this, Paul often became spirited and would justify his role in the fight for Kampung Serani as follows:

While I fought the cause of Noah's Ark and of Kampung Serani, it was just not an Eurasian affair, it was mine too. It was my school. I studied there, and my wife's great grandfather [F. Pasqual] was a teacher there. My children have his blood. Do you mean that I have no say in anything? I am part of it. I am in it. But they argued over it. In a way they wanted to push me out, because I am too outspoken.

When I met Paul again in 1993, the pending lawsuit to evict him was another enormous pressure on him and his family. Apart from their sense of insecurity over their remaining days at Kampung Serani, at the center of the lawsuit was a bitter dispute between Paul and his mother-in-law. Paul and Pauline did not own the house at 356A Leandros Lane. Title to the house was registered in the name of Paul's mother-in-law.

The house was originally built in the late nineteenth century by J. Pasqual, Pauline's great-grandfather, who taught at the Noah's Ark school. For over a century, different members of the Pasqual family had lived in the house. The third daughter of J. Pasqual, the wife of I. Rajan, Pauline's uncle, was in charge of the house until she died in 1973, whereupon Paul and Pauline were invited to move in with Pauline's uncle.

When Paul and Pauline moved into the house, title to the house had been transferred to I. Rajan.[18] According to Paul, Pauline's uncle had wanted to make a will to leave the house to Paul and Pauline to ensure that other clan members would not dispute their right to continue living there. Paul had instead suggested that the house be bequeathed to Pauline's mother as she was the next most senior member of the Pasqual family alive at that time. As Pauline's mother already owned a house, it was understood that her possession would be in name only and that Pauline and Paul would be able to continue living there for as long as they wanted. As a result, a will was made in 1969, naming Paul's mother-in-law as the owner of the house.

In 1992, when Company Highview was actively buying out the *kampung* residents, the developer approached Pauline's mother with an offer of RM25,000 in compensation for the house.[19] Pauline's mother agreed to this offer without consulting Paul and Pauline and signed over her interest to the developer in June 1992.[20]

This action resulted in a rift between Paul and his mother-in-law. In this family feud, it was perhaps Pauline who suffered most, as she was torn between her loyalty to Paul and her duty to her mother. There were significant tensions between Paul and Pauline but, remarkably, Pauline endured in quiet spirit and had no contact with her mother who lived only a few minutes away from Kampung Serani.[21]

In the Bishop's court proceedings to evict Paul and his family, affidavits signed by his mother-in-law attesting that Paul and family did not have her consent in residing at the premise were used as court evidence. In bitter jest, Paul said, "Now the Bishop is taking me to court using my mother-in-law as his witness."

In reviewing the Church's position throughout the conflict and its decision to take legal action against the residents, Paul said:

> . . . from the human, social and religious point of view, we are your flock, we look upon you, the priest, the Bishop, as our shepherd. At least you must call us all together . . . and get our feedback before you make an agreement. If it had happened that way, I think it would have had definitely helped out very much. But the pain is this, throughout the history of the *kampung* the Church hierarchy and the residents never had to resort to civil law. But now the Church has unashamedly used the courts to get us out—the very people who built and kept the Church for you. How do you come to terms with that?

---

[18] I. Rajan had three tenants staying with him when Paul and Pauline first moved in. Only the Dashan family stayed on as Paul's tenant until 1994.

[19] The mother-in-law finally received RM27,000 as compensation for the house.

[20] I have to note that this account is entirely based on Paul and Pauline's version of the dispute. I did not approach Paul's mother-in-law, as emotions were so volatile between them during my fieldwork that I felt any form of meddling would only serve to aggravate the situation.

[21] In March 1995, after the Kampung Serani saga was over, I received a letter from Paul that he had "made peace" with his mother-in-law. He wrote, "After all, she'll be 89 in April this year and I feel it is not worth keeping any more grudge. . . Life is too short for bearing grudges and ill feelings." Letter dated March 28, 1995.

In his criticism of the Church's attitude towards the residents, Paul used the past contributions by the *kampung* residents' ancestors to criticize the Church for its lack of accountability to the *kampung* community. He highlighted that it was the early settlers who built the Church and their financial contributions that enabled the Church to grow. In verifying his argument, he often quoted the claim made by an elderly *kampung* resident, whom he called "Auntie Emily," that the *kampung* land was given to the Church for Eurasians.[22] Paul also used the example of Pauline's own father, whom Paul said had contributed a month of his salary for renovations to the Pulau Tikus parish Church. He further claimed that the residents, as well as Catholics living in the vicinity of the Church, had made similar contributions.

Apart from this, Paul, like many of the *kampung* residents, maintained that Kampung Serani used to be a "purely Eurasian *kampung*" at least until the 1950s. Falling back on his own experience, Paul explained that when he first became a member of the Pulau Tikus parish, the congregation consisted largely of Eurasians from Kampung Serani and the vicinity. In addition, Paul argued that during those days, the Church would not allow Eurasian residents of the village to sell their houses to non-Eurasians. Paul referred to two house-owners in Kampung Serani who had to sell their houses to the Church because they could not find any Eurasian buyers for their properties.[23]

The *kampung* conflict severely affected Paul's relationship with the Church. He stopped attending Church services when developments escalated in 1990 and was resigned to the fact that, "If I am dead today, it doesn't matter if the Church doesn't want to bury me." In 1992, Pauline and their children also stopped attending Church.

Paul rationalized his stance as not "quarrelling with God," but that his problem lay with the Church establishment itself. He had come to view the Bishop as follows:

> The Bishop has also become a developer. How do you expect us to think highly of them. So has the Bishop succumbed to money politics?[24] You know, you are supposed to build treasure in heaven not on earth! You cannot serve God and Mammon at the same time. You are supposed to be above business and to be a servant of God working for the spiritual welfare of the people, which does not only mean, seeing to their spiritual needs. A hungry man will be an angry man and a man in that state will not be able to sit down and pray. What more for families without roofs over their heads? In fact, as you are preaching to me you are destroying me. . . . You ask me to offer you the sign of peace in church, to my brothers and sisters. You call me a brother and a sister and you take me to court?

[22] This "Auntie Emily" was born in 1901. She passed away in late 1980 after the *kampung* conflict had begun.

[23] An exception was the Yeap family, who moved into Kampung Serani in 1963, after another Catholic parish interceded on behalf of the Chinese family. Here again, Paul used the fact that the Church had initially opposed the entry of this Chinese family into Kampung Serani as evidence that only Eurasians were allowed to live in the *kampung* during those early days.

[24] See Chapter Three for an explanation on the meaning of this term and its popular usage in Malaysia.

In June 1994, Paul and his family moved out of Kampung Serani and became tenants in new premises in a western suburb of Penang Island.

SIBLINGS IN DISCORD[25]

Next to Paul and Pauline's house stood a blue double-story house: number 356C Leandros Lane. In this house lived Anthony D'Mello and his wife, Agnes Ling, who was part Eurasian and part Chinese. They had six children. Anthony D'Mello was not only a neighbor of Paul and Pauline but also a relation. Anthony, a maternal cousin of Pauline, was also a great-grandson of J. Pasqual, the school teacher at Noah's Ark.

The D'Mello family forged its links with Kampung Serani when Anthony's father, C. D'Mello, a textile-store owner from Klang, married Rida, a granddaughter of J. Pasqual. For a while, C. D'Mello and his wife lived in Klang[26] after their marriage, but they returned to Kampung Serani after the Japanese war. On their return, C. D'Mello bought the house at 356C in the village, which subsequently became the family home. Incidentally, buying the house also led to Anthony and Agnes's marriage, by virtue of the fact that Agnes was the daughter of the D'Mello's new house-tenant.

The house became a family trust property in a will made by C. D'Mello before he died in 1978, just two years prior to the eruption of the Kampung Serani conflict. In the will, the eldest of his ten children, a daughter, was made the principal trustee of the house. It was this legacy of shared possession of the family house that became the source of dissension among the D'Mello siblings during the Kampung Serani conflict.

In 1981, Company Dreamland had approached the principal trustee of the house with an offer of RM49,000 as compensation.[27] By this time, three of Anthony's siblings had died, leaving seven siblings (five girls and two boys) as co-owners of the family house. The five sisters wanted to accept Company Dreamland's offer, but Anthony and his brother, who were residing at the house, opposed it. When a compromise could not be reached among the siblings, the sisters filed a lawsuit[28] challenging the two brothers' decision in court. However, the sisters lost the case and the matter was laid to rest, as by this time development plans in Kampung Serani had subsided due to the mid-1980s recession. Although the relationship between the siblings soured after this incident, they still managed to maintain cordial relations. However, this cordiality was shattered in the early 1990s following the escalated developments in Kampung Serani.

This time, Company Highview offered RM70,000 to the principal trustee of the house, to be shared equally among the seven siblings. This time round, all of Anthony's siblings, including his brother, who had left the family house, wanted to accept the offer. Anthony found himself in sole opposition to his other siblings' decision.

---

[25] Information and quotations in this section are based on my recorded interview with Anthony and Agnes on April 25, 1993. Additional reference sources will be specified individually.

[26] Klang is a port town located in the state of Selangor, in Peninsular Malaysia.

[27] By this time, the principal trustee was the second daughter of C. D'Mello, as the eldest had passed away.

[28] I was not able to obtain the details of the legal proceedings of the case.

Anthony explained that he had initially sympathized with his siblings' wishes as "they were aged and they wanted to be able to spend the money while they still could." However, with four of his children still going to school, Anthony had his own family to think of. He asserted, "If you ask me, I find it difficult to buy a house, even if it is RM25,000, what more when houses at least now cost over RM100,000. RM10,000 is only barely enough to pay for a house deposit." Anthony explained that he was not opposed to receiving cash compensation at this stage, but wanted to negotiate for an amount around RM100,000. He rationalized that with this amount, his siblings could still have their RM10,000 each, while he could have about RM40,000 to enable him to find alternative housing for his family. Anthony felt justified to a bigger portion of the compensation as he was the one who had been maintaining the house over the years. Using this rationale, Anthony tried to persuade his siblings to be more patient.

However, the atmosphere in Kampung Serani was moving against Anthony's plans. During this period, more and more residents were settling for cash compensation every day. Anthony's siblings became increasingly agitated and decided to sign over their individual beneficial interests in the family house to the developer some time in mid-1992, without informing Anthony. Anthony only came to know of his siblings' actions through a letter issued by the developer's lawyer.

The family feud deepened when the Church and the developer used the accord with the other siblings and took Anthony to court on the grounds that he had no right to the house he was living in.[29] The turn of events enraged Anthony, causing him to harden his stance to a point where he no longer wanted to accept cash compensation. He said:

> They can say that I am illegal. They can say this house belongs to them. We want to be relocated here. If possible we want a low-cost house where we can live in this place. We want Kampung Serani to be still standing here. Let it be even a small community. We still want this piece of land, let it be part of it, or even, one-tenth of it, at least we have a Kampung Serani. I don't mind even if I don't get a cent even. Worse comes to worst, if we lose and the court decides the house is finally to be only worth RM15,000, well, let them pay that and we can divide by seven.

Indeed, both the developer and the PEA had a taste of Anthony's hard-line stance from this point on. For instance, when the lawsuit was still pending in 1993, Anthony was solicited several times by the developer's "agents" to go to the developer's office for negotiations. Nonetheless, Anthony was adamant that the developer should make the effort to come and see him and not vice versa. Finally, Company Highview had to make a compromise by setting up a meeting with Anthony at a nearby restaurant where negotiations still fell through.[30]

---

[29] This lawsuit was instituted by the Bishop under Order 26A of the (Malaysian) Subordinate Courts Rules (P.U. (A) 328/1980). I have no details on the legal technicalities, but on April 4, 1994, the court ruled in favor of the Bishop, whereupon Anthony's lawyers filed an appeal against the court's ruling. On May 18, 1994, the High Court dismissed the former judgement and ordered a fresh hearing on the case. The case was not heard, as it was eventually settled out of court.

[30] He was offered RM70,000 at this meeting.

Anthony was equally hard on the PEA, such as when he recounted an incident in which he actually "chased" a PEA leader out of his house when this person tried to persuade Anthony to accept the cash compensation offered by Company Highview. Not surprisingly, Anthony was the last of the remaining residents to leave Kampung Serani. As things turned out, Anthony's hard-line stance actually worked in his favor in the final negotiations with the developer. From among the three remaining house owners, Anthony received the highest compensation.[31] Perhaps another contributing factor to making Anthony a more effective negotiator was his knowledge of the construction industry. Anthony worked as a land surveyor with a civil engineering company that builds roads and highways.

Apart from the family feud, Anthony and his wife Agnes were troubled about their relationship with the Church. Anthony first stopped going to Church sometime in 1992, followed by Agnes. Although Anthony was plagued with guilt over "failing his Catholic duties," he said he could not overcome his anger over the Church's attitude in the whole affair. He spoke of his agony:

My father and I, we have served the Church for so long, for over fifty years. And now they [the Church] have combined with PEA to get rid of us. But the whole truth is that the Bishop is summoning us to court. Not the developer. I must make this clear to you. This is nothing to do with Company Highview, where the court case is concerned. . . . So the Bishop is the landowner saying that we are illegals [sic] staying here. How can they say we are illegals [sic]? We have been living here for over fifty years.

When I talked to Anthony, he had on numerous occasions asserted that the land on which Kampung Serani stood was *"wakaf* land" (religious endowment land) which, he claimed, was meant for the poor Eurasian parishioners of the Church. Anthony maintained that such land could not be sold by the Church. This view was shared by Anthony's wife, Agnes, who added that the donor of the *kampung* land was a wealthy Englishman.

Regarding the evocation of Eurasian heritage by the PEA, Anthony queried the meaning of "heritage" espoused by the Association. He said:

The PEA made a deal with the Bishop and the developer, Company Highview. That was why they agreed to demolish Noah's Ark, which was a heritage. Why demolish this? Because the PEA will get a free club. A free club for PEA! But prior to this, the PEA talked very big about it. They said that Noah's Ark should not be demolished and they would fight till the end. Where is the heritage now? There is no heritage of Noah's Ark. There is no Kampung Serani left! The one thing that can support Kampung Serani is the Portuguese Settlement in Melaka. We don't have anything else, to be honest with you. It should be Kampung Cina instead of Kampung Serani, because the Chinese have bought over.[32] We have been betrayed by the PEA and the Church. Not by the developer. The developer only wants to develop.

---

[31] He received RM130,000.

[32] *Cina* is the Malay word for Chinese.

Anthony's wife, Agnes, a Eurasian of part-Chinese descent, had lived in Kampung Serani for thirty years. Agnes's association with the village, which began in 1963 when she was ten years old, had a lot to do with her parent's mixed marriage. Her mother had moved to Kampung Serani specifically because she wanted to bring up her children in a Eurasian community.

The marriage of Agnes's mother, a Eurasian of Anglo-Portuguese descent, to her father, a Chinese, was met with strong opposition, particularly on the part of her father's family.[33] The main cause of antagonism was Agnes's father's conversion from Buddhism to Catholicism upon his marriage. So great was the hostility over religious and cultural differences in the mixed marriage, that on his death there was yet a last wrangle between Agnes's mother and her husband's family over whether he should be buried as a Buddhist or a Catholic.[34] A consequence of this acrimonious situation was that halfway through the marriage, an arrangement was reached whereby Agnes's father went back to live with his parents, and had resorted only to visits with his wife and children. It was at this point that Agnes's mother decided that she would bring up her children in a Eurasian community and moved into Kampung Serani, as a tenant of Anthony's father, C. D'Mello.[35] Therefore, to Agnes, Kampung Serani became a place where she could forge and secure her Eurasian identity. Considering her background, it is not surprising that Agnes was passionate in defending her Eurasian identity. She said:

> There are people who say to me that I am a Chinese married to a Eurasian. But I can say to them that my mother is a Eurasian. My father is a Chinese no doubt, and I carry a Chinese surname, but I still consider myself a Eurasian, as I am still having the Eurasian blood.

To further illustrate Agnes's Eurasian self-identification, I quote a comment she made regarding the residents in Kampung Serani:

> In the 1960s, the residents living in Kampung Serani were all Eurasians. The only Chinese here was the Yeap family.

Agnes expressed particular rancor over the "heritage house" deal between the PEA and the developer. In her words:

> People think that the PEA represents the Eurasians. They think PEA is going to fight for this Eurasian community. They [the PEA leaders] think that in the name of Eurasians they can say everything for us. We never instruct them to say anything for us, but they think that they can put every word into our mouths. The PEA has got no say in Kampung Serani because they have not been staying here before. You are using us to get your clubhouse, your own clubhouse, for your benefit! It is not giving us the benefit. So I say, they have no right, they have got no right!

---

[33] Agnes's mother was the offspring in the marriage between a local Eurasian woman of Portuguese descent whose maiden surname was Stewart, and a Englishman with the surname of Head, who came from Plymouth, England.

[34] He was finally buried according to Catholic rites.

[35] This information is based on an interview with Agnes's mother on April 25, 1993.

In the process of the conflict, both Anthony and Agnes had given up their lifetime membership in the PEA. They boycotted all functions organized by the PEA, and vowed never to have anything to do with the Association.

Anthony and Agnes finally moved out of Kampung Serani in September 1994. Anthony and family are now living on the mainland in the state of Penang, where they have bought a house.[36]

THE UNRELENTING KINSMEN[37]

Anthony and Agnes had two long-standing tenants at their house, tenants who were also their kinsmen. One of the tenants was Abraham Ling, the elder brother of Agnes. The other tenant was Colin Pestana, a nephew of Anthony.

Between the two kinsmen, Abraham Ling was the longer-standing tenant. Abraham's association with the D'Mello house began in 1963 when he was seventeen, at which time his mother moved in as a tenant. After his mother and other siblings had moved out, Abraham continued on as a tenant and raised his own family in Kampung Serani. Abraham married a Chinese woman, Joceline, and they had two sons.

Like his sister, Abraham identified strongly as a Eurasian resident in Kampung Serani, and would refer to the pioneers of the *kampung* community as his "ancestors." In asserting his Eurasian identity, he first argued against the existing definition of the Eurasian through patrilineal descent, saying such a practice was a "mistake" as many Eurasians married out of their community. In addition, Abraham specifically established his Portuguese roots, which he traced through his mother's own maternal line:

> Although I am having a surname [Ling], my mother however, is a real type of Eurasian. She is a Portuguese-type of Eurasian because she is a Miss Stewart [this was the surname of his maternal grandmother, who was a Eurasian of Portuguese descent, and not his mother's surname which was Head, following her English father]. I still uphold my mother's surname and I am very proud of it.

Abraham shared the view of his neighbors that the *kampung* land was religious endowment land, held in trust by the Church for poor Eurasians. However, he claimed that the land was donated to the Church by the British government. Like Paul, Abraham often evoked the memory of the late resident, "Auntie Emily," in substantiating his accounts of Kampung Serani's past. For instance, Abraham claimed that Auntie Emily had told the story of how early *kampung* residents had each donated half-a-month of their salaries for the construction of the Pulau Tikus parish Church in the late 1800s. On this basis, Abraham accused the Church of abandoning the residents, now that it no longer needed their support.

---

[36] Housing prices on the mainland area of Penang are much lower than prices on the island.

[37] The information on Abraham and quotations in this section are based on my interview with Abraham, recorded on June 21, 1993. The information on Colin Pestana is based on my conversation with him on October 3, 1993.

Abraham was also one of the activists who contributed greatly to the residents' fight against eviction, and served as the second elected Secretary of the Residents' Association in 1987. On several occasions Abraham, who worked at the Postal Service Department, efficiently used his position as a civil servant to the advantage of the *kampung* residents in the course of the conflict.

The first of these occasions took place in 1980, when the conflict began. Some time in the middle of 1980, the residents found themselves in a dilemma when the Church refused to collect their ground rent payments. They feared that this situation could eventually be used to allege that they were illegal tenants having not paid their ground rent. Abraham was quick to resolve the dilemma, by suggesting that the residents send their ground rent payments by registered mail, so that they would have a record of trying to pay their ground rent. This also acted to raise the residents' awareness of the importance of keeping records of all transactions pertaining to their houses throughout the conflict.[38]

Apart from this, Abraham also took the initiative in contacting the local police station at Pulau Tikus during the first bulldozing attempt on Mary Carrier's house. Abraham explained that he requested police presence to ensure the safety of the residents, as the developer had brought thugs along to the demolition site. Abraham took the initiative, as he felt that the police would pay more heed to his request since he was a government servant. Nonetheless, the police did not turn up.[39] Disappointed and angry at their attitude, Abraham pursued the matter and lodged a complaint against the local police at Police Headquarters in Penang.[40]

Like his other *kampung* compatriots, Abraham was bitter that the Church initiated legal proceedings against him. Abraham was particularly furious over affidavit-evidence against him signed by the priest, who was also the Chairperson of the Church's Financial Commission. The affidavit-evidence had alleged that Abraham's tenancy at the D'Mello house was without the Church's permission or knowledge.[41]

Abraham viewed this allegation as "a false statement," because he maintained that the priest knew him and his family personally. Abraham viewed the priest's statement as evidence that "the Church has no more principles." So strong was Abraham's reaction over the affidavit-evidence that he confronted the priest over it. Abraham described this encounter:

> I went to see him in the Church one morning. I said to him, "You are dirty, your heart is not clean. You should strip off your robe. You are the dirtiest man I have ever come across."

---

[38] During my fieldwork, I found that all the residents had kept good records of the correspondence and other documents pertaining to their houses throughout the conflict. This effort proved especially helpful when it came to the preparation of their affidavits-in-reply in the lawsuits against them.

[39] Abraham recounted how the local police station responded that it could not send any personnel to the scene, as no police patrol cars were available at that moment. Incidentally, the police station is just about a five minute walk from Kampung Serani.

[40] Subsequent to this complaint, some police inspectors paid a visit to the residents and left their telephone contact numbers for the residents.

[41] The lawsuit against Abraham was among the cases dismissed by the High Court on February 9, 1994 (see Chapter Four).

Abraham explained his resolution over his action: "I didn't care if I was to be excommunicated from the Church, because I felt that justice was not done." After the incident, Abraham stopped attending the Pulau Tikus parish Church, explaining that it caused him too much distress. "Each time I saw the faces of the priests, my blood boiled," he told me.

Abraham said he felt most frustrated that the Church and the developer had only recognized the PEA, and not the *kampung* residents.

> They only recognized the PEA, that is all. They only talk to the PEA, not to the people here. That is why I said, where is the justice? What has the PEA to do with the issue? But the Church believed that they can only talk to the PEA leaders.

Similarly, like his neighbors, Abraham had much to say about the PEA's deal over the clubhouse.

> It is not necessary for the PEA to get a clubhouse here. Why? Did any one of them, any of the PEA leaders ever live in this area and deserve the clubhouse? If they had given us the land instead, we could build some decent flats for the people here.[42]

Abraham pointed out that during the "protest gathering" outside the Noah's Ark, no *kampung* residents were given the chance to speak to the press. On the campaign to preserve Noah's Ark and its outcome, Abraham remarked:

> We were all making fools of ourselves during the protest, that was all. The building is gone, no more. It is dead and gone! There is no such thing as a Kampung Serani anymore. Then they talk of a "heritage house" here when all those high class people are coming to stay. . . . If you talk about Eurasian heritage, what heritage can we talk about now? The only heritage left is Melaka, where we have our own Portuguese Settlement, other than that, there is nothing more.

In late 1994, Abraham reached a settlement with the developer and moved out.[43]

Another unrelenting kinsmen in the D'Mello house was Anthony's nephew, Colin Pestana. Colin was also related to Pauline and Paul, as he was a great great-grandson of J. Pasqual. Colin was, in fact, born in Kampung Serani at the house in which Paul and Pauline lived, but had moved out of Kampung Serani together with his parents in 1973. He returned to the village in 1978, whereupon he became a tenant of his uncle, Anthony D'Mello.

Colin's return to Kampung Serani was facilitated by a priest at the Pulau Tikus parish Church. This was because Colin, a craftsman skilled in stained glass work, had helped with renovations at the Pulau Tikus parish Church in the 1970s, and in

---

[42] In fact, the mother of one of the PEA leaders was said to have once lived in Kampung Serani.

[43] Abraham was the only resident during my fieldwork who already owned a low-cost house that he purchased through a low-interest government loan scheme. I have no information on the amount of compensation Abraham received.

the process had established a good rapport with the parish priest. In 1978, Colin was temporarily unemployed and needed a place to stay. He approached the priest for permission to build an extension on his uncle's house, where he could live. Colin recounted how the priest gave him the permission, and even provided him with some of the building materials to make the extension.

Colin was married to Marie, an Indian Catholic, and they had a daughter who was born towards the end of my fieldwork. In addition, Colin had two other children from a previous marriage, as well as his father, living with him.[44]

Despite the background of Colin's tenancy at the D'Mello house, the Church instituted court proceedings against Colin as well, alleging that his tenancy was illegal as it was without the Church's permission. The Church refuted Colin's defense arguing that the parish priest, now deceased, had no authority to issue tenancy permission.

As it turned out, Colin lost his case in the Bishop's lawsuit against him, and was evicted some time in April 1994.[45] However, Colin managed to get some compensation from Company Highview before moving out.[46] To the *kampung* residents' surprise, Colin purchased an apartment unit in a newly completed apartment development located just opposite Kampung Serani on Leandros Lane.[47]

THE DERELICT

The morning of March 12, 1992, is a day never to be forgotten by Mary Carrier, a sixty-six year old resident at number 356 in Kampung Serani. It was on this morning that the bulldozer demolished part of her house. Mary recounted the incident:

> I think it was about nine o'clock. I was speaking to a Mr. Cheah, the house developer [possibly a contractor] opposite my house [referring to the Delima Apartment project[48]]. He was watching his workers at work. Then, I heard a rumbling sound, and this bulldozer came right to my garden! I thought he wanted to cross over to the back portion of my house where the lady had sold off already. But this Mr. Cheah, whom I was talking to, said, "Auntie, you move, he is going to bulldoze your house!" So I ran to that mango tree, away from there. He gave one, two, three bashes and the verandah came down onto my stairs, so I couldn't go up to my house. I later asked Mr. Cheah for an affidavit since he witnessed the incident, but he said that as a developer himself, he could not write an affidavit against another developer.

The second bulldozing, on March 26, 1992, finally brought Mary's house crumbling down, making her homeless. She first took up an offer from her neighbors, Paul and Pauline, and lived with them for over a year before moving out some time in May 1993.[49] From this point, Mary began moving around, staying with

---

[44] Colin's father had suffered from mental illness for a great number of years.

[45] I have no details of the court's rulings.

[46] Colin received RM8,000 from the developer.

[47] The apartment unit cost RM168,000. I received this information from Paul in a letter dated April 7, 1994. On this, Paul commented, "So Kampung Serani folks not that poor after all!"

[48] This was the apartment project from which Colin Pestana had bought a unit.

[49] A misunderstanding between them caused this move.

friends who would take her in for short periods at a time. This moving around eventually took a toll on Mary's health, and towards the end of 1993, she fell rather ill. Finally, when Mary's health deteriorated, her sister, who lived in a southern suburb in Penang Island, took her in.

For Mary, life had never been easy, but until her house was bulldozed she at least had a house to live in. Through the benevolence of her father's good friend, Mary had come into possession of the house in Kampung Serani when her father died in 1942.

Mary's father, the son of a marriage between a British officer from the British East India Company and a local Chinese woman, was an accounting clerk with a British trading company. He married Mary's mother, a Hakka Chinese, and they had two daughters, of which Mary was the elder. Mary's father was a rather improvident man and when he died, left his family destitute.

At the time of her father's death, Mary and family were renting a house in Leandros Lane, located just opposite Kampung Serani. Widowed and without a job, Mary's mother found it difficult to pay the rent. Mary explained how her mother's plight led a good friend of her father to sell them the house at Kampung Serani for a mere "sixty British currency."

Soon after moving into Kampung Serani, Mary became the breadwinner for her family. She found a job making *bedak* in a cottage industry.[50] Further adversity occurred when, at age nineteen, Mary entered into a disastrous brief marriage that left her with two children to bring up on her own. Mary had married a Malay who was teaching at the school near Kampung Serani. Theirs was what Mary called a "bus-stop" romance. They happened to share a similar work schedule and had met while waiting for the bus just beside the Pulau Tikus Church. Her husband converted from Islam to Catholicism upon their marriage in 1946.[51] Three years later, after two sons, he left Mary.[52] A single mother, Mary had taken up a string of jobs, from working at school cafeterias to army co-operative shops, to support her children.

After the bulldozing, Mary's two sons, who no longer lived in Penang, had both offered to take her in, but Mary repeatedly turned down their offers. She explained that it was because she did not want to move out of Kampung Serani.[53] Part of Mary's attachment to Kampung Serani was her desire to be near the Church. Mary was still faithfully attending mass during my fieldwork.

In fact, Mary was the only one among the remaining residents during my fieldwork who laid no blame for the Kampung Serani conflict on the Bishop. She believed that the Bishop had nothing to do with the development deal. Instead, she chose to blame the Financial Commission of the Church for the *kampung*

---

[50] *Bedak*, a type of face powder, is made from rice.

[51] In Malaysia, Malays are by definition Muslims. The act of a Malay person renouncing his Islamic faith and converting to another religion would be inconceivable in present-day Malaysia. The "Islamization" process in Malaysia has in part led to constraints on a Malay person to at least adhere nominally to the Islamic faith. For instance, a Malay person automatically comes under the Shari'a Law, and there are various Islamic bodies, set up by the state, which govern the conduct of Muslims in Malaysia. For details, see, Norani Othman, ed., *Shari'a Law and the Modern Nation-State: A Malaysian Symposium* (Kuala Lumpur: Sisters In Islam (SIS) Forum (Malaysia) Berhad, 1994).

[52] This man reverted to his Muslim faith.

[53] One son had become a trade unionist and the other a schoolteacher.

conflict. In particular, Mary singled out the priest who was the chairperson of the Commission as the one responsible. When Mary's house was first bulldozed, she called on the priest to inspect the damage. She received no sympathy but was instead turned away. Frustrated, Mary resorted to insinuation to get back at the priest. She described one of her attempts:

> I used to help the Church a lot. Why not? We used to help, mop, clean, and all that. That was why, one day when we were sitting down under Father's window, I was saying, "There is nothing like the Westerner priests who came. They left home, family, and country to serve God. Everything they gave up. They are so different from the local priests we have today." I intentionally talked loudly so that the Father could hear me.

Mary viewed the bulldozing of her house as a case of victimization. She said:

> Because they think I am a fool. They couldn't do it to others because they have children, have family. So, they think, "she is only an old lady, never mind, we can frighten her." It shows how mad after money they are. To get rich quick!

In addition, Mary commented on the developer:

> I don't think developers have got the right to pull down people's houses. They are supposed to build, right? Not destroy!

Mary recounted that before her house was bulldozed, a PEA leader had asked her to accept a RM30,000 settlement from the developer, but she had refused. When asked to comment on the PEA, in a fit of laughter Mary exclaimed:

> What can I say? They started out to help us, but it went wrong somewhere! After the Eurasians have gone, then they want to get a Eurasian club in here. You will get the PEA there [referring to the clubhouse], then you get all the rich people around it. What Kampung Serani? What a joke! When they hammered Noah's Ark, they all just kept quiet.

Although Mary was advised by the other residents to take up a lawsuit against the developer to compensate for the loss of her house, she refused to pursue the matter throughout the time I was in the field. She eventually pursued the matter and accepted an offer of RM35,000 from the developer in 1999, halfway through her lawsuit against the Church and the developer.[54]

---

[54] *The Star*, June 9, 1999, p. 20.

A Chinese Family in Kampung Serani[55]

The house at 350B Leandros Lane was the largest of the three houses remaining in Kampung Serani during my fieldwork. Painted pale blue and rather run-down, it was built raised above the ground like a typical Malay house.

It was in November 1963 that Magdelene Yeap, a widow with four children, first moved into the house. Popularly known to her friends as the "Catholic auntie," Magdelene's move into the house made her the first and only Chinese living in Kampung Serani.

Magdelene recounted that her purchase of the house was initially met with opposition from the Pulau Tikus parish priests on the grounds that she was not Eurasian. She could only finalize the purchase of the house after a priest from another parish of which she was a member made a plea on her behalf to the Pulau Tikus Church.

Magdelene explained that the primary reason that prompted her to purchase the house was because it stood on Church land. She believed that living on Church land meant that she would not have to worry about being evicted. She recounted the advice she received before she bought the house from a fellow Catholic, who lived across Kampung Serani on Leandros Lane and who also happened to be an officer with the Penang City Council:[56]

> He said to me, "Catholic Auntie, you need not have any fear, you can stay here until your grandchildren's time and the house would not be torn down. You would not be evicted." So I bought it. How could I know that some day they would develop it. If I knew this house was to be demolished I would not have bought it. During those days, everyone was saying it was Church land. How can they demolish the houses here? This land cannot be sold.

For Magdelene, living in Kampung Serani was synonymous with living in a Catholic community. First and foremost, she saw her Eurasian neighbors as fellow Catholics.

Among the houses still standing, Magdelene's house had the largest number of people living in it. Two of her sons and their families, as well as two large tenant-families, were living in the house.

Magdelene's eldest son had suffered a stroke some years back and had been unable to work ever since. He had two children and his wife had taken up work as a washer woman to bring in an income for her family. The family was largely dependent on the second son, Matthew, who was an office worker. Matthew himself had three children.

It was also Matthew who took on the task of negotiating with the developer on behalf of the family during the conflict. Matthew, a rather soft-spoken man, recounted how he had on two occasions turned down the offer of a RM40,000

---

[55] Information and the quotations in this section are based on my recorded interview with the Yeap family on August 1, 1993. This interview was conducted mainly in the Hokkien dialect and all translations are mine.

[56] This man, now deceased, was much recalled by many of the *kampung* residents. Being a Penang City Council Health Inspector, and a fellow Catholic, he was highly regarded by the *kampung* residents.

settlement, as he considered it insufficient to enable his family to buy another house.

Like their neighbors, the Yeap family also faced lawsuits from the Bishop, who was trying to evict them. In fact, Matthew and his mother were named in separate lawsuits. In the lawsuit against Matthew, he was alleged to be an illegal tenant in his mother's house, because his tenancy was said to be without the Church's permission. As much as Matthew was offended by the ludicrousness of these allegations, he was also much bemused by them. He said, "How could my stay with my mother be considered illegal?" Matthew likened the Bishop's court action to the Church's "washing its dirty linen in public." Whilst acknowledging that theirs was the only Chinese family in Kampung Serani, Matthew could nevertheless justify their right to reside there:

> We are Chinese, we can't say anything. Only we like to say we have lived here for over thirty years already. As long as we are Christians we stay here together. It is the Catholic identity which is important.

On assessing the PEA's role, Matthew alluded to the "protest gathering" outside the Noah's Ark:

> Actually it was for the PEA, but the PEA said it was for all the *kampung* people. I don't know how they operate. They told us to go and protest. It was all because of the Noah's Ark and the PEA wanted to get their clubhouse. They didn't care about the *kampung* people. I did not know then. It is too late now. It is not fair. It is for their own greed, for PEA to get a clubhouse. A clubhouse is not important, isn't it right to say so? The priority must be for those who stay here.

During the course of the conflict, Matthew stopped going to Church. As he explained:

> I find it very hard to go to Church, to go for confession anymore. It is like I don't trust the priests anymore. They can't be bothered with us. My children have also stopped going to Church. I let them be. When we as parents no longer go, we can't force our children to go either.

The Yeap family finally settled with the developer for RM110,000 in October 1994. They were able to purchase another *kampung* house in a housing estate in Penang Island where they remain ground tenants at their new residence.

ETHNIC INDIANS IN KAMPUNG SERANI[57]

The remaining house-tenants living in Kampung Serani were all ethnically Indian and belonged to one of three extended families—the Dashan, the Rath, and

---

[57] Information and the quotations in this section are based on my recorded interview with: the Dashan family on August 12, 1993; the Rath family on August 8, 1993 and August 12, 1993; and the Yagambaram family on August 8, 1993. Additional reference sources will be specified individually.

the Yagambaram families. Among these Indian tenant families, the Dashan family had the longest association with Kampung Serani, spanning two generations. Their association began in 1952 when Meena Dashan, an Indian woman of Catholic faith, moved into Kampung Serani.

Originally from Rangoon, Burma, Meena migrated to Penang where she met and married a South Indian immigrant and a fellow Catholic. Some time after the marriage, Meena's husband left her and went back to India, where he found another wife. Meena's plight led a close friend (who was Colin Pestana's mother) to arrange for Meena to live in the extension at the back of the house at 356A Leandros Lane. Thus, Meena Dashan became a tenant of I. Rajan, Paul and Pauline's uncle.

Meena had a son, Khrisna Dashan, who continued to be a tenant on the premises after his mother died. Khrisna worked as a gardener at the Headquarters of the Royal Australian Air Force (RAAF) in Penang Island, and that was how he met Lalitha, whom he married in 1962.[58] Lalitha was the daughter of one of Khrisna's fellow workers. It was upon Lalitha's marriage to Khrisna that she came to live in Kampung Serani.

Unfortunately, Lalitha discovered after her marriage that her husband was a philanderer. Khrisna took four other "wives" after his marriage to Lalitha, though only the last of these liaisons lasted. Finally, eight years into their marriage, Khrisna left Lalitha and their two sons. Lalitha continued to be a tenant at Paul and Pauline's house, and brought up her sons in Kampung Serani.

Khrisna's desertion of his wife, however, did not mean he deserted Kampung Serani. Khrisna together with his last "wife" became tenants in one of the Kampung Serani houses. Khrisna even built himself a shed on the village grounds in 1980, without seeking permission from the Church.[59] Although he lived in close proximity to Lalitha and his sons, he never visited them throughout the time he lived in Kampung Serani. It was Lalitha who brought up their two children by working as a washerwoman and domestic help.

Lalitha's eldest son, Nathan, was an articulate, angry thirty-year old man. He ran a small business as a mechanical tool supplier. Eventually, Nathan became the developer's negotiator and representative within the *kampung* community.

Throughout my fieldwork, I found that Nathan could be charming one minute, but angry and abusive the next. He was very susceptible to fits of anger that would lead him to burst into verbal onslaughts. Perhaps it was Nathan's impetuousness and his proclivity to verbal abuse that caused the other *kampung* residents to perceive him as a sort of "ruffian." Nathan was not apologetic about his rash nature and described to me how he had verbally abused two priests in the course of the *kampung* conflict.

The first of these incidents occurred when Nathan confronted the priest who had signed an affidavit alleging that Lalitha's tenancy in Paul's house was illegal. Enraged, Nathan went to the parish where the priest, the chairperson of the Financial Commission, had been transferred and verbally abused the priest. The next confrontation occurred when the remaining shed in Kampung Serani was demolished. The evening after the demolition, Nathan was at the site to help his

---

[58] The RAAF stopped its operations in Penang in 1984.

[59] In 1990, Khrisna was quick to accept a RM10,000 compensation by Company Highview and moved out before events escalated in the Kampung Serani conflict.

friends salvage what they could from the wreckage. When a Pulau Tikus parish priest made the unprecedented gesture of visiting the demolished site, Nathan could not control his temper. He hurled verbal insults at the priest, who quickly departed from the scene.

Nathan vented his anger not only at the Church, but also at the developer. In early 1992, when Company Highview was buying out the *kampung* residents, Nathan was not approached. Nathan's response was to barge into the developer's office to make his presence known. He claimed that he kicked up a fuss during this intrusion and broke some furniture in the developer's office before leaving.

While I speculate that responses like Nathan's were what the Church was most apprehensive of, the developer was instead able to exploit the situation, and ended up winning Nathan over to its side. When I talked to Nathan in August 1993, he was constantly referring to the developer as his "good friend." At this stage, Nathan lay the entire blame for the conflict on the Church. He said:

> I don't blame the developer, to be honest. It is the Bishop whom I don't give my respect anymore. So, I won't blame the developer, it is their job.

Nathan explained that he was offered compensation of RM8,000 by the developer, but he was still trying to negotiate for RM2,000 more. Convinced that he would be able to negotiate for a better price, Nathan was not worried about the Bishop's court proceedings to evict his family.[60] During my fieldwork, Nathan was in fact acting as a "mediator" for the developer in negotiating with the Rath family, who were tenants of Magdelene Yeap, and the owners of the remaining shed in Kampung Serani. Nathan explained he was asked by the developer to convince the Rath's family to accept a RM4,000 compensation offer for the shed, as well as for their tenancy at the Yeap family house. When the Rath family lost their court case on the remaining shed, the developer again deployed Nathan to use the opportunity to persuade them to accept RM5,000 in compensation for their tenancy at the Yeap family house and to leave Kampung Serani.

Nathan was candid about the fact that he had made a deal with the developer over the Rath family. The developer had agreed to pay Nathan an additional RM2,000 compensation if he managed to persuade the Rath family to accept the developer's offer. Nathan, however, was to be disappointed. The Rath family persistently refused to accept the developer's offer.

Arthur Rath, a *kacang putih*[61] hawker who had migrated from South India, headed the Rath family. Arthur was married to Angelica Santino, who was also from India. They were both Catholics by birth. Arthur and Angelica had six children—five boys and one girl—all of whom were living with them. Two of the sons were married with children of their own. The Rath household comprised thirteen people. Among their children was a technician, a telephone operator, an office worker, a ticketing clerk at a travel agency, and a vegetable seller.

Arthur first moved in as a tenant at 350B Leandros Lane in 1961, even before Magdelene Yeap bought the house. It was because of his large family that Arthur had asked a parish priest for permission to build the shed for his two married sons

---

[60] The Bishop's lawsuit against Lalitha was among the cases dismissed by the High Court on February 9, 1994.

[61] *Kacang putih* is the Malay word for chick-pea.

to live in. Arthur explained that the priest had even refused to take ground rent for the shed because the priest felt that Arthur was too poor.

On the morning of August 5, 1993, some time after Arthur lost the court case over the shed, the developer sent in a bulldozer. The Rath family was unprepared for the shed's demolition, although they had already been given notice of the developer's intentions after they lost their appeal.[62] Arthur and his family explained that they were confident that Company Highview would not carry out the demolition, as they were still negotiating with the developer for a settlement that included their tenancy at the Yeap residence.

When the bulldozer arrived that morning, the Rath family pleaded for a two-hour delay so that they could salvage their belongings. While this discussion was going on, Arthur's third son, Luke, rushed to their lawyer's office where the lawyer tried to obtain a court order to delay the demolition. The Rath family's lawyer had in fact procured a court order for a delay until 4:00 p.m. from the court bailiff. However, by the time Luke returned to the *kampung* site with the order, the shed had been demolished.

Another Indian tenant in Magdelene Yeap's house was the family of Annabel Yagambaram. Like the Raths, Annabel was already a house-tenant of the former owner when Magdelene Yeap bought the house. Annabel's tenancy in Kampung Serani began in 1960, when her husband, a school gardener, was transferred to the St. Xavier's branch school in Pulau Tikus. Their tenancy at the house was facilitated by Annabel's brother-in-law, who knew the former Eurasian owner, as they were fellow Church members at the Pulau Tikus parish.

At the time of the Kampung Serani conflict, Annabel had three of her children living with her. Among her children, the eldest daughter, Hilary, was married with a child. Her husband, Alberto, a postal clerk, also lived with his mother-in-law. The Yagambaram family was comprised of seven people in total.

Hilary and her husband, Alberto, took on the task of negotiating with the developer. In 1991, the developer offered RM6,000 as compensation to the family, but Hilary said she turned down the offer as the amount was too little to enable them to "do anything with it."

Hilary's husband was pessimistic that the *kampung* residents' reference to Portuguese-Eurasian heritage would have any effect:

> The government does not believe in archives and heritage. They favor Vision 2020 and it is in the government policy for development. We cannot be arguing with old tradition and heritage. Development has to go along. We are only tenants. If development comes along, we cannot do anything about it. We are not owners. By law, we have no right to gain in this development. It is only because of human compassion that they may give us something.

Finally, in late 1994, the Rath family received RM20,000 while Annabel Yagambaram's family received RM15,000 as compensation settlements from the developer.[63] They are still tenants at their new residences.

---

[62] The Rath family initially lost their case on July 5, 1993. They lost their appeal on July 29, 1993 and were given notice by the developer to absent themselves from the premises.

[63] Letter from Matthew Yeap, dated July 25, 1995.

Each of these Indian families, like their Eurasian neighbors, had long-standing associations with Kampung Serani. From their point of view, their ethnicity had never posed a problem to their stay in the village. They were all Catholics and, like the Yeap family, had understood Catholicism to be the common denominator that they shared with their Eurasian neighbors. When Eurasian cultural heritage became an issue in the conflict, these non-Eurasian residents were, therefore, not distressed by it. All of them rather nonchalantly expressed their concurrence with the evocation of the Eurasian heritage and identity. Below is a remark made by Fernando, the second son of Arthur Rath, that exemplifies this sentiment among the non-Eurasian residents:

> When the PEA came, they told us, "Let one body voice out, not every individual go and voice out. . . ." We are Indians here and since this is a Eurasian *kampung* we are happy to let the Eurasians speak out. We thought that the Eurasians would stick together and fight their cause.

CONCLUSION

To conclude this chapter, I would like to note some of the more important points raised in the foregoing discussion. To begin with, there is the ethnic composition of the residents. We have seen that the *kampung* residents were not ethnically homogeneous, but consisted of Eurasians as well as non-Eurasians. In addition, the Eurasian residents were themselves not necessarily, nor exclusively, of Portuguese descent. Rather, these residents had ancestors who were of various European and Asian origins.

Apart from the ethnic heterogeneity of the residents, the circumstances leading to their association with Kampung Serani were equally diverse. For Eurasian residents like Anthony D'Mello, Pauline D'Aranjo, and Colin Pestana, their residence at Kampung Serani was primarily due to family genealogy, as previous generations of their families had lived in Kampung Serani. For other Eurasians like Paul, Mary, Agnes, and Abraham, the Eurasian identity of Kampung Serani was an important factor in their personal association with the village. Particularly for Paul, Agnes, and Abraham, Kampung Serani was the place where they forged their personal identities as Eurasians. For the non-Eurasian families, their background as Catholics was a primary reason for taking-up residence at Kampung Serani.

Despite these diverse circumstances, the residents, Eurasians and non-Eurasians alike, were united by two things: first, a recognition of the historical association between Eurasian heritage and identity and Kampung Serani; and second, their Catholic faith.

Their battle to stay on in Kampung Serani meant that they were not only embroiled in a fight against the developer, but also with the Church, which was both their landowner and religious foundation. In addition, they had to contend with the PEA, their erstwhile mediator who in the end became their competitor. For some of the residents, the conflict also resulted in family dissension, as family members fought between themselves over occupancy and ownership rights.

Their experience shows that the Kampung Serani conflict was not simply a battle over terms of compensation. The residents were equally arduous in contending with other parties to the conflict whom they considered had misrepresented and disregarded their rights, cultural heritage, and identity as the descendants of the early settlers of Kampung Serani. For instance, there were two particular events in the conflict that they reacted strongly to. These were the allegations in the lawsuits that they were illegal tenants and the PEA "clubhouse" deal. They perceived the "illegal tenant" allegations to be not only false but unjust in view of their long-standing association with Kampung Serani and the Church. As we have seen, the courts ruled that they were in fact legal tenants. Regarding the PEA "clubhouse" deal, the residents were critical of the PEA's cultural assertions and challenged the Association's rights to gain the "clubhouse." They unanimously viewed the PEA "clubhouse" deal to be at their expense, and also that the Association had "sold out" the Noah's Ark building for its self-interest. According to them, in doing so, the PEA was untrue to the Association's earlier commitment to Portuguese-Eurasian culture and heritage.

To contest these events, the residents began to articulate competing discourses as they endeavored to assert their personal beliefs, as well as their historical and cultural understanding of Kampung Serani. The historical imaginary of Kampung Serani as the pioneer settlement for the Portuguese Eurasians in Pulau Tikus constituted an important component of their discourses. Noticeably, they deliberately and strategically appropriated the historical and cultural understandings of Kampung Serani. They reinterpreted and reconstructed these understandings in order to support their arguments during the conflict. For instance, their insistence on the endowment status of the *kampung* land, said to be exclusively meant for the Eurasian community, was undoubtedly reconstructed from the history of Kampung Serani, as there remained no concrete evidence for these claims. Furthermore, these claims were marked by inconsistencies, as they each differed in their individual interpretations as to who had donated the land to the Church.

We have also seen how the contestations over cultural representation eventually shifted to issues of personal identity, as the Eurasian identity of the residents became another contested terrain in the conflict. Paul, the leading spokesperson, had his role as the *kampung* representative disputed on the grounds that he was not a Eurasian. On the other hand, Eurasians of part-Eurasian descent like the Lings, responded to the conflict by affirming their Eurasian identity in which they specifically sought to reclaim their Portuguese roots.

The residents' responses and narratives in the foregoing discussion indicate that they were not passive victims in the conflict, but were actually as resourceful and active as producers of cultural meanings as their adversaries in the conflict. Indeed, they constructed a multiplicity of competing cultural narratives in the course of the conflict, all based on their personal sensibilities, experiences, and priorities. Yet, apparently, their "voices" were somehow "silenced" in the course of the conflict, while the PEA's voice gained dominance and won a "heritage house" for the Association.

We have so far seen the particular and competing cultural meanings constructed by the *kampung* residents from the location's historical, social, and personal particularities as they responded to the changing circumstances of the conflict. The next chapter will further examine the constitution of difference in the cultural articulations between the PEA and the residents in the conflict. It will explore how and why the PEA constructed a set of differing discourses in the cultural politics of the Kampung Serani conflict.

CHAPTER SIX

THE POLITICS OF PORTUGUESE-EURASIAN IDENTITY CONSTRUCTIONS IN THE KAMPUNG SERANI CONFLICT

This chapter explores the connections between the Penang Eurasian Association's arguments in the Kampung Serani conflict and the broader constructions of a distinct Portuguese-Eurasian identity around the themes of Malayness and indigenousness. The aim is to understand how the Association made use of national and regional discourses on Portuguese-Eurasian identity to silence the residents' demands for low-cost housing and persuade the developer and the Church to include a Eurasian "heritage house" as part of the redeveloped *kampung* site.

This chapter draws on the events of the Kampung Serani conflict discussed in Chapter Four to analyze the conflict in terms of national discourses on Portuguese-Eurasian identity in recent Malaysian history. In doing so, I wish to illustrate how national discourses of nation, ethnicity, and modernity in Malaysia had particular effects on groups and individuals depending on their class, ethnic background, and geographical location. I will show how the new schemas of nation, ethnicity, and class in Malaysia created possibilities for, as well as challenges to, the Portuguese-Eurasian community. Enterprising and visionary elites or trustees of the Portuguese-Eurasian community were quick to seize these opportunities and take up the formidable task of advancing the class and identity interests of their community in Malaysian society. These broader dynamics had definitive consequences for the Kampung Serani conflict as the leaders of the PEA appropriated and reworked the larger discourses of Portuguese-Eurasian identity to legitimate their role and to achieve their goals in the conflict. These analyses reiterate my larger argument that the actions, dreams, and articulations of Portuguese-Eurasian identity by the actors in the Kampung Serani conflict were intertwined with the broader political, economic, cultural, and spatial dynamics involved in the Malaysian quest for modernity.

This chapter is divided into three sections. The first section traces the origins of the rearticulations of Portuguese-Eurasian identity back to the Portuguese Settlement in Melaka, and provides important background for my analysis of the PEA's reworking of discourses of Portuguese-Eurasian heritage and identity in the Kampung Serani conflict. I discuss two texts written by Portuguese-Eurasian community leaders during the 1980s that have since become the foundation for many arguments concerning the relationship between Portuguese-Eurasian and Malay cultural identities. These arguments were important to the community's eventual acceptance into the Amanah Saham Nasional (National Unit Trust) scheme.

The second section offers an interpretation of the Portuguese-Eurasian community's acceptance into the privileged ASN scheme in 1984, an acceptance which promised class mobility and the recognition of *bumiputera* status for the community. I discuss the political motivation behind the Portuguese-Eurasian claim of Malayness and the ways in which this debate was shaped by the shifting conceptualizations of Malay identity. As I show, the Portuguese-Eurasian community ultimately benefited from the political fragmentation within the Malay elite since the mid-1980s, divisions which enabled minority groups such as the Portuguese-Eurasian and Thai communities to win concessions from the government.

In the third section, I discuss the political significance of the Portuguese-Eurasian community's acceptance into the ASN for the Penang Eurasian Association, and the role this has allowed them to "legitimately" play as community representatives in the Kampung Serani conflict. As explained in Chapter Four, admission to the scheme is regulated by a set of bureaucratic stipulations, one of which gives the power to vet applications to the various Eurasian Associations and the Regidor—the government-appointed community leader of the Portuguese Settlement in Melaka.[1] The acceptance of Portuguese Eurasians into the ASN legitimated the position of these Eurasian Associations and the Regidor, although Portuguese Eurasians are yet to be officially categorized as indigenous or *bumiputera*. As a result, the PEA was able to effectively silence the residents and modify the redevelopment plans of the *kampung* site.

IDENTITY POLITICS: SPECIFICITIES OF THE PORTUGUESE SETTLEMENT IN MELAKA[2]

In Malaysia, the Melakan Portuguese Eurasians have long been considered a distinctive Eurasian community. There are believed to be the descendants of the first Eurasian population in the country, established during the Portuguese rule of Melaka from 1511-1641.[3] Therefore, it is not surprising that Melakan Eurasians

---

[1] There are four officially registered Eurasian Associations in the country: the Penang Eurasian Association, the Eurasian Association of Kedah, the Eurasian Association of Selangor and the Federal Territory, and the Regidor (and his committee) in the Portuguese Settlement in Melaka.

[2] Melaka is also spelt as "Malacca." The latter spelling was commonly used during the British colonial era. Throughout this book, I adopt the Malay spelling of "Melaka" unless quoting citations or referring to names of organizations that adopt this colonial version of spelling.

[3] See E. Allard, "Social Organization of Eurasians in the Malaya Federation," *Current Anthropology* 15,5 (1964): 422; and Chan Kok Eng, "The Eurasians of Melaka," in *Melaka: The Transformation of a Malay Capital, C.1400-1980*, vol. II, ed. Kernial Singh Sandhu and Paul Wheatley (Kuala Lumpur: Oxford University Press, 1983), p. 264. The Portuguese were the first of the European powers to rule Melaka. According to Malay Annals, the Portuguese made initial contact with Melaka in 1509. See Chong Yoke Lin Linda, "The Portuguese-Eurasians (Serani of Penang)," in *Malaysian Ethnic Relations*, ed. S. Gardner (Penang: School of Social Sciences, Universiti Sains Malaysia, 1975), p. 115. The next colonial power in Malaya were the Dutch, who ruled Melaka from 1641 to 1795, and again from 1818 to 1823. The British were the third colonial power, and ruled Melaka from 1795 to 1818, and from 1824 until 1957, when the country gained independence. See Barbara Andaya and Leonard Andaya, *A History of Malaysia* (London: Macmillan, 1982), pp. 108, 114.

strongly identify with their Portuguese heritage.[4] They are further distinguished by the fact that they live largely on a piece of land known as the Portuguese Settlement. The Melakan Portuguese Settlement was created in 1933 by the British government.[5] It currently has a population of about two thousand, which makes it the country's largest single geographical concentration of Portuguese Eurasians.[6] Another feature of the Portuguese Settlement is that it is predominantly a fishing community.[7]

These geographical and social characteristics of the Portuguese Settlement have contributed to the development and maintenance of particular cultural and linguistic practices over time. For instance, this is the only Eurasian community in Malaysia which speaks Kristang (a form of Portuguese patois) and celebrates festivals such as San Pedro (which commemorates the patron saint of fishermen).[8] Roman Catholicism is another important marker of Portuguese heritage, and one that distinguishes them from Anglo-Eurasians, who are, by and large, Protestant.[9] Other than these distinctive traits, an important factor that unites the residents in the Portuguese Settlement is their engagement in a long-standing fight to safeguard the land of the Settlement. This fight began when the state government alienated several land parcels from the Settlement in the 1960s. The Portuguese Settlement became a property of the Melakan state government after independence and its

---

[4] See Chan Kok Eng, "The Eurasians of Melaka," p. 267; Ronald Daus, *Portuguese-Eurasian Communities in Southeast Asia* (Singapore: Institute of Southeast Asian Studies, 1989), p. 9; Myrna Braga-Blake, ed., *Singapore Eurasians: Memories and Hopes* (Singapore: Times Edition, 1992), p. 25; John Colliers, "The Estado da India in Southeast Asia," in *The First Portuguese Colonial Empire*, ed. Malyn Newitt (Exeter: University of Exeter, 1986), p. 50; C. Jack-Hinton, "Malacca and Goa and the Question of Race Relations in the Portuguese Overseas Provinces," paper presented at the International Conference in Asian History, Kuala Lumpur, August 5-10, 1968, p. 20; C. R. Boxer, *Portuguese Colonial Empire, 1415-1825* (Oxford: Clarendon Press, 1963), p. 2; Alan Baxter, *A Grammar of Kristang (Malacca Creole Portuguese)*, Pacific Linguistics Series B-95 (Canberra: Australian National University, Department of Linguistics, Research School of Pacific Affairs, 1988), p. 2; M. J. Pintado, *A Stroll through Ancient Malacca and a Glimpse at her Historical Sites* (Macau: Instituto Cultural de Macau, 1990), p. 4; and Fr. Manuel Teixeira, *The Portuguese Missions in Malacca and Singapore (1511-1958)*, vol. III (Singapore and Lisboa: Agencia Geral Do, 1963), p. 18.

[5] Bernard Sta Maria, *My People, My Country* (Melaka: The Malacca Portuguese Development Centre Publication, 1982), pp. 128, 135.

[6] Daus, *Portuguese-Eurasian Communities*, pp. 17-18; Chan Kok Eng, "The Eurasians of Melaka," p. 273.

[7] The Melakan Eurasians have been associated with the fishing occupation for several generations. See Peter J. Begbie, *The Malayan Peninsula: Embracing its History, Manners and Customs of the Inhabitants, Politics, Natural History, etc. from its Earliest Records* (Madras: Vepery Mission Press, 1834).

[8] See Chan Kok Eng, "The Eurasians of Melaka"; Baxter, *A Grammar of Kristang*; Daus, *Portuguese-Eurasian Communities*; Allard, "Social Organization of Eurasians." Kristang/Cristao, the Portuguese patois, is referred to by different names such as: *Papia Kristang* ("Christian speech"); *bahasa Serani* ("Serani language"); *bahasa Katholik* (Catholic language); *bahasa geragau* ("shrimp language," as speakers are well-known for catching a small shrimp—zool Acetes—found in shallow waters close to shore); *Malaqueiro, Malaquense, Malaques,* and *Malaquenho;* or *dialecto Portuguese de Malacca.*

[9] See Chan Kok Eng, "The Eurasians of Melaka," p. 267; Allard, "Social Organization of Eurasians," p. 422.

residents have been living under Temporary Occupation License since that time.[10] The land alienation sparked off fears among the settlers that they would eventually lose their land to other development projects. Their pleas to the state government to return the land and to grant them permanent titles were persistently turned down.[11]

As part of their fight, the residents set up the Portuguese Cultural Society in 1967 in order to instill a sense of pride within the community regarding their history and cultural heritage.[12] Part of the Society's activities was to establish the Tropa de Malacca in 1969, a cultural troupe specializing in the performance of traditional Portuguese dances and songs.[13] More recently, the Tropa de Malacca has represented the Portuguese-Eurasian community at various festivals throughout the country and has been invited by Eurasian Associations from outside Melaka to perform at their functions.

The community's fight to safeguard the Settlement land eventually led to their direct involvement in formal politics. In the 1969 General Election, the founder of the Portuguese Cultural Society won a state legislative assembly seat as a member of the opposition Democratic Action Party (DAP). He was subsequently reelected for two more terms in the 1974 and 1978.[14] This politician played a vital role in organizing a campaign to save the Portuguese Settlement during the 1970s, when a massive new land reclamation project was proposed as part of the redevelopment of the Customs and Excise Department's staff quarters.[15] During this campaign, a "Save the Portuguese Community Committee" was set up to lobby the government at both the state and federal levels. At the height of this campaign, the community established the Malacca Portuguese Development Trust and through the Trust built the Malacca Portuguese Development Center in the Settlement in 1981.[16]

These events in the Melakan Portuguese Settlement coincided with the start of Mahathir's term as Prime Minister. In his capacity as the Management Trustee of the Malacca Portuguese Development Trust, the Melakan Eurasian politician sent the newly elected Prime Minister a congratulatory note.[17] Although this move can

---

[10] There are both government and privately built houses in the Settlement. Tenancy in the government houses is regulated by an administrative committee which is headed by the Regidor. However, the Regidor also represents the interests of his people before the state government and negotiates the terms of lease, water, electricity supply and bus routes with the state government. See Chan Kok Eng, "The Eurasians of Melaka," p. 273; Sta Maria, *My People, My Country*, p. 132; and Daus, *Portuguese-Eurasian Communities*, p. 17.

[11] Chan Kok Eng, "The Eurasians of Melaka," p. 274.

[12] The shifting identity of the Portuguese-Eurasian community of Melaka through the projection of new public images via music and dance has been noted by some scholars. See Margaret Sarkissian, "Cultural Chameleons: Portuguese Eurasian Strategies for Survival in Post-colonial Malaysia," *Journal of Southeast Asian Studies* 28,2 (1997): 249-262.

[13] Ibid., p. 277; and *The Star*, September 27, 1993, p. 10.

[14] He was a member of the State Legislative Assembly for the Bandar Hilir constituency. See Sta Maria, *My People, My Country*, p. 193; Chan Kok Eng, "The Eurasians of Melaka," p. 274.

[15] The Customs' quarters were first built in 1953 during British rule. See Sta Maria, *My People, My Country*, pp. 142-143.

[16] Ibid., pp. 232, 227. The Portuguese Development Center conducts tutorial classes and vocational training for school dropouts and the unemployed, besides organizing fishermen. It has set up a university Loan Scheme and other socio-economic projects for the community.

[17] Ibid., p. 266

be interpreted as no more than part and parcel of Malaysian political protocol, the community received a reply from the Prime Minister stating that he would "give appropriate attention to the Portuguese Community."[18] In that same year, the Deputy Prime Minister became the first Malaysian Cabinet Minister to visit the Melakan Portuguese Settlement.[19]

The awakening of a Portuguese-Eurasian identity among the Melakan Eurasians had repercussions for the wider Eurasian community. This is not surprising, given that many of the Portuguese Eurasians in Negeri Sembilan, the Federal Territory, and Selangor are migrants from Melaka.[20] Even the substantial Portuguese-Eurasian population in the northern states of Kedah and Penang, who trace their ancestry to the Island of Phuket in Thailand, were affected by the events in Melaka.[21] Two publications from the early 1980s are testimony to the strength and spread of this cultural resurgence. 1981 and 1982 saw the publication of seminal texts written by Portuguese-Eurasian community leaders. The first was a pamphlet on the history of the Portuguese-Eurasian community of the northern states, and the second a text on the cultural heritage of the Melakan Portuguese-Eurasian community.

THE AWAKENING OF PORTUGUESE-EURASIAN IDENTITY—TWO TEXTUAL ANALYSES

The author of the first text was serving as the President of the Kedah Eurasian Association when he published his memoir. Titled *Bygone Eurasia: The Life Story of the Eurasians of Malaya*, the author, James Augustine, reasserts that the ancestors of the northern Eurasians fled the island of Phuket in 1778 and arrived in Kuala Kedah (Port Kedah) in 1781 before moving on to Penang.[22] Their flight from Phuket, Augustine alleges, was due to religious persecution when an usurper of the Thai throne by the name of "Phya Tak" conquered Ligor in 1778 and ordered the massacre of all Christians.[23] According to Augustine, these Eurasian religious refugees in Kuala Kedah, who spoke a mixture of Malay, Portuguese and Siamese,

---

[18] Ibid., 255. For a reprint of the Prime Minister's letter to the Malacca Portuguese Development Trust, dated July 7, 1981. See ibid., p. 226.

[19] During this visit, the federal government promised to provide a grant for the construction of a community hall and other amenities in the Settlement. Ibid., p. 255.

[20] See Chan Kok Eng, "A Study in the Social Geography of the Malacca Portuguese Eurasians" (MA thesis, University of Malaya, 1969), p. 65; Chan Kok Eng, "The Eurasians of Melaka," pp. 267-270.

[21] Teixeira, *The Portuguese Missions*, p. 328.

[22] James F. Augustine, *Bygone Eurasia: The Life Story of the Eurasians of Malaya* (Kuala Lumpur: Rajiv Printers, 1981), p. 10.

[23] While Augustine refers to the Thai usurper as "Phya Tak," John Cady, in his account of Southeast Asian history, explains that for a short period between 1778 and 1781 the Thai throne was taken over by a Chinese robber by the name of "Phya Taksin." See John F. Cady, *Southeast Asia: Its Historical Development* (New York: McGraw-Hill, 1964), p. 292. In contrast to Augustine's claim about Christian persecution in Phuket as the cause for the Eurasian out-migration during the latter part of the eighteenth century, Jennifer Cushman instead cites devastation wrought by the intermittent Burmese attacks and the continued raids on the island by Malay and Chinese pirates as the reasons for emigration. See Jennifer Cushman, *Family and State: The Formation of a Sino-Thai Tin-mining Dynasty, 1797-1932*, ed. Craig Reynolds (Singapore, Oxford, and New York: Oxford University Press, 1991), p. 8.

were well treated by the Sultan of Kedah and were even given a church and a religious center during their stay in the state.[24] They moved to Penang in 1786 when Francis Light (the "founder" of Penang) took over the island, whereupon they settled in Georgetown in the vicinity of Fort Cornwallis.

Augustine is, however, silent about a second Eurasian migrant group from Phuket who, according to a Catholic missionary text, immigrated directly to Penang in 1809 and settled in the Pulau Tikus area.[25] It is to this second batch of Eurasian migrants from Phuket whom the Kampung Serani residents trace their ancestry. Nonetheless, despite Augustine's silence on this subsequent group of Eurasian migrants who settled in Pulau Tikus, the PEA's arguments in the Kampung Serani conflict were significantly influenced by this text. Three of Augustine's assertions taken up by the PEA were: firstly, the importance of Christian missionary education and the use of Malay as the medium of teaching in the missionary schools; secondly, the role of Eurasian teachers as the "backbone of the [teaching] staff" in the "education of girls in Malaya"; and thirdly, a claim that the first president of the United Malays National Organization (UMNO), the late Dato Onn Jaafar, had "placed on record" his belief that Eurasians could justly claim to be "sons of the soil."[26]

The emphasis on the Eurasian contribution to education is a distinctive feature of the northern states. Unlike their Melakan counterparts who are associated with the fishing industry, northern Eurasians are known for their involvement in the teaching profession. There are other differences of note here too. In particular, Augustine's use of the more general term "Eurasians" to refer to Eurasians of Portuguese descent in the northern states.[27] In my opinion his usage of the more general term is due to the difficulty associated with claiming exclusive Portuguese descent for these northern Eurasians. Historically, the beginnings of a Portuguese-Eurasian community in the north coincided with the onset of British rule.[28] This

---

[24] Augustine, *Bygone Eurasia*, p. 18. The existence of the church in Kuala Kedah—the St. Michael Church—and the benevolence of the Sultan of Kedah were noted in the writings of two Catholic missionaries. See Rev. Felix George Lee, *The Catholic Church in Malaya* (Singapore: Eastern Universities Press, 1963), pp. 45-46; and Teixeira, *The Portuguese Missions*, pp. 327-328.

[25] Teixeira notes the immigration of this second batch of Eurasians from Phuket in his documentation of Portuguese Missions in Malaya. See Teixeira, *The Portuguese Missions*, p. 328. According to him, these migrants, led by a Portuguese priest by the name of Father Pasqual, fled Phuket in 1809 and came directly to Penang, as a boat was sent for them by the Vicar of the Church of the Assumption in Georgetown. These immigrants settled in the area of Pulau Tikus where the Catholic missions had set-up a seminary called College General. Ibid., p. 329.

[26] Augustine, *Bygone Eurasia*, pp. 19, 26. Dato Onn Jaafar was the first President of UMNO from its inauguration in 1946 to 1951. Ironically, his departure from UMNO was related to his suggestion of opening the party membership to all ethnic groups in the country.

[27] The term "Eurasian" was introduced by the British in 1820 when it became an official population category for all persons born of mixed-blood between Europeans and Asians. See Braga-Blake, *Singapore Eurasians*, p. 11; Judith Nagata, *Malaysian Mosaic: Perspectives from a Poly-Ethnic Society*, (Vancouver: University of British Columbia Press, 1979), p. 24; Allard, "The Social Organization of Eurasians," p. 422; and Daus, *Portuguese-Eurasian Communities*, p. 68. In 1931, the Population Census defined a Eurasian as the product of "inter-marriage" between European and Asiatic, or European and Eurasian, individuals. See Chan Kok Eng, "The Eurasians of Melaka," p. 279ff. Since 1957, census enumeration for Eurasians has used this guideline. However, Eurasians are placed under the category of "Others."

[28] The British East India Company occupied Penang on behalf of the English Crown in 1786.

led to the establishment of a significant Anglo-Eurasian population through the subsequent intermarriage between the various Eurasian groups. Consequently, northern Eurasians have never been associated with an exclusive Portuguese ancestry but are instead known for their heterogeneous origins.[29]

Let us now turn to the second text, which appeared a year after the first memoir. *My People, My Country* was written by Bernard Sta Maria, the aforementioned Melakan politician, and published by the Malacca Portuguese Development Center. It offers a comprehensive chronicle of Portuguese-Eurasian history in the country from 1509 to 1981. Published just after the Deputy Prime Minister's visit to the Melakan Portuguese Settlement, Sta Maria highlights the visit and draws attention to the Minister's designation of the Melakan Eurasians as "Malaysians of Portuguese descent." He interprets this new designation as signaling the dawn of "a new era and a new identity for the Portuguese Eurasians."[30]

In contrast to Augustine, Sta Maria particularizes the Melakan Eurasians as Portuguese Eurasians. Indeed, he places great emphasis on the Portuguese-Eurasian history in Melaka that dates back to the sixteenth century in order to assert their Portuguese identity. He uses the Portuguese-Eurasian historical experience in Melaka as the basis for three specific constructions of Portuguese-Eurasian identity.

Firstly, he claims that the authentic racial roots of Portuguese Eurasians are Portuguese and Malay. He arrives at this conclusion by noting that the first interracial unions could have only occurred between Portuguese men and either Malay or Indonesian women, given that Melaka was a Malay center at that time.[31] Sta Maria goes to great length to substantiate this claim and to ignore other genealogical ancestries implicitly by citing a wide range of references to prove that the Melakan Portuguese Eurasians are primarily Portuguese and Malay in origin.[32]

Sta Maria draws on several literary and textual sources to support his argument. He cites a Catholic missionary, the Reverend M. J. Pintado, who wrote that the "Portuguese descendants in Malaysia" should be referred to as "Luzo-Malays" because of their racial origins.[33] To further prove his point, Sta Maria highlights two colonial texts: C. M. Turnbull's *The Straits Settlements 1826-67* and Isabella Bird's *The Golden Chersonese and the Way Thither*, which use the term "Malay-Portuguese" to refer to the "Portuguese descendants" in Malaya.[34] In this way, the contemporary construction of Portuguese descent simultaneously affirms both the specificity of Portuguese heritage while claiming a common ancestry with the Malay community by virtue of a shared Melakan connection.

---

[29] See Khoo Kay Kim, "Malaysian Historiography: A Further Look," *Kajian Malaysia*, 10,1 (1992): 56; Nagata, *Malaysian Mosaic*, p. 40; Allard, "The Social Organization of Eurasians," p. 422.

[30] Sta Maria, *My People, My Country*, p. 255.

[31] Ibid., pp. 22-54.

[32] Sta Maria adopts the argument that the Portuguese encouraged their men to marry local women because Portuguese imperial expansion was, in part, inspired by Catholicism and, as such, was less "racially" conscious than other European expansionist powers. See Sta Maria, *My People, My Country*, p. 19; and Colliers, "The Estado da India."

[33] Sta Maria, *My People, My Country*, p. 26 (his spelling and emphasis).

[34] Ibid., pp. 95, 97. See C. M. Turnbull, *The Straits Settlement 1826-1867: Indian Presidency to Crown Colony* (London: Athlone Press, 1972) and Isabella L. Bird, *The Golden Chersonese and the Way Thither* (Kuala Lumpur: Oxford University Press, 1967 [1883]).

The significance of this historical connection between the Portuguese-Eurasian and Malay communities should not be overlooked. Melaka was founded between 1400 and 1401 and is closely identified with the origins of Malay civilization.[35] Throughout its first century, Melaka was ruled by a Malay sultanate, and it has been suggested that because the Portuguese's main interests in Melaka was as a naval and commercial base, its rule of Melaka from 1511-1641 hardly altered the administrative structure of the former sultanate.[36] Some analysts go so far as to argue that Melaka is the foundation of Malay polity, culture, and identity.[37] Melaka is thus a symbol of Malay culture and identity. It is not surprising then that Portuguese Eurasians ground their claims to Malayness in their historical presence there.

Sta Maria's second assertion is that Portuguese-Eurasian culture and language have assimilated elements of Malay culture and language. He bases his argument once again on the Portuguese-Eurasian historical presence in the predominantly Malay world of Melaka:

> In the process of time, living and sharing, in an environment of differing cultures, dominated primarily by the indigenous Malay culture, it was inevitable that a fusion of the two cultures after 400 years, would cause to emerge a culture, unique not only to the descendants of the Malacca Portuguese Community but also to the state and country; a culture where the basic elements of Iberian Portuguese Culture are conspicuous yet tied strongly to the influences of the indigenous Malay culture.[38]

Sta Maria argues that the structure of the Kristang patois spoken by the Melakan Portuguese Eurasians is similar to the basic forms of the Malay language. He further cites the works of two foreign scholars—Edger C. Knowlton, Jr. and Antonio Rego—to argue that over five hundred words from the Portuguese language have contributed to the evolution of Malaysia's national language, Bahasa Malaysia.[39] His referencing, however, is highly selective and highlights the political nature of the document. For example, a rather different picture is gleaned from two more recent research projects conducted in the Melaka Portuguese Settlement which show that Malay is seldom spoken by Melakan Portuguese Eurasians.[40]

Regardless of the accuracy of statements about the closeness between Malay and Portuguese-Eurasian cultures and languages, their close association continues to be an important platform in the political campaign waged by some members of the Portuguese-Eurasian community in Melaka to allow Portuguese Eurasians to join

---

[35] Andaya and Andaya, *A History of Malaysia*, p. 37.

[36] Colliers, "The Estado da India," p. 49.

[37] Clive S. Kessler, "Archaism and Modernity: Contemporary Malay Political Culture," In *Fragmented Vision: Culture and Politics in Contemporary Malaysia*, ed. Joel S. Kahn and Loh Kok Wah (Sydney: Allen & Unwin, 1992), p. 136. See also Anthony C. Milner, *Kerajaan: Malay Political Culture on the Eve of Colonial Rule* (Tucson: University of Arizona Press, 1982).

[38] Sta Maria, *My People, My Country*, pp. 197-198.

[39] Ibid., p. 211. See Edger C. Knowlton, "Malaysian Portuguese," *Linguist* 26,8-9 (1964): 211-213, 239-141. Rego's work is in the Portuguese language and is cited in Baxter, *A Grammar of Kristang*, p. 1.

[40] Chan Kok Eng, "The Eurasians of Melaka," p. 276 and Baxter, *A Grammar of Kristang*, p. 14.

UMNO. The following statement, quoted in *The Star* newspaper, was made by a Melakan Portuguese-Eurasian leader in 1993, following great optimism among the non-Malay population in Malaysia with the commitment to a Malaysian Nation under the national Vision 2020:

> The Portuguese community in Malacca should be allowed to join UMNO because the people are culturally closer to the Malays than the people of modern day Portugal, a scholar said. He said that there had been very little contact between the community and Portugal during the past 450 years. . . . "Whatever little direct contact we had did not have any major influence on us," he said. "What is significant in *Kristang* culture are things like *branyo (Joget lambak)*, *Mata Kantiga (pantuns)*, wearing of *sarong kebaya* and chewing of betel leaves which are still practised [sic] by the elders," he added.[41] He said even Cristao—the community's spoken language—was based on the Malay term of phonetics. [He] said in view of this, the Malacca Portuguese community should be referred to as *Luso-Malays*. (Luso is from the race of Lusitamos, the original inhabitants of Portugal).[42]

Sta Maria's third tenet is his claim that the Melakan Portuguese Settlement is the "cultural core-area" or "the Mecca" for all Portuguese Eurasians in Malaysia and that Portuguese Eurasians can trace their origins to Melaka.[43] This claim is highly problematic. As noted earlier, many Eurasians in the northern states of Malaysia do not share the same history with their counterparts in Melaka. Sta Maria attempts to overcome this obstacle by speculating that the ancestors of the northern Eurasians (who came from Phuket to Kuala Kedah) were probably those Portuguese Eurasians who fled Melaka due to the persecution of Catholics by the Dutch when they took over Melaka in 1641. He refers to the Eurasian immigrants from Phuket as "[t]he Malacca Portuguese of Kuala Kedah."[44] Unfortunately, this explanation is not supported by other historical sources and remains pure conjecture on his part.

Nevertheless, despite their different histories and cultural assertions, the various Eurasian Associations from the other states, including the Penang Eurasian Association, have been actively promoting the Portuguese heritage of their

---

[41] Kristang, sometimes spelled Cristao, is the Portuguese patois spoken by the Melakan Eurasians, but the word is frequently used to refer to the community itself (for details, see footnote 8 of this chapter). *Joget lambak* and *pantuns* are forms of Malay dance and poetry, and the *sarong kebaya* is a type of female attire commonly associated with the Malays, but not exclusively worn by them. The practice of chewing betel leaves, though believed to be a Malay habit, is also commonly found among the older generation of other ethnic groups in Malaysia.

[42] See *The Star*, February 25, 1993 under the headline, "Expert: Let Portuguese join UMNO" (emphasis in original).

[43] Sta Maria, *My People, My Country*, pp. 140, 147.

[44] Sta Maria made his argument based on missionary writings which claim severe persecution of Catholics by the Dutch when they took over Melaka. See ibid., pp. 140, 147. See also Teixeira, *The Portuguese Missions*, p. 295; Lee, *The Catholic Church in Malaya*, pp. 43-44; and J. P. Francois, *Historical Guide of Malacca* (Singapore: Malacca Historical Society Printers Ltd., 1936), pp. 84-88. However, other scholars have argued that the persecution of Catholics by the Dutch was only sporadic, ranging from occasional condemnation to general unofficial toleration. See Andaya and Andaya, *A History of Malaysia*, p. 211; and Baxter, *A Grammar of Kristang*, p. 7.

individual communities by emphasizing a historical connection to Melaka and reproducing other claims of the Melakan Eurasians. Indeed, due to their regulatory role in processing the Eurasian applications to the ASN unit trust scheme, these Eurasian Associations have become ever more adroit at appropriating national themes on Portuguese-Eurasian identity. The following statement was made in 1993 in the wake of the National Vision 2020:

> We want to go back to history in the 1500s. So we are very Malaysian in descent. In fact we are not fifty percent fifty percent [referring to half European and half Asian descent] because if we are, we would not look like us today, brown and Malay looking. Look at our color! We would prefer the name Luso-Malays or rather Luso-Malaysians.[45]

A promotional pamphlet advertising a Conference, Exhibition, Food and Cultural Fair, organized by the Eurasian Association of Selangor in 1993, is filled with illustrations of Portuguese-Eurasian heritage in Melaka, including the Portuguese Fort, the Portuguese armada, and the "traditional" Portuguese dance. The Program of the Cultural Fair similarly featured Portuguese customs, including "the songs and dances of Old Portuguese Malacca." The pre-eminence given to Portuguese heritage is even more noteworthy given the broad appeal that the Eurasian Association of Selangor was seeking:

> The Malaysian-Eurasian people is [sic] a unique community that embraces almost every race that lives in Malaysia and we are proud to state that we are TRUE MALAYSIANS. We invite you to witness the History, the customs and the traditions of the Malaysian-Eurasian and our contribution to the harmonious and affluent standard of living the Malaysian people enjoy today. ... We ... hope your interest and support will help us realise (sic) our Vision as we enter the 2000s.[46]

The above discussion of seminal texts has established the character of the recent constructions of Portuguese-Eurasian identity. On some occasions cultural distinctiveness is embraced (for example, in the formation of the Tropa de Malacca and the various attempts to stress the contribution to education of northern Eurasians), while at other times, it is played down (in claiming genealogical, cultural, and linguistic closeness to the Malay community). The growing articulation of Portuguese-Eurasian identity during the past twenty-five years has been integral to a number of political campaigns, initially to preserve the Portuguese Settlement in Melaka, and then, more recently, to have the community recognized as *bumiputera*.

However, this leaves unanswered the question of why Portuguese-Eurasian identity has been constructed in these terms. To address this question, we need to consider existing conceptualizations of Malay identity in the context of the

---

[45] Interview with A. S., a PEA leader, on October 5, 1993.

[46] Source: Pamphlet titled "Our Heritage"—a Conference, Exhibition, Food and Cultural Fair, organized by The Selangor and Federal Territory Eurasian Association, July 31 and August 1, 1993. Emphasis in original.

redefinition of the Malay nation and the impact this has had on the direction and shape of the politics of Portuguese-Eurasian identity in Malaysia.

ASSESSING CLAIMS OF PORTUGUESE-EURASIAN IDENTITY: HISTORY, RACE, CULTURE, AND MALAYNESS

In Chapter Three I noted the constitutional definition of Malay identity, the bureaucratic stipulations surrounding the official endowment of *bumiputera* status, and the special social and economic privileges for Malays and *bumiputera* groups in Malaysia. Needless to say, *bumiputera* status in Malaysian society is therefore inherently bound up with cultural status as well as opportunities for class or social mobility. In order to be accorded Malay-*bumiputera* status, one must be a Muslim, a habitual speaker of Malay, and practice Malay customs. Given this background, it was almost inevitable that other groups within Malaysia who aspire to *bumiputera* status and privileges would seek to construct their claims for officially recognized ethnic identity in terms congruent with the established definitions.

The above discussion clearly demonstrates the manner in which Portuguese-Eurasian history, language, and customs were used and manipulated to construct a concept of Portuguese-Malayness compatible with the existing conceptualizations of Malay identity.

Apart from the official demarcations of cultural distinctiveness (in terms of religion, language, and customs), there is among Malaysian citizens a popular belief in the notion of race and racial difference.[47] As noted in Chapter Three, the racial definition of ethnicity in Malaysian society, which presumes inherent biological and cultural differences, is rooted in the late nineteenth-century scientific racism practiced by the British colonial government.[48] The ideology of race argues that Malaysia's different ethnic groups are distinguishable by their distinct racial origins or "blood." This difference is manifest in individual physiological characteristics such as facial features, skin color, and so on. In this context, it is not difficult to see why the current constructions of Portuguese-Eurasian identity place such great emphasis on their part-Malay origin to claim Malayness.

Clearly, the rhetorical explanations of racial origins and cultural and linguistic distinctiveness in the recent constructions of the Portuguese-Eurasian identity are influenced by the existing arbitrary demarcations of cultural and racial traits in the conceptualization of Malay identity in Malaysia.

While we have established the congruity between the Portuguese Eurasians' emphases on historical, racial, cultural, and linguistic traits and the existing conceptualizations of Malay identity, a glaring incoherence remains—that is, the factor of Islam. We know that the Portuguese Eurasians are not Muslims, whereas

---

[47] It has been noted that "Malay," as well as other ethnic identities in Malaysia, is not only defined by the identification of discrete cultural characteristics, but also by the ideology of race. In appraising this trend, Joel Kahn points out that scientists have long proven that human beings cannot be easily divided into discrete racial groupings and as such the notion of race is but an ideological construct. Likewise, he equates the demarcation of a handful of discrete cultural characteristics in defining ethnicity as just as problematic as the use of "race." See Joel S. Kahn, "Class, Ethnicity and Diversity: Some Remarks on Malay Culture in Malaysia," in *Fragmented Vision*, p. 161.

[48] See Charles Hirschman, "The Making of Race in Colonial Malaya: Political Economy and Racial Ideology," *Sociological Forum* 1,2 (1986): 330-361.

Islam is an important Malay identity marker. Why then do they bother to claim Malayness when they are instead known for their total adherence to Catholicism?

I suggest that this peculiar move is related to recently shifting notions of Malayness, in particular the opening up in the 1990s of the Malaysian nation to include other ethnic groups. I noted in Chapter Three that some scholars have observed a trend in the politics of Malay identity, since the period of rising discord among the Malays during the 1980s, in which factors such as history and tradition were given more prominence than religion. I suggest that the emergence of this trend in Malay identity politics, which escalated with the reimagining of the Malaysian nation under the national Vision 2020 plan, was in part an encouragement for Portuguese Eurasians who are non-Muslims to use their history and cultural practices to lay claims to Malayness.

I will next consider those wider political and social developments within a rapidly modernizing Malaysia. They provide the political backdrop for the maneuvers of an elite section of the Eurasian community, which was seeking privileges from the government in the early 1980s.

ENTRY INTO THE ASN: EXIGENCIES OF MALAY POLITICS

"We would like to be accepted as *bumiputeras* because if the Thais can, why can't we?"[49]

My point of departure is the emergence of a Eurasian group that lobbied the government for Eurasian eligibility for the Amanah Saham Nasional investment scheme, reserved only for *bumiputeras* in the early 1980s. This lobbying group had its beginnings in the state of Kedah when another minority group—the Thais—were given the ASN. Kedah was the state in the north of the country where Eurasians were first established. Incidentally, Kedah has a large Thai minority population.[50] In the early 1980s the Thais, who are a non-Malay, non-Muslim, and non-*bumiputera* group, were given access to the ASN investment scheme.[51] Inevitably, the Thais' access to the ASN came to the knowledge of the Eurasian Association of Kedah which was at that time headed by James F. Augustine, the author of the memoir *Bygone Eurasia*. The leaders of the Association responded by initiating a lobbying group to persuade the government to extend the same privilege to the Eurasians in the state.[52] To understand why the Eurasian leaders in Kedah reacted in such a manner, we need to consider two things. First, we need to understand the significance of the government's decision to open to the Thais a scheme designed to benefit Malays and *bumiputeras*. We have noted that the Malay identity is largely politically defined and regulated. As Clive Kessler remarked, an individual's "social existence as a Malay" is "essentially a political

---

[49] Interview with A. S. on October 18, 1993.

[50] Apart from Kedah, Thais are also found along the Malaysian-Thai border in the states of Perak, Perlis, and Kelantan. This information is based on a statement made by the Chairman of the Malaysian Thai Association in *The Star*, October 4, 1993, p. 16.

[51] Interview with A. S. on October 5, 1993. This PEA leader was originally from Kedah and was acting as the Secretary of the Association during this period.

[52] Ibid.

condition of involvement with rule."[53] At the core of this political condition is "a relationship between the Malays as subjects and the rulers as their leaders who endowed them with a full Malay or completed Malay identity."[54] Therefore, the government's action in conferring a Malay/*bumiputera* privilege on the Thais was unavoidably a sign of a liberalization in the official definition of Malay and *bumiputera* identities. Not surprisingly, this provoked a response from other minority groups who sought similar inclusion in the ASN scheme.

A second matter to be considered is the similarities that exist between the Thais and the Eurasian community in Kedah. Both are minority groups who migrated from Thailand and who practice a mixture of Thai/Eurasian and Malay customs. (Some southern Thais are Muslims. This does not concern us here, as they are already officially categorized as Malays and considered as *bumiputeras*.)[55] In addition, the Thai community speaks a language that is a hybrid of Malay and Siamese.[56] In early descriptions of the Kedah Eurasians, it is noted that they spoke a mixture of Malay, Siamese, and Portuguese.[57] Given these similarities, it is not difficult to see why the Eurasians of Kedah reacted to the Thais' access to the ASN by demanding that they too be given the same privileges. Indeed, the pattern was repeated in 1993 when Portuguese Eurasians demanded the right to join UMNO following the entry of Thais and the non-Muslim *bumiputeras* of Sabah into the once exclusively Malay political party.

However, the ASN lobbying group in Kedah was not the only politically active group amongst the Portuguese-Eurasian leadership. Parallel with the political ferment in Kedah was the heightened political atmosphere amongst the Melaka Eurasians. In 1982, their political representative—the author of *My People, My Country*, Bernard Sta Maria—switched his political affiliation and joined the Gerakan party, a member of the National Alliance. As a result, his constituency seat went to the National Alliance in the General Elections that year.[58] As we know, two years later, in 1984, the privileged ASN unit trust scheme was opened up to the Portuguese Eurasians.

It is reasonable to assume that all these developments contributed to the decision to make Portuguese Eurasians eligible for the ASN. However, the question remains as to why the government chose to open up a privilege once reserved only for Malays and *bumiputeras* to the Portuguese Eurasians who are non-Malays and non-*bumiputeras* at this particular time. In order to understand the reason behind the government's decision, we need to consider the country's larger political context during this period.

As discussed in Chapter Three, one of the central problems, since the early 1980s, has been the political and cultural fragmentation of the Malay community, in the rapidly industrializing and modernizing Malaysian society. The period spanning from the early 1980s through to 1987, in particular, was marked by a fractious and unsettled political climate. The rifts in the Malay political

---

[53] Kessler, "Archaism and Modernity," p. 136.

[54] Ibid.

[55] See Nagata, *Malaysian Mosaic*, p. 50.

[56] Ibid., p. 50.

[57] See Augustine, *Bygone Eurasia*, pp. 10, 18; and Chong Yoke Lin Linda, "The Portuguese-Eurasians (Serani of Penang)," p. 123.

[58] Unfortunately, he died shortly after his political switch.

leadership began in 1981, when Dr. Mahathir came to power, and culminated in 1987 when his UMNO party split into two opposing groups. Accompanying this political feud was the resurgence of Islamic revivalist movements, which further split the Malay community and threatened the ruling party politically. In addition, there was growing disaffection among the Malay middle class towards the government's modernist but undemocratic practices, disaffection which led to heightened political tension among the Malays.

The emergence of a major Malay political opposition, coupled with the splintering of the Malay community, created keen competition between the two Malay parties to win supporters. One strategic way for the government to gain clear advantage over its new opponent was, therefore, to increase the pool of "Malay" supporters by accepting new members from selected minority groups which could demonstrate a cultural, social, or linguistic affinity with the Malays. Undoubtedly, an effective way for the government to gain political support from these minority groups was to endow them with the special privileges reserved for Malays and *bumiputeras*. Their ulterior motive was the subtle message that there were other groups in the country to whom the state could extend its patronage, if the Malay electorate was not duly loyal to the government.

For these reasons alone, the Thais and the Portuguese Eurasians were eminently suitable target groups for this political strategy. In addition, an investigation of the politically strategic importance of these two minority groups in Kedah, given the context of Malay disunity, further strengthens my hypothesis.

Kedah is the traditional "rice-bowl" state of the country, and also the home of the parliamentary seat of the Prime Minister.[59] Consequently, since Mahathir came to power in 1981, Kedah has gained considerable political prestige. Kedah has an extraordinary high number of minority groups.[60] The Thai community is Kedah's largest minority group; about half of the country's Thai population of 50,000 is found in Kedah alone.[61] Their substantial population gave the Thais in Kedah a political prominence not to be overlooked by a government in search of new political supporters. This political significance did not go unnoticed; besides acceptance into the ASN, UMNO specifically offered the Thai minority membership in its party.

As regards the Portuguese Eurasians, their entry into the ASN was most directly a repercussion of the acceptance of the Thai community into the scheme. Nevertheless, they were an equally suitable target, as they are also a substantial minority population numbering 15,345 persons, according to the 1980 Population

---

[59] The Prime Minister is the parliamentary representative of the Kubang Pasu electorate in Kedah.

[60] According to the 1980 Population Census, Kedah led the other states of Malaysia in terms of its minority population size, which totaled eighteen thousand. In second place was Sarawak, with a total of thirteen thousand, while Penang ranked third, with a total of eleven thousand. See Malaysia, *Malaysia Year Book 1990-91* (Kuala Lumpur: Berita Publishing Sdn. Bhd, 1990), p. 77.

[61] This information is based on a statement made by the Chairman of the Thai Association in *The Star*, October 4, 1993, p. 16. This number was inclusive of Thai-Muslims who are not classified as Thais but as Malays in the country's Population Census.

Survey.[62] In addition, I suggest that the prominence of the Melakan Portuguese Eurasians as a unique historic group strengthened their suitability in the government's eyes.[63]

From the perspective of the Portuguese-Eurasian leaders who lobbied for acceptance into the national unit trust scheme, their victory was an important symbol of the community's patronage by the government. This encouraged the community leaders to further assert their Malayness and to lobby for additional *bumiputera* status and privileges. This legitimation of the leaders of the Eurasian community significantly enhanced the PEA's position in the Kampung Serani conflict.

In the next section I discuss how the PEA appropriated the constructions of Portuguese-Eurasian identity at the national level to further its own local political legitimacy.

REPRODUCTION OF PORTUGUESE-EURASIAN IDENTITY IN PENANG

You see what happened is that everyone who is a Catholic and a Eurasian, he/she is considered Portuguese and can qualify for the ASN.[64]

The Penang Eurasian Association gained increasing legitimacy as the guardian of Eurasian culture and identity when it assumed a regulatory role in processing Eurasian applications to the Amanah Saham Nasional unit trust scheme.[65] Since taking on this new role, there was an increasing number of university graduates and professionals on the PEA executive committee.[66] One PEA leader, interviewed in 1993, described this change in the following terms:

We used to have people with the fisher of men mentality who ran the show. It was only in 1980s that professionals like [name of persons] and others joined. It is us who can give it a vision and steer the boat.[67]

Indeed one of the initial concerns of the new leadership was to inscribe the Portuguese-Eurasian heritage in the Pulau Tikus area.[68] As part of this, a formal

---

[62] Presumably, those who qualify as Portuguese Eurasians would have to be the Eurasians who adhere to the Catholic religion. See Penang Eurasian Association, "Penang Eurasian Community Population Survey 1987," Research Paper, 1987, p. i.

[63] There are about three thousand Eurasians in Melaka.

[64] Interview with A. S., PEA leader, on October 18, 1993.

[65] According to the 1980 Population Census, there were 2,501 Eurasians in Penang, forming about 16 percent of the total Eurasian population of 15,435 in Malaysia. Penang Eurasian Association, "Penang Eurasian Community Population Survey 1987," p. i.

[66] The PEA was formed in 1919 as a recreational club. Prior to its formation, a group of elite Penang Eurasians had formed a Penang Recreation Club in 1916. This club was opened to the "upper ten" of Indian and Chinese communities but was destroyed during the war. Interview with A.S., October 5, 1993. See also Khoo Su Nin, *Streets of Georgetown, Penang: An Illustrated Guide to Penang's City Streets and Historic Attractions* (Penang: Janus Print & Resources, 1993), p. 84.

[67] Interview with A. S. on October 5, 1993.

[68] During my interview with A. S., this PEA leader also revealed that he was in the process of writing a book on the history of the Portuguese Eurasians in Pulau Tikus.

request was made to the Penang State Government in 1988 to rename three roads in the area after prominent members of the early Portuguese-Eurasian community. The three particular roads—College Square, College Avenue, and College Lane—were chosen because they were named after the Catholic College Seminary demolished in 1982. The Association argued that without the seminary building the names by themselves no longer captured the Portuguese-Eurasian heritage of the area. The PEA proposed that College Square be renamed Martina Rozells Square, College Avenue be renamed Jeremiah Avenue, and College Lane (located next to the Church and Kampung Serani) be renamed Pasqual Lane.[69] These changes were justified as follows: Martina Rozells was the Eurasian wife of Francis Light (the "founder" of Penang) and thus, the "first lady of modern Penang"; Jeremiah was a prominent settler in Pulau Tikus;[70] and Pasqual was the Portuguese priest who led the second group of migrants from Phuket to settle in Pulau Tikus area in 1809.[71]

The proposal is yet to be approved, but the submission reveals the Association's standing interest in the Portuguese heritage of Pulau Tikus. This is not surprising given the area's status as the pioneer settlement of Portuguese Eurasians in Penang. In addition, Pulau Tikus is the only remaining Eurasian historic site in Penang where a substantial Eurasian population is still found.[72]

Apart from activities focused on the Pulau Tikus area specifically, the Association has been involved in the general promotion of Portuguese heritage amongst Penang Eurasians. For example, in 1991 the Association established a community center called Kaza Eurasian in a rented building. This move marked the first time ever that the PEA had established a premises for its activities. One of the first activities offered at the community center was a Kristang language class, introduced to encourage the learning of the Portuguese patois. This was a peculiar move on the part of the Association as Kristang is the mother tongue of the Portuguese Eurasians of Melaka and is not spoken in Penang. None of the residents of Kampung Serani, for example, knew or spoke Kristang. Instead, English was the lingua franca of the village. In addition, the community center organized a program to send Eurasian youths from Penang to the Portuguese Settlement in Melaka specifically to learn "traditional Portuguese" cultural songs and dances.[73] At the same time, social functions were organized by the new Executive Committee,

---

[69] Interview with A. S. on October 5, 1993.

[70] According to my interview with the grandson of Jeremiah, he had donated the cemetery land located along Kelawei Road to the Eurasian community. Interview with C. J. on October 6, 1993.

[71] See Anthony E. Sibert, "Preserve 'Noah's Ark,'" Typescript, n.d. I was told that the name Pasqual was originally De Pascoa—a Portuguese name—but was changed to Pasqual by the French Missionaries who took over the administration of the Pulau Tikus Church. Interview with A. S. on October 5, 1993.

[72] For information on locations in Georgetown once associated with the Eurasian community, see Khoo Su Nin, *Streets of Georgetown*, pp. 76, 90-91, 118, 158. A survey carried out by the Penang Eurasian Association on the Penang Eurasian population in 1987 showed that the largest number of Eurasians (19.7 percent) lived in its southern metropolitan towns of Green Gardens, Island Glades, East/West Jelutong, Gelugor, Bukit Dumbar, Minden Heights, and Brown Gardens, followed by 16.7 percent in the northern metropolitan town of Tanjung Bunga. Penang Eurasian Association, "Penang Eurasian Community Population Survey 1987," p. 2.

[73] Interview with A. S. on October 18, 1993.

including the revival of the Eurasians' once famed New Year's Eve dance party.[74] In 1993, the Kaza Eurasian center moved into the more spacious surroundings of a rented government bungalow. The Chief Minister of Penang was the guest of honor at the opening ceremony, which featured a performance by the Tropa de Malacca.

The presence at this official ceremony of this renowned cultural troupe from Melaka, coupled with the promotion of "traditional" Portuguese cultural practices, indicates a strong intention on the part of the PEA to establish a link between the Penang and the Melaka Eurasian communities. While historically this link is very tenuous, it makes sense in terms of contemporary cultural politics in Malaysia. The Portuguese-Eurasian history of Melaka is the only credible basis for the construction of a Eurasian identity that lays claims to indigenousness or Malayness. As noted earlier in the chapter, the leadership of the PEA is heavily embroiled in constructing a Portuguese-Eurasian identity around the terms "Luso-Malay" or "Luso-Malaysian." However, in order for the PEA to attach themselves to this debate, they needed to demonstrate a connection to Melaka.

Unfortunately for the PEA, this proved problematic on two fronts. Firstly, the push to establish an exclusive Portuguese heritage among the Eurasian community of Penang is unconvincing. As discussed earlier, Penang is known for its heterogeneous Eurasian population, which includes Eurasian immigrant groups such as the Anglo-Indians.[75] Even in Kampung Serani—the supposed Portuguese-Eurasian nucleus—many of the inhabitants were not exclusively Eurasians of Portuguese descent and claimed Portuguese descent on the basis of a single Portuguese-Eurasian ancestor.

Secondly, on the basis of interviews conducted during my fieldwork, it seems that some Portuguese Eurasians of Penang disagreed with the PEA's construction of Portuguese-Eurasian identity. In particular, they were opposed to the PEA's strong orientation towards Melaka and to the suggestion of an inherent Malayness within Portuguese-Eurasian identity. Many instead emphasized their "Europeanness":

The Malaccan Eurasians were brought up the Malay way. But we in Penang were brought up by the Portuguese way, the European way.[76]

The Penang Portuguese-descent Eurasians are closer to Europeans. I say they are more European because they are English-educated. Also, they are very good in sports. We have no communication with the Melakan Portuguese Eurasians; we could not even communicate with them as they used Portuguese.[77]

Despite the contested nature of PEA's construction of Portuguese-Eurasian heritage in Penang, its position, status, and highly articulate leadership has

---

[74] This was supposed to be a renowned Eurasian event during the British era. See Braga-Blake, *Singapore Eurasians*, p. 21.

[75] See Allard, "The Social Organization of Eurasians," p. 422. The Anglo-Indians, who worked mainly as railway staff, were known to have settled mainly in Penang, and many married Chinese women in succeeding generations. Ibid., p. 422. It has also been noted that Eurasians in Georgetown were mostly Anglo-Indians and Anglo-Chinese. See Nagata, *Malaysian Mosaic*, p. 40.

[76] Interview with R. A. on September 23, 1993.

[77] Interview with C. J. on October 6, 1993.

served to legitimate its own problematic constructions. I now turn to a discussion of the arguments put forward by the Association during the Kampung Serani conflict.

DECIPHERING THE PEA'S DISCOURSE IN THE KAMPUNG SERANI CONFLICT: LEGITIMACY, OPPORTUNITY, AND STRATEGY

The Penang Eurasian Association was first invited to mediate in the Kampung Serani conflict in 1984, but did not take on this role until 1991. Both 1984 and 1991 are highly significant dates in terms of the Association's entry into Portuguese-Eurasian identity politics. In 1984, the PEA began its regulatory role in processing Eurasian applicants for the Amanah Saham Nasional unit trust investment scheme. 1991 witnessed the Association's promotion of Portuguese heritage and its special interest in the Pulau Tikus area. We have established that the PEA's regulatory role in the privileged unit trust scheme brought it increasing legitimacy as the guardian of Eurasian culture and identity in Penang. This influence and stature did not go unnoticed. It was one of the competing developers—Company Golden-Heights—who first offered the Association a clubhouse in order to get the PEA's support so it could win the development contract from the Church. Also, it was the PEA's position as representative of the Eurasian community in Penang that allowed it to become involved in the Kampung Serani conflict, initially on behalf of the *kampung*'s residents and in order to safeguard Eurasian heritage in Penang.

Despite its role as spokesperson or representative which the Kampung Serani residents initially drew upon, the Association often maintained a different position from the residents on the issue of Portuguese-Eurasian cultural heritage and identity. I want to discuss two events during the conflict when the PEA produced quite different accounts of Portuguese-Eurasian cultural heritage and identity than the residents did. These differences, I argue, are explained by the PEA's mobilization of national and regional discourses about Portuguese-Eurasian identity, in contrast to the residents' more localized discourse.

The first event occurred during the PEA's public campaign to highlight the historical and cultural significance of the Noah's Ark building. In Chapter Four, I described the three distinctive claims that the PEA made in relation to Noah's Ark during the campaign. These were: firstly, an emphasis on the Eurasian contribution to modern education; secondly, an assertion of the basic Malayness of Eurasians because of their use of the Malay language; and thirdly, the contention that Pulau Tikus Eurasians originated from Melaka. These arguments initially appeared in an article written by a PEA leader and were later reproduced in speeches delivered during the public protest outside the Noah's Ark building in 1992.

The emphasis on the Eurasian contribution to national modern education—the first claim—was most likely influenced by the importance of missionary education to Eurasians in the states of Kedah and Penang and the Eurasian contribution to the "education of girls" in Malaysia, as pointed out in Augustine's *Bygone Eurasia*. This construction of cultural heritage also highlights the Eurasian involvement in teaching, which continues to this day, as many Penang Eurasians are teachers, indicated by the many academics on the executive committee of the PEA.[78]

---

[78] According to the 1987 PEA Survey, the majority of Penang Eurasians worked in the private sector (25.1 percent) followed by those who worked in the government or quasi-government sector (10.2 percent). Out of those who were engaged in the second occupational sector, 32.4

Noah's Ark, the first school in Pulau Tikus run by the Christian missions, provided an ideal vehicle for conveying the importance of the "Eurasian contribution to the modern education of the country."[79] It is my contention that the use of the word "modern" was not accidental, but deliberately chosen to resonate with the country's aspiration to become modern. Eurasian Associations outside Melaka, including the Penang Eurasian Association, have demonstrated an adroitness in appropriating pertinent themes from the national Vision 2020 (see Chapter Three) in order to identify their specific contributions to the nation. This appropriation further emphasizes the achievements and uniqueness of Portuguese-Eurasian culture. The desire by the PEA to draw upon Malaysia's modernizing aspirations in order to support its own position was clearly demonstrated by the Association in a draft of the Memorandum of Understanding (MOU) it drew up to formalize the agreement over the heritage house between the Church, the developer, and the Association:

> Malaysia is developing and changing at a rapid pace, in line with Vision 2020 that aims to make Malaysia an industrialized nation. These developments bring many new changes in our human and physical environment. In such a situation it is important that we preserve what is good in our lives and not destroy, uncritically, in the name of development. A case in point is the development of land associated with particular communities whose cultural heritage is attached to the land. In such cases, concrete ways must be made to ensure that their cultural and historical link to the land is maintained in the development process.[80]

The PEA's second claim was that the use of Malay as the medium of instruction in the Noah's Ark school in Pulau Tikus is evidence of the essential Malayness of local Portuguese Eurasians. Here once again the memoir *Bygone Eurasia* is a valuable resource, pointing out as it does that the medium of teaching in the early Christian missionary schools was Malay. The PEA noted not only that the Noah's Ark school was one of the early Christian missionary schools in Penang, but that the language of the Eurasians of Pulau Tikus shared many of the linguistic features of Malay. The PEA thereby tried to demonstrate that the Portuguese Eurasians of Penang conformed to the view of Portuguese-Eurasian identity promoted by leaders of the Melakan Portuguese-Eurasian community. That is, the PEA tried to establish a genealogical connection to the Malay community on the basis of linguistic proximity.

The final claim of the PEA, that the ancestors of the Pulau Tikus Portuguese Eurasians who immigrated from Phuket were originally from Melaka, was similar to the claims in Sta Maria's *My People, My Country*. Again, the Eurasian leaders reproduced this claim to allege that the ancestors of the Pulau Tikus Eurasians first settled in the Celebes before they went to Phuket, in contrast to the author's claim that they fled from Melaka directly to Phuket (see Chapter Four). The PEA's

---

percent worked in the field of education. See Penang Eurasian Association, "Penang Eurasian Community Population Survey 1987," p. 6.

[79] See Sibert, "Preserve 'Noah's Ark.'"

[80] "Draft of MOU" in the Penang Eurasian Association, "Annual General Meeting Report, 1993," p. 26.

effort to evoke Melaka as the residents' ancestral home was a means to validate its claim that Penang's Portuguese-Eurasian heritage is inherently part Malay by virtue of its connection to the Melakan Portuguese-Eurasian community.

How did these arguments benefit the Penang Eurasian Association in the Kampung Serani conflict? I contend that the PEA's appropriation of the national debate on Portuguese-Eurasian identity advantaged the Association in two ways. Firstly, it strengthened Noah's Ark as an important Eurasian cultural symbol. Secondly, it consolidated the PEA's position as the legitimate guardian of Eurasian cultural heritage and identity in Penang. As noted in Chapter Four, the campaign won the Association much public support, which placed it in an ever stronger bargaining position in the conflict. It was precisely the effectiveness of the campaign that forced Company Highview to recognize the heritage value of Noah's Ark and to concede to the PEA's request for a compensatory building.

The second event involved the PEA's ability to discredit villagers who did not meet their definition of Portuguese Eurasians. This meant that in the Noah's Ark campaign, the PEA successfully opposed a group of residents led by Paul, the *kampung* spokesperson, who disputed the Association's right to a clubhouse. The leaders of the Association argued that Paul was not Eurasian on the grounds of his Indian origins in order to discredit his role as the villagers' representative. Their ability to question Paul's Eurasian identity was, I argue, inevitably connected to their engagement in the national constructions of the Portuguese-Eurasian identity. We have established that a central feature in constructions of the Portuguese-Eurasian identity is the singling out of Portuguese descent in order to justify Malay "racial" origins. Furthermore, this arbitrary singling out of Portuguese descent is formalized in the bureaucratic stipulations of the ASN scheme, regulated by the various Eurasian Associations and the Regidor in Melaka. This regulatory role has given the PEA the power to determine who is and who is not a Portuguese-Eurasian person, within the context of the existing construction of Portuguese-Eurasian identity.

In sum, in the Kampung Serani conflict, the PEA exploited its engagement with national constructions of an indigenous Portuguese-Eurasian identity in at least three ways. Firstly, it used the legitimacy gained as the guardian of Eurasian culture in Penang to justify its role in the conflict and its demand for a compensatory building from the Church and developer. Secondly, it appropriated the arguments of national and regional debates to strengthen its claims on the heritage value of Noah's Ark to effectively realize its demand. Thirdly, it used its regulatory role in the privileged Amanah Saham Nasional scheme to silence opposition voices and to gain authority as the only legitimate Eurasian representative in the conflict.

CONCLUSION

This chapter has demonstrated the close connection between the broader constructions of a distinct Portuguese-Eurasian identity amidst the shifting ethnic and class politics in Malaysian society and the nature and persuasiveness of the Penang Eurasian Association's arguments in the Kampung Serani conflict. It has argued that the political leverage of a distinct Portuguese-Eurasian identity rested on an underlying Malayness which had its foundation in the long historical presence of the Melakan Portuguese Eurasians and the political developments faced by the Portuguese Settlement in Melaka in the early 1980s.

Despite the long association of Portuguese Eurasians with Melaka, their aspiration for *bumiputera* status and class mobility via access to the privileged Amanah Saham Nasional scheme were realized only because of larger political exigencies surrounding the fragmentation of the ruling Malay elite and middle classes in a rapidly modernizing Malaysian society. This fragmentation created space for a more flexible conceptualization of Malay identity as the government sought to gather political support from minority groups who could lay claim to Malay identity.

Admission to the privileged ASN investment scheme not only encouraged Portuguese Eurasians to make more vocal claims based on their supposed Malayness, but directly empowered elite segments of the community, in particular the various Eurasian Associations and the Regidor in Melaka. Not only could these Associations vet ASN applicants, but as a consequence they were given a new role, that of facilitators of class mobility and guardians of Portuguese-Eurasian culture and identity.

In this context, the PEA was able to assume the role of mediator in the Kampung Serani conflict in 1991. Through the exploitation of their legitimate role as guardian of Eurasian society, culture, and identity, and their reworking of national and regional discourses about Portuguese-Eurasian identity, the Association leaders were able to disenfranchise the residents of their negotiation rights and to alter the redevelopment plans of Kampung Serani. While the agenda of the national debate about Portuguese-Eurasian identity sought to push for full *bumiputera* status, the PEA exploited this discourse to achieve its own ambition of possessing a building which would express Eurasian heritage and identity in modern Penang.

This analysis clearly demonstrates the need to locate the divergent cultural production in the Kampung Serani conflict within larger political-economic and ethnic identity processes. The contrasting articulations of Portuguese-Eurasian cultural identity in the Kampung Serani conflict were the outcome of political, class, and social practices underlying the struggles of residents and the Penang Eurasian Association, first with the Church and the developer, and subsequently among themselves, to attain their differing goals for the *kampung* site.

Having examined the interaction between local, regional, and national forces in molding the PEA's and the residents' arguments about Portuguese-Eurasian heritage and identity in the conflict, we are still left with the question of why the PEA desperately wanted a "heritage house" to showcase Eurasian culture and identity in Penang. Why did Company Highview and the Church concede to the PEA's demands, and not the residents' requests for low-cost flats on the redeveloped site? In addition, we are still in the dark over why the Church, a non-commercial establishment, entered into a joint venture with a private developer. Why was the competing developer, Company Golden-Heights, so interested in the *kampung* site? To understand these issues we need to turn to the complex articulation between changes in the cityscape and the divergent conceptions of modernity among various groups in the city of Georgetown during the early 1990s, a period in Malaysia of relative prosperity and the promise of modernity.

CHAPTER SEVEN

THE JUGGERNAUT OF GROWTH AND THE KAMPUNG SERANI CONFLICT

This chapter outlines recent political, economic, cultural, and spatial dynamics within Penang in order to provide a context for understanding the actions and decisions of the Church and the Penang Eurasian Association in the Kampung Serani conflict. I argue that the Church's and the PEA's decisions during this dispute must be understood in the context of Penang's rapid economic growth and the state government's endorsement of the national push for modernization and urban development (encoded in policies such as "Penang: Into the 21st Century"). I show how the particular forces of economic liberalization and urban growth, in tandem with an enthrallment with modernity, created particular constraints as well as opportunities for the social, class, and identity positions of the Church and the PEA, forcing them to respond within their own sets of contingencies and circumstances, all of which contributed to shape the events of the Kampung Serani conflict.

My analysis begins with an introduction to Penang, including its geography, political administration, demography, political economy, and development history. The second section outlines Penang's economic growth over the last fifteen years and the state government's aspiration to develop Penang into northern Malaysia's high-technology, industrial, and cultural center. Rapid economic growth led to the intensification of property development activities in the state, which in turn resulted in a dramatic transformation of the urban skyline.

The final section traces these development transformations in the specific locale of Pulau Tikus. Long considered a middle-class area, it was not until the construction boom of the 1980s and 1990s that Pulau Tikus experienced dramatic high-rise and commercial developments. My discussion here illustrates how the redevelopment of Pulau Tikus, while in line with many residents' contemporary aspirations for a modern, industrialized Penang, brought the interests and aspirations of the *kampung* residents into conflict with those of the Church and members of the Penang Eurasian Association.

GEOGRAPHY, POLITICAL ADMINISTRATION, AND DEMOGRAPHY

Geography

Penang is situated to the north-west of peninsular Malaysia and is the second smallest state of the country. It has a total land area of 1,031 square kilometers, which is less than one percent of Malaysia's total land mass.[1] The state consists of the island of Penang and a strip of land across the mainland which is known as Province Wellesley or Seberang Perai.

There are a total of five administrative districts in Penang (see Map 7.1 in Appendix N).[2] Two of these administrative districts—the Northeast District and Southwest District—are located on the island.[3] The remaining three administrative districts—Seberang Perai North, Seberang Perai Central, and Seberang Perai South—are located on the mainland.

The capital of Penang, Georgetown, falls within the Northeast District.[4] The Pulau Tikus area (where Kampung Serani stood) lies within the Georgetown City limits and is shown in Map 7.2 in Appendix O. There are no official boundaries which delineate Pulau Tikus as a specific locale. Officially, it is subsumed within the Northeast administrative district and within the Georgetown City limits. Therefore, in geographically defining the area, I have adopted a social definition of Pulau Tikus common among Penangites. According to this definition, Pulau Tikus is bounded by the following roads: Jalan Pangkor, Lebuhraya Peel, Jalan Macalister, Jalan Utama (Western Road), Jalan Gottlieb, Jalan Bagan Jermal, and Persiaran Gurney (Gurney Drive). Map 7.3 delineates the location of the Pulau Tikus area (see Appendix P).[5]

Urban areas in Penang were originally defined according to the city limits of Georgetown and the designated towns of Butterworth and Bukit Mertajam on the mainland.[6] Since the mid-1980s, new, sprawling residential areas and townships have erased Penang's earlier city and town limits, giving rise to a "metropolitan region."[7] On the mainland, the metropolitan region includes the towns of Seberang Perai and Bukit Mertajam, as well as surrounding built-up areas. On the island, this newly defined metropolitan region consists of areas linking Georgetown and its suburban towns. This means that the metropolitan region on Penang Island extends from Georgetown to the following towns: Tanjung Bunga in the north, Air Itam and Paya Terubong in the west, and Bayan Lepas and Teluk Kumbar in the south (for the location of these towns, see Map 7.4 in Appendix Q).

---

[1] Penang Development Corporation, *Statistics Penang Malaysia*, n.d.

[2] Each district is further divided into towns and *mukims* (land outside town areas). Each town is divided into sections, and within each section, numbers are assigned to every piece of surveyed land. Similarly, surveyed land lots in each *mukim* are assigned a number.

[3] The size of the Northeast District is roughly 119 square kilometers, while the Southwest District is approximately 173 square kilometers. Majlis Perbandaran Pulau Pinang, *Maklumat Asas Majlis Perbandaran Pulau Pinang [Basic Information on the Penang City Council]* (Penang: Majlis Perbandaran Pulau Pinang, 1989), p. 1.

[4] The size of Georgetown is about 25 square kilometers. Ibid.

[5] *Jalan* is equivalent to Road, and *Lebuhraya* means Avenue.

[6] In Malaysia, regions with a population of ten thousand citizens or more are designated as urban. All regions with a population below ten thousand are designated as rural (P. J. Rimmer and George C. H. Cho, "Urbanization of the Malays since Independence: Evidence from West Malaysia, 1957 and 1970," *Journal of Southeast Asian Studies* 12,2 (1981): 351.

[7] Goh Ban Lee, "The Foundation of Urban Planning in Georgetown and Adelaide," *Kajian Malaysia* 6,1 (1988): 46.

Political Administration

The five districts in Penang are administered by the state's two local planning authorities: the Majlis Perbandaran Pulau Pinang (the Penang City Council) and the Majlis Perbandaran Seberang Perai (the Seberang Perai Municipal Council). The Penang City Council is the planning authority on Penang Island and administers the Northeast and the Southwest Districts, while the Seberang Perai Municipal Council's jurisdiction covers the remaining districts of Seberang Perai North, Seberang Perai Central, and Seberang Perai South on the mainland.[8]

These two authorities[9] have a mandate under the Town and Country Planning Act, 1976 (T&CPA, 1976).[10] However, they are not autonomous bodies and are administered by the Chief Minister, as specified in Local Government Act, 1976 (Act 171),[11] which provides the state government with supreme powers in all planning matters.

Municipal councilors for the two local authorities are appointed by the Chief Minister, based on recommendations by the State Office. The councilors are appointed on a political party basis—a clear indication that planning decisions in the state are intertwined with party politics. The councilors in the Penang City Council are dominated by Gerakan political party members, while the councilors in the Seberang Perai Municipal Council are predominantly from UMNO.[12]

---

[8] These two local authorities were created as a result of the restructuring of local authorities under the Local Government (Temporary Provisions) Act 124, 1973. Prior to 1974, Penang Island was administered by two local government structures: the City Council of Georgetown City, which administered the city area, and the various Rural District Councils, which administered the other districts in the state. For a history of local authority in Penang, see Jurgen Ruland, *Urban Development in Southeast Asia: Regional Cities and Local Government* (Boulder, CO: Westview Press, 1992); Mat Lazin bin Awang, "An Evaluation of the Functions of the City Council of Georgetown, Penang, 1957-1966" (Graduation Exercise of School of Humanities, Universiti Sains Malaysia, 1974); and Choo Eng Guan, "A Study of the Administrative Process of the City Council of Georgetown" (Bachelor of Economics Graduation Exercise, Faculty of Economics and Administration, Universiti Malaya, 1970).

[9] The Town and Country Planning Act, 1976, provides for the two-tier planning system—that is, strategic planning and detailed technical planning. See Goh Ban Lee, "Evolusi Perancangan Bandar di Pulau Pinang [The Evolution of Urban Planning in Penang]," *Kajian Malaysia* 2,2 (1984): 22. The Penang Structure Plan, which interprets national and regional policies in the context of physical planning, was completed in the 1980s. Three local plans for the northern towns of Tanjung Bunga, Tanjung Tokong, and Teluk Bahang were completed in 1993.

[10] Under Section 58 of the T&CPA, 1976, the local authority can make rules to: regulate the development of land or buildings in accordance with proper planning; control density, height, plot ratio, floor area, design appearance, car park provisions, set backs, open spaces; and so on. For a discussion of the development control process under the T&CPA, 1976, see Ong Swee Teik, "The New Process in Development Control under the Town and Country Planning Act 1976," paper delivered at National Planning Conference on "The Role of Town Planners in Society," Penang, September 9-10, 1986.

[11] The transfer of all functions of the local council to the Chief Minister took place in 1966 under the City Council of Georgetown (Transfer of Functions) Order, 1966. Prior to the transfer of functions, there were local government elections in Penang, and the Georgetown City Council was headed by a Mayor. The mayoral system was abolished in 1965, when the federal government banned all local elections. See Ruland, *Urban Development*, p. 211; Choo Eng Guan, "A Study of the Administrative Process," p. 7; and Mat Lazin bin Awang, "An Evaluation of the Functions," p. 13.

[12] In 1993, of the total forty-eight municipal councilors in Penang (twenty-four on each council), twenty-six were from the United Malay National Organization (UMNO), fifteen from Gerakan,

Demography

Penang differs from the other states in Malaysia in that the majority of its population are Chinese Malaysians. In 1990, of the total population of 1.15 million people, 52.9 percent were Chinese, 34.5 percent were Malay, and 11.5 percent were Indian. An additional 1.1 percent of the population is classified as other minority groups, within which is included a total of 2,501 Eurasians (see Table 7.1).

Table 7.1 [13]
Penang's Population and Ethnic Composition for 1990

Ethnicity	Malay	Chinese	Indian	Others	Total
Population (100,000's)	399.2	607.4	131.1	12.7	1,150.4
Percentage	34.5	52.9	11.5	1.1	100.0

In 1990, 49 percent of Penang's population lived on the island while 51 percent lived on the mainland. In that same year, the ethnic demographics of the island closely resembled those of the state as a whole. The Chinese community constituted 52 percent of the total population of Penang Island, while the Malay and Indian communities accounted for 35 percent and 12 percent, respectively.[14] Overall, the Chinese were the most urbanized group in the state and made up 55.9 percent of the total metropolitan population, in contrast to the Malay and Indian communities, which constituted 30.4 percent and 12.4 percent, respectively (see Table 7.2).

Table 7.2[15]
Penang: Population of Metropolitan Region by Ethnicity for 1990

Ethnicity	Population (in hundred thousands)	%
Malay	261.1	30.4
Chinese	481.9	55.9
Indian	107.2	12.4
Other	11.3	1.3
TOTAL	861.5	100.0

---

four from the Malaysian Chinese Association (MCA), and three from the Malaysian Indian Congress (MIC). The dominance of the UMNO in federal politics has often meant that councilors from the Seberang Perai Municipal Council have better access to the federal government.

[13] Penang Development Corporation, *Statistics Penang Malaysia.*

[14] In 1970, 55.8 percent of Penang's population lived on the island. See Institute of Strategic and International Studies (ISIS) and Penang Development Corporation, "Penang Strategic Development Plan, 1991-2000" (Final Report to the Penang State Government, 1991), pp. 1-3. There is a long-term plan to house 40 percent of the state's population on the island and 60 percent on the mainland.

[15] Adapted from ISIS and Penang Development Corporation, "Penang Strategic Development Plan," pp. 3-13, Table 3.5

The urban nature of the island's Chinese majority, with rates of urbanization higher than Malays and other ethnic groups, has strong repercussions for Penang's political economy.

THE POLITICAL ECONOMY OF PENANG

Penang's ruling political party is the Gerakan party,[16] which first came to power in 1969 as an opposition party. Since then, it has ruled without interruption, though in 1972, Gerakan switched its political affiliation to become a member of the National Alliance. The party's position of Chief Minister has always been held by a Chinese Malaysian. This situation has been made possible by the state's Chinese majority, and this fact makes Penang the only state in West Malaysia to be administered by a non-Malay political leader.[17] The Chinese in Penang also hold much of the state's economic power. A state report reveals that in 1989, Chinese owned 49.4 percent of the total share of capital in Penang's corporate sector, while Malays only owned 2.1 percent.[18]

This situation indicates that Penang fell significantly behind in achieving one of the goals of the New Economic Policy (NEP)—to increase the Malay or *bumiputera* share of corporate sector ownership from 2.4 percent in 1970 to 30 percent by 1990.[19] Thus, there is much pressure on the state government to speed up the commercialization and urbanization of the Malays.[20] Fuelling this pressure are the new goals of the New Development Policy (NDP), which aims to rapidly develop an active *bumiputera* commercial and industrial community (see Chapter Three).

The organizations pushing for greater Malay participation in Penang's economy and urbanization are the Penang branch of UMNO and the federal government. The Penang branch of UMNO has frequently voiced its concern that Malays should not be left out of the state's development. UMNO state politicians have used their better access to powerful federal authorities to push for various special programs to help Malays catch up to the achievements of the non-Malays.

Inevitably, this has led to a certain amount of tension between UMNO and Gerakan, the two major partners in the National Alliance which forms the state government. This tension increased after 1992 when the Gerakan government was returned to power only with the support of UMNO. In that election, UMNO held twelve of the twenty seats won by the National Alliance, while Gerakan only won

---

[16] Gerakan is the multi-racial party in the National Alliance, but a majority of its members are of Chinese descent.

[17] The Head of Penang State is the Yang-Di-Pertua Negeri Pulau Pinang, who is appointed by the federal government.

[18] See ISIS and Penang Development Corporation, "Penang Strategic Development Plan," pp. 2-22, Table 2.8; and *New Straits Times*, October 20, 1993, p. 10.

[19] At the national level, the *bumiputera* proportion of share capital rose from 1.5 percent in 1969 to 19.4 percent in 1988. See K. S. Jomo, *Beyond the New Economic Policy?: Malaysia in the Nineties* (Asian Studies Association of Australia, 1990), pp. 9-10.

[20] Under the New Economic Policy, the encouragement of *bumiputera* participation in urban activities, the establishment of new growth centers, and the creation of a Malay commercial and industrial community were seen as the principal means to accelerate the process of restructuring Malaysian society.

seven seats and the MIC won the remaining one seat.[21] This unusually poor performance by Gerakan led to an unprecedented controversy within the winning coalition as to whether the political head of the state should come from Gerakan or from UMNO. The controversy was finally resolved by appointing a UMNO member of the State Legislative Assembly as Deputy Chief Minister, while retaining a Gerakan member in the position of Chief Minister.[22]

Given Penang's dismal performance in the New Economic Policy, Gerakan's weaker political position enabled the Penang branch of UMNO and the federal government to step up their pressure on the state to strengthen its commitment to the goals of the new NDP and the federal government initiative "Vision 2020." It is no coincidence that the early 1990s saw a greater involvement of federal agencies in Penang's urban development. The tension between the state and the federal governments over the issue of Malay participation in the urban economy significantly influenced the politics of development and ethnic representation in contemporary Penang. Continued economic growth during the early 1990s, combined with an increasingly affluent social class with increasing potential for consumption, further complicated the struggle for urban space and ethnic representation in Penang. In order to comprehend the complexities of these struggles, we need to understand both the historical foundation of the state's economic development, and the various interests with a stake in the island's recent economic boom. These wider politics of urban development, as I will show, had direct repercussions on the Kampung Serani conflict, because the Pulau Tikus area where the village was located became an attractive site for property developers, commercial enterprises, and the upper-income elites of Penang.

Development History

Penang was occupied by the East India Company on behalf of the English Crown in 1786.[23] Penang and its mainland became part of a single administrative

---

[21] The 1994 State Election saw a growing reactionary disposition among Penangites as they gave thirty-two State Legislative Assembly seats to the National Alliance, leaving the opposition party—the Democratic Action Party (DAP)—with only a single seat. In the 1999 State Election, PAS (Pan-Malaysia Islamic Party) and the new opposition party, Keadilan, won a seat each. The following is a breakdown of Penang's State Legislative Assembly seats held by political parties from 1986 to 1999:

Year	Gerakan	MCA	MIC	UMNO	DAP	Keadilan	PAS	Total
1986	9	2	-	12	10			33
1990	7	-	1	12	13			33
1995	11	9	-	12	1			33
1999	8	9	1	12	1	1	1	33

[22] This arrangement led to constant taunting from the opposition political party (which incidentally won thirteen of the State Legislative Assembly seats that year) that the "de facto" head of the state was the UMNO Deputy Chief Minister. See *The Star*, July 8, 1993, p. 13; and *New Straits Times*, July 2, 1993, p. 9.

[23] The Sultan of Kedah, who acknowledged the suzerainty of the King of Siam, was the nominal ruler of the island, but ceded Penang to England in 1781. England's suzerainty over Penang was not formalized until the Treaty of Bangkok between England and Siam was signed in 1826.

unit called the Straits Settlements (which included Singapore and Melaka) in 1826, and remained under the control of the British authorities in India until it was transferred to the Colonial Office in 1867.[24]

Penang's history as a British Crown Colony and its status as a free port contributed to its economic growth, at least until the early twentieth century. Its economic growth—largely in the area of commerce and trade—attracted various immigrant groups to the state, ranging from South Indians, Ceylonese, and Burmese, to Chinese, Thais, and Europeans (especially Christian missionaries).[25] These groups established their own communities and neighborhoods, and this multi-cultural heritage is still evident in the eclectic style of architecture found in Georgetown today.

While Penang's economy fared rather well during the colonial period, problems began to appear during the early Independence era. This started with the disruption of trade with its neighboring countries due to the Indonesian confrontation in the 1960s. The greatest setback came in 1969 when the federal government withdrew Penang's free-port status. The revocation of this status greatly affected the economy, so much so that by 1970 Penang's per capita GDP was 12 percent below the national average of RM1,183, and the unemployment rate was as high as 15 percent.[26]

This state of affairs called for an alternative development strategy. The Penang Master Plan Study, commissioned by the federal government, provided such an alternative. This report, completed in 1970, became known as the Nathan Report (after the consultant, Robert Nathan). The major thrust of the report was that the state needed to enhance its global economic links through industrialization and tourism.[27] In line with the twin objectives of the New Economic Policy—to eradicate poverty and restructure society—the development strategy of the Penang Master Plan became the basis of Penang's development throughout the 1970s and 1980s.

Subsequently, the state government began a program of massive industrialization in the 1970s which saw the setting up of Free Trade Zones (now called Free Industrial Zones) to attract export-oriented manufacturing industries to the state, aiding its economic growth. This successfully established Penang's industrial base: from one industrial estate with thirty-one factories employing 2,784 people in 1970, Penang now has four industrial estates and four Free Industrial

---

[24] Barbara Andaya and Leonard Andaya, *A History of Malaysia* (London: Macmillan, 1982), p. 122.

[25] See Judith Nagata, *Malaysian Mosaic: Perspectives from a Poly-Ethnic Society* (Vancouver: University of British Columbia Press, 1979), pp. 21-23; and Patrick Low, ed., "Trends in Southeast Asia (No. 2): Proceedings and Background Paper of Seminar on Trends in Malaysia" (Singapore: Institute of Southeast Asian Studies, 1972), pp. 125-126.

[26] Helen E. S. Nesadurai, "The Free Trade Zone in Penang, Malaysia: Performance and Prospects," *Southeast Asian Journal of Social Science* 19,1&2 (1991): 107.

[27] See Penang Development Corporation, *Penang: Looking Back, Looking Ahead. 20 Years of Progress* (Penang: Penang Development Corporation, 1990), p. 10. In 1962, the Penang State government had engaged a Colombo Plan Advisor, A. M. Munro, to prepare a Master Plan for the state that was completed in 1964. This plan was not implemented as it did not have the support of the federal government. See Lee Lik Meng, Abdul Mutalib Abdullah, and Alip Rahim, *Town Planning in Malaysia: History and Legislation* (Penang: School of Housing, Building and Planning, University Sains Malaysia, 1990), p 37; Goh Ban Lee, "The Foundation of Urban Planning," p. 68; and Ruland, *Urban Development*, p. 236.

Zones serving a total of 637 factories which employ 162,703 workers.[28] In addition, the manufacturing sector's contribution to the state's GDP jumped from 13 percent in 1970 to 46 percent in 1990 (see Table 7.3 below).

Table 7.3[29]
Penang's GDP 1970-2000 (1978 prices, RM million)
(In parentheses = %;   * = projection)

Economic Sectors	1970	1980	1990	2000*
Agriculture, Livestock, Forestry & Fishing	264 (19.5)	223 (6.5)	189 (3.3)	209 (1.8)
Mining & Quarrying	2 (0.2)	18 (0.5)	26 (0.5)	22 (0.2)
Manufacturing	172 (12.7)	1,399 (41)	2,668 (46)	5,894 (50.1)
Construction	78 (5.8)	143 (4.2)	170 (2.9)	254 (2.2)
Electricity, Gas & Water	42 (3.1)	68 (2.0)	116 (2.0)	229 (2.0)
Transport, Storage & Communications	101 (7.5)	313 (9.2)	648 (11.2)	1,387 (11.8)
Wholesale & Retail Trade, Hotels & Restaurants	361 (26.7)	565 (16.6)	731 (12.6)	1,531 (13.0)
Finance, Insurance, Real Estate & Business Services	131 (9.7)	269 (7.9)	540 (9.3)	1,115 (9.5)
Government Services	58 (4.3)	322 (9.4)	563 (9.7)	843 (7.2)
Other Services	142 (10.5)	93 (2.7)	143 (2.5)	270 (2.3)
TOTAL	1,351	3,413	5,795	11,754
Increase over ten years#	-	152%	71%	103%
Ratio over 1970 GDP Value#	1.00	2.52	4.30	8.70

Penang's Vision into the Twenty-First Century

From a position of comparative disadvantage in the late 1960s, Penang has achieved an impressive level of economic growth, at times even surpassing the national average. Between 1991-1993, its economy grew by 9.7 percent per annum—

---

[28] Boonler Somchit, "Meeting Penang's Needs for More Trained Manpower and Overcoming Skills Shortage—The PSDC Experience," paper presented at the International Conference on Penang 2002: Into the 21st Century, Penang, July 26-27, 1994, p. 1

[29] Reproduced from Penang State Government, *Penang into the 21st Century: A Strategic Plan to Build a Fully Developed, Post-Industrial Society* (Penang: Penang State Government, 1992), p. 19, Table 2. Additional figures ("Increase over Ten Years" and "Ratio over 1970 GDP Value") are obtained from Koh Tsu Koon, "Preparing for the Next Major Transformation Towards an Advanced Industrialised Economy for Penang." Keynote address at the International Conference on Penang 2002: Into the 21st Century, Penang, July 26-27, 1994, p. 24.

higher than the national average of 8.1 percent.[30] In 1993, Penang's per capita GDP of RM11,000 was 28 percent higher than the national average.[31] RM11,000 is equivalent to US$4,400, and thus brings Penang close to the US$5,000 per capita GDP qualification for a "developed country," as defined by the World Bank.[32]

In November 1990, Penang became the first state in the country to formulate and unveil its own strategic development plan in line with the national "Vision 2020." "Penang into the 21st Century" offers a vision of Penang in the next century as a fully industrialized and highly cultured city. Its goals are to establish Penang as a center for manufacturing, tourism, business, education, professional services, transportation, and technology, as well as a center for culture and the arts.[33] The ultimate ambition is to establish Penang as the regional center of the nascent Indonesia-Thailand-Malaysia Growth Triangle (the "Northern Growth Triangle").[34]

This strategy statement gives responsibility for the promotion of Penang as a state rich in culture to the tourism sector—already targeted for growth under the Penang Master Plan.[35] In accordance with this, the Penang State Culture and Tourism Committee was given additional state support. In particular, the state sponsored the preservation of historic buildings in Georgetown and supported the Committee's long-standing promotion of Penang's multi-ethnic heritage and colonial legacy as a means of enhancing Penang's cultural attractions.[36]

In order to achieve another of its goals, the state government launched a campaign to encourage Malaysian professionals working overseas—in particular, Malaysian engineers and scientists—to return to work in Penang.[37] The "High Tech Career Opportunity in a Resort Environment" campaign sought to address the acute shortage of skilled labor in Penang and actively promoted Penang as a blend of the old (a "quaint old world") with the new (quality infrastructure and high tech

---

[30] Ali Abul Hassan bin Sulaiman, "Penang's Economic Performance and Future Prospects: Challenges, Issues and Developments," paper presented at the International Conference on Penang 2002: Into the 21st Century, Penang, July 26-27, 1994, p. 2.

[31] Ibid.

[32] Koh Tsu Koon, "Preparing for the Next Major Transformation," p. 12.

[33] See Koh Tsu Koon, "Preparing for the Next Major Transformation"; Kang Chin Seng, "Making Penang a Center of Education: Challenges and Opportunities in the Age of Knowledge," paper presented at the International Conference on Penang 2002: Into the 21st Century, Penang, July 26-27, 1994; and Boonler Somchit, "Meeting Penang's Needs."

[34] The concept of the Northern Growth Triangle was agreed to in principle by the countries involved in July 1993, pending detailed recommendations by the Asian Development Bank. See *New Straits Times*, May 23, 1993, p. 1.

[35] Tourism is a large revenue source for Penang. In 1992, the chairperson of the State Culture and Tourism Committee announced that revenue from tourism-related sectors reached RM1.3 million, making it the second highest income source, after the industrial sector. See *New Straits Times*, March 9, 1993, p. 8.

[36] See Kee Phaik Cheen, "Tourism and Leisure Industries in Penang: Challenges, Responses and Opportunities for Growth and Development," paper presented at the International Conference on Penang 2002: Into the 21st Century, Penang, July 26-27, 1994, p. 4. The State Tourism Committee invited French, Australian, and Japanese conservation experts to help with this urban conservation effort.

[37] About twelve thousand scientists and engineers are currently working in Penang, but the state projected a need for a supply of three thousand engineers and scientists per year. See Koh Tsu Koon, "Preparing for the Next Major Transformation," p. 17.

career opportunities).[38] Penang's labor structure and its anticipated manpower demand are indicated in Tables 7.4 and 7.5 below.[39]

Table 7.4[40]

Percentage Distribution of Employed Persons by Occupation Groups, 1989

Occupation Groups	Percent
Professional, Technical & Related Workers	6.5
Administrative & Managerial Workers	2.3
Clerical & Related Workers	11.5
Sales & Related Workers	13.2
Service Workers	13.3
Agriculture, Animal Husbandry, Forestry, Fishermen & Hunters	7.2
Production, Transport Equipment Operators, & Laborers	46.0
TOTAL	100.0

Table 7.5[41]

Penang: Manpower Demand (by Job Category)

Year	Managerial & Research	Supervisory & Technical	Clerical & Sales	General Workers	Skilled Workers	Unskilled Workers	TOTAL
1992	615	2,027	783	755	11,556	2,630	18,367
1993	729	2,283	1,241	794	9,710	909	15,666
1994	424	1,123	1,061	521	2,131	5,087	10,347
Subtotal	1,768	5,433	3,085	2,071	23,397	8,626	44,380
Plus employment expected from Penang Development Corporation's new projects							7,708
TOTAL							52,088

As the material in the next section shows, the rapid economic growth in the late 1980s and the launch of the state's vision, "Penang into the 21st Century," brought about an intensification of new construction in the early 1990s, accompanied by the emergence of new class and consumption trends. What distinguished this more recent construction boom was an emphasis on high-rise construction, such as

---

[38] Human Resource Development Council of Penang State Government, *High Tech Career in a Resort Environment* (Penang: Human Resource Development Council of Penang State Government, n.d.), p. 15.

[39] There was a nationwide labor shortage in the 1990s. The national unemployment rate was at a record low of 3.3 percent in 1993.

[40] Penang Development Corporation, *Statistics Penang Malaysia.*

[41] *1994 Survey by the Manpower Monitoring Committee of the Penang Human Resources Development Council,* cited in Boonler Somchit, "Meeting Penang's Needs," p. 2, Table 1.

condominiums, and their favorable association with concepts of prosperity, class exclusivity, and cultural distinctiveness.

Growth of a New Cityscape

In Penang, urban development activities are concentrated on the island rather than on the mainland, which is characterized, at least in many people's perceptions, by heavier industries and cheaper housing. Unlike other island cities, such as Singapore, the center of Georgetown, with its rows of double-story Straits Chinese shop-houses, has not changed much since the British colonial days. The retention of these older buildings in Penang is mainly due to the Rent Control Act, 1966 which, prior to its repeal in 2000, made redevelopment of these properties difficult. Consequently, much of the development on the island has occurred on the periphery of the city and in the larger metropolitan area.

The Rent Control Act, 1966 applied to all buildings built before February 1, 1948. It was enacted after the war to protect tenants from escalating rents due to an acute shortage of buildings. The Act limited the rents of these pre-war buildings and stipulated that landlords must apply to a Rent Tribunal for permission to redevelop their premises. In addition, it assisted tenants who legally challenged any Rent Tribunal decision which approved development. This Act was repealed in January 2000. The repeal of the Rent Control Act has had significant social impact on Penang, as the state owns the country's largest number of buildings under rent control.[42] A citizen's movement, the Save Our Selves (SOS) movement, has been formed to involve the general public in consultation and provide feedback, as well as to look for solutions to the problems of housing and social inequity arising from the repeal of the Rent Control Act.[43]

Before the mid-1970s, Penang's cityscape was predominantly characterized by landed properties and low-rise commercial buildings. When the tallest public housing project on the island was built between 1968 and the early 1970s, it was noted that "seventeen and eighteen storey flats were almost unheard of."[44] During those days, high-rises were associated with low-cost public housing and commonly referred to as "flats."[45]

The property boom of the early 1980s saw the beginning of high-rise construction, due to increasing land shortages and changing consumption patterns of Penangites. The economic recession in the mid-1980s severely hit the property development industry and brought these developments to a halt. It was only in the late 1980s that the property development sector was revitalized. This time, in concert with the national move towards economic liberalization and the hope for modernity, consumers and developers exhibited a new interest in high-rise

---

[42] Penang state has twelve thousand buildings under rent control out of the country's total number of 39,000. See *New Straits Times*, June 2, 1993, p. 1.

[43] The SOS movement runs a coordination center for residents affected by the repeal of the Rent Control Act (1966) at 67, Noordin Street, Georgetown, Penang.

[44] N. Jagatheesan, "Industrialised Housing—An Appraisal," in *Aspects of Housing in Malaysia*, ed. Tan Soo Hai and Hamzah Sendut, South East Asia Low Cost Housing Study Monograph (Ontario, Canada: International Development Research Center and University Science Malaysia, n.d.), p. 205.

[45] See Tan Soo Hai and Hamzah Sendut, eds., *Aspects of Housing in Malaysia*.

buildings for both high-status residential and commercial premises. Since the Rent Control Act was still in force during the 1980s, these developments took place largely on the periphery of Georgetown, in areas like Pulau Tikus and in the larger metropolitan region. However, following the federal government's announcement in 1993 of a concrete plan to gradually phase out the Rent Control Act, the Penang state Rent Tribunal relaxed its tough stand against urban renewal and approved several redevelopment plans for rent-controlled premises.[46] As a result, several new commercial high-rises appeared in Georgetown's city core.

Paving the way for the arrival of urban high-rises as the new architectural aesthetic in Penang was the completion of two high-profile state projects. These are the mammoth sixty-five story KOMTAR (Tun Abdul Razak Complex) project in the city center and the 13.5 kilometer-long Penang Bridge that connects the island to the mainland. The KOMTAR project features a geodesic dome and claims to be the "only one of its kind in Southeast Asia," while the Penang Bridge is reputed to be "the third longest of its kind in the world."[47] The completion of these modern icons was marked by elaborate celebrations, and images of the two monuments have subsequently adorned many state government publications. The KOMTAR project was undertaken and managed by the Penang Development Corporation (PDC)—the state body originally set up to spearhead industrial development.

The condominium symbolized the contemporary, fashionable status of a modern and upper-middle-class lifestyle in Penang. The unprecedented growth of condominium projects during the 1990s has prompted at least one feature article in a Malaysian newspaper with captions titled, "Georgetown fast turning into a city of condominiums."[48] The condominium or "condo" was introduced by property developers in Malaysia during the late 1970s, and endorsed by the government in the Fourth Malaysia Plan as a measure to optimize land usage.[49] But the concept only gained popularity with the Malaysian public in the latter half of the 1980s due to the country's growing affluence.[50] In Malaysia, the term condominium typically implies a luxurious dwelling with shared facilities such as swimming pools, leisure facilities, and a twenty-four hour security service.[51] When the condominium was first introduced in the country, it was marketed to the very well-to-do. Subsequently, the "semi-luxurious" condominium, or "apartment," has become popular among members of the upper-middle class.

In Penang, property developers were the most aggressive in constructing and promoting the condominium. Most of these condominium developments took place in the Pulau Tikus area and along the coastal belt of the northern metropolitan area.

---

[46] See *New Straits Times*, June 2, 1993, p. 1.

[47] The KOMTAR project was initiated in 1974, while the Penang Bridge project was implemented in 1981. See Penang Development Corporation, *Penang: Looking Back, Looking Ahead: 20 Years of Progress* (Penang: Penang Development Corporation, 1990), pp. 31, 47.

[48] *The Star*, Business Section, June 25, 1993, p. 11.

[49] The word condominium is said to be derived from the Latin words "dominion" meaning control and "con" meaning one or more persons. See Halim Abdullah, *Everything the Condominium Developer Should Have Told You, But Didn't* (Petaling Jaya, Malaysia: Pelanduk Publications, 1992), p. 3.

[50] See *Property Malaysia*, (June-July 1993), p. 17.

[51] See Halim Abdullah, *Everything the Condominium Developer Should Have Told You*, p. 3.

These developments took advantage of the panoramic views of the mainland and Georgetown offered from these areas.

However, some state and federal agencies were also involved in condominium construction. In 1993, the state government announced plans to replace existing government quarters in Georgetown city (mostly in the form of double-story terrace housing) with condominium schemes. The proposed condominium developments were a solution to the government's lack of staff housing and the rising property prices on the island.[52] The Penang Development Corporation also ventured into the condominium construction game, despite its responsibility to provide low-cost housing.[53] The PDC constructed its first medium-cost apartment project on the island in 1993, and announced that it would no longer undertake low-cost housing on the island due to high construction costs. This annoyed many private developers, who saw the PDC's involvement in medium-cost apartments as in direct competition with their own activities and interests (see Chapter Eight).[54]

Another builder of condominiums was the Penang Regional Development Authority (PERDA)—a federal statutory body (under the Ministry of Land and Regional Development) created in 1983 to redress the developmental imbalances between urban Penang and its rural areas.[55] Originally PERDA's frame of reference was rural development in Penang. However, it has increasingly moved into urban development. In 1993, PERDA constructed what it called the "country's first low-cost apartments" in the southern metropolitan town of Teluk Kumbar. Since PERDA is a federal authority associated with the promotion of Malay class interests in Penang, this testified to federal concern over whether Penang's Malay community was able to afford apartments.[56]

The condominium was not the only high-rise development to emerge at this time. Commercial high-rise buildings also began to appear in Penang—especially on the periphery of Georgetown and in Pulau Tikus—marking rapid growth in the state's business, office, and retail sectors. These buildings were characterized by their height and multifunctional "integrated development," meaning that they combined retail, office, and residential uses under one roof. In 1993, I documented a total of thirteen ongoing and newly completed commercial high-rises in Georgetown and Pulau Tikus (see Table 7.6 below).[57] Once again, private developers were most aggressive here, and hence there was a significant investment of Taiwanese and Singaporean capital in the larger projects (see Chapter Eight).

Commercial properties were not the only developments during this period. Education and tourism-related developments also sprouted in response to this era of

---

[52] The first "package" of the state's condominium construction was tendered out to private developers in 1993. See *The Star*, February 26, 1993, p. 14; and *The Star*, August 18, 1993, p. 10.

[53] Up until 1993, the PDC had built 6,700 units of low-cost housing in Penang—with four thousand units located on the island and the rest on mainland. See *Malaysian Business*, August 16-31, Advertisement Supplement (1992), p. 311.

[54] The PDC still develops low-cost housing on the mainland.

[55] In 1993, the Chairman of PERDA was the Deputy Chief Minister of Penang, an UMNO politician.

[56] Each of PERDA's apartment units has three rooms with a built-up area of 580 square feet, some 50 square feet larger than the average low-cost flat. See *New Straits Times*, February 19, 1993, p. 11.

[57] The tallest of these commercial projects was the thirty-one story MBf Tower.

rising affluence and consumer spending.[58] Tapping into the state's aspiration to become a regional education center, four large private college campuses (two on the island and two on the mainland) were built.[59] Not surprisingly, the Penang Development Corporation and the Penang Regional Development Authority were involved. PDC collaborated with a property development company and the Penang Bumiputera Foundation to develop the Penang International Higher Education and Information Technology Center, close to the industrial zone and the local university in the southern metropolitan town of Bukit Jambul. This was part of the state government's plan to turn this area into an education, research, and training center to serve the needs of a nearby future high-technology industrial park—the Penang Technoplex.

Table 7.6
Fieldwork Documentation of Newly Constructed Office Complexes in Georgetown and Pulau Tikus, 1993

Name of Projects	Location
1. Wisma/Complex Tahwa	Sultan Ahmad Shah Road
2. Wisma Penang Garden (additional block)	Sultan Ahmad Shah Road
3. MBf Tower	Sultan Ahmad Shah Road
4. Wisma Argyll	Argyll Street
5. Harbor Trade Center	Macallum Street
6. Wisma LCI	Larut Road
7. Urban Development Authority	Larut Road
8. Prime Plaza	Burma Road (Georgetown)
9. Axis	Cantonment Road (Pulau Tikus)
10. Fortune Heights	Cantonment Road (Pulau Tikus)
11. Canton Square	Cantonment Road (Pulau Tikus)
12. MBf Office	Cantonment Road (Pulau Tikus)
13. New Bob Plaza	Gottlieb Road (Pulau Tikus)

The creation of new townships by federal authorities such as the Penang Regional Development Authority was also a prominent feature of Penang's modern aspirations, during the early to mid 1990s, to help Malays to keep pace with the era of progress and development. One of PERDA's largest developments from this period is the 320-hectare township, Bandar Baru PERDA, being built on the mainland. The township contains an educational center, an Institute of Technology, and a Polytechnic school. Other federal agencies are also involved in the push to guarantee a place for the Malay community in a "modern" Penang. For example, the

---

[58] A survey by the Malaysian Institute of Economic Research revealed that the Index of Consumer Sentiments rose to 125.1 percent in the last quarter of 1992. See *The Star*, Business Section, January 25, 1993, p. 5

[59] These were the Penang International Higher Education and Information Technology Center and the Tunku Abdul Razak College on the island, and the Adorna-Royal Melbourne Institute of Technology and the MARA Institute of Technology and Polytechnic on the mainland.

Urban Development Authority (UDA)[60] developed a new Malay township in the northern metropolitan town of Tanjung Tokong. MARA, the Majlis Amanah Rakyat (Council of Trust for Indigenous People),[61] also constructed several business and trading establishments, as well as entrepreneur-training centers, on the mainland.[62]

There were also significant developments of the tourism and leisure infrastructure in line with both national and state emphases on the promotion of tourism.[63] The importance of the tourism industry in the state, together with the promotion of Penang as a "resort environment" in order to attract skilled workers, led to a surge in the level of investment in hotels and leisure resorts. For instance, four new city and eight new beach hotels and "resorts" were built in the northern metropolitan area and in the tourist belt from Batu Ferringhi to Teluk Bahang.[64] PERNAS (National Corporation) and the UDA had investments in two of the new beach hotels.[65] Facilitated by economic deregulation at the national level, which allowed total foreign capital ownership in hotels and tourist projects, Taiwanese, Hong Kong, Singaporean, Indonesian, and American capital became active in hotel development in Penang.[66]

The "condotel" first emerged at this time. These are condominium projects that offer their units for rent and provide the same services as those found in hotels. In 1993, there were three condotels in operation, all on the northern coastline of Penang Island.[67] Golf courses were another major tourism and leisure development

---

[60] UDA, a semi-government agency under the Ministry of Public Enterprise, was set up in 1971 to implement urban projects in the field of commerce, industry, and housing which would help achieve the objectives of the New Economic Policy.

[61] MARA is a statutory body under the Ministry of National and Rural Development. It was set up in 1966, following the first Bumiputera Economic Conference in 1965. Its objective is to motivate, guide, train, and assist *bumiputeras* to participate in commercial and industrial activities.

[62] See *The Star*, March 10, 1993, p. 14.

[63] A National Tourism Plan identified under the Sixth Malaysian Plan (1991-1994) saw the promotion of both foreign and domestic tourism in the country in the early 1990s. See Malaysia, *Sixth Malaysia Plan, 1991-1995* (Kuala Lumpur: Government Printers, 1991), p. 233.

[64] The new city hotels are: the Equatorial Hotel (the airport hotel), the Grand Continental Hotel, the Sunway Hotel, and the Berjaya Georgetown Hotel. The new beach hotels are: the Mutiara Resort, the Ferringhi Resort, the Bayview Pacific Hotel, the Parkroyal Hotel, the Crown Prince Hotel, the Park Paradise Hotel, and the Sandycroft Hotel.

[65] PERNAS, together with American capital, owns the Mutiara Hotel in Penang. See Malaysia, *Property Market Report 1989* (Kuala Lumpur: Ministry of Finance, 1989), p. A-44. UDA has share-equity in the Parkroyal Hotel in Penang through its investment company Paremba, a substantial shareholder of Landmarks Limited, which owns the said hotel. See *Far Eastern Economic Review*, November 15, 1990, p. 90; and Malaysia, *Property Market Report 1990* (Kuala Lumpur: Ministry of Finance, 1990), p. A-103. For details of Paremba, an UMNO investment arm, see Edmund Terence Gomez, *Politics in Business: UMNO's Corporate Investments* (Kuala Lumpur: Forum, 1990).

[66] In the early 1990s in Penang, Indonesian capital developed a new beach hotel and Taiwanese capital opened a new town hotel. See Malaysia, *Property Market Report 1991* (Kuala Lumpur: Ministry of Finance, 1991), p. A-100; and Malaysia, *Property Market Report 1992* (Kuala Lumpur: Ministry of Finance, 1992), p. A-94. Prior to 1990, three hotels (two beach and one town) in Penang were sold to Hong Kong and Singaporean investors. See Malaysia, *Property Market Report 1989*, pp. A-78, A-91.

[67] These are the Mount Pleasure, the Desa Mar Vista, and the Sri Sayang condotels.

that attracted investment at this time.[68] As late as 1993, Penang had only three golf courses—the Bukit Jambul Golf Course and the Bukit Gantung Golf Course on the island; and the Bukit Jawi Golf Resort on the mainland. During 1993, three new golf courses were under construction on the mainland and development plans for three more golf courses on the island were approved.[69] Local and Japanese capital, as well as the UDA, were involved in these developments. The increasing number of golf course developments in Penang caused protests from political and environmental groups. The state's opposition political party—the Democratic Action Party—challenged the development approval of the three new golf courses in the state assembly.[70] In addition, two local non-governmental groups hosted a "No-Golf Day" in Penang, an event which was part of a world-wide campaign against the development of golf courses, organized by the Japan-based "Global Network for Anti-Golf Course Action."[71]

Others condemned aspects of Penang's construction frenzy. One influential group was the Penang Heritage Trust (PHT), which began to lobby for the preservation of "heritage" buildings in old Georgetown. The PHT was formed in 1985 to preserve architectural and cultural heritage sites when heritage buildings throughout Georgetown began to be demolished by property developers. Comprised largely of professionals and elite members of Penang society, the PHT has been successful in winning a level of government sponsorship where its endeavors have corresponded with the state's plan to promote the heritage and cultural attractions of Penang. The PHT was the force behind the identification of the central heritage area of Penang (the Acheen Street-Armenian Street enclave). Importantly, this area has a historical legacy of being a Malay urban space in Penang. As part of this project, the PHT restored a historic building in the area—the Syed Alatas Mansion built in

---

[68] The development of golf courses in Penang coincided with a national boom in golfing activities. The number of golf courses in Malaysia grew from a total of sixty-three in 1990 to 153 in 1993. See Malaysia, *Social Economic Development Trends Bulletin 1980-90* (Kuala Lumpur: Department of Statistics, 1989), p. 153; and *New Straits Times*, April 11, 1993, p. 12. Even the state of Sarawak in East Malaysia was not spared; it opened its first golf course in 1993. See *The Star*, Business Section, July 8, 1993, p. 4. In 1993, the golfing mania became a controversy when commercial airplane pilots lodged an official complaint against night golfing activities near the Kuala Lumpur International Airport. The pilots told of their nightmarish experiences of landing at the airport in the glare of floodlights from ten nearby golf courses. Apparently, the floodlights from these golf courses not only temporarily blinded the pilots but also looked like airport approach lights. See *New Straits Times*, July 11, 1993, pp. 1, 5; *New Straits Times*, July 16, 1993, p. 1.

[69] The golf courses under construction were: the Kristal Golf Resort, owned by Japanese capital, the Penang Golf Resort, owned by the UDA and private capital, and the Mutiara Perdana Country Golf Club, owned by local capital (information gathered from their various advertisement supplements). The intended golf course developments would take place in Gertak Sanggul, Balik Pulau, and Teluk Bahang—all areas within Penang's Southwest District. The development in Balik Pulau involved Japanese capital. See Malaysia, *Property Market Report 1990*, p. A-103.

[70] In responding to the Democratic Action Party's opposition, an UMNO state assemblyman argued that "when each hole brings RM1 million to [the] state coffer, the opposition party should not oppose golf courses in Penang." He emphasized that "foreigners like Americans and Japanese" would think that the locals were "left behind" if they came to a place without amenities like the "condominium, shopping complexes or golf courses." He added that "We do not want the 'rakyat [people]' to appear 'bodoh [foolish]' not knowing how to play golf. . . ." See *The Star*, December 12, 1992.

[71] *The Star*, April 30, 1993, p. 17.

the 1880s—and turned it into a Heritage Training Center to teach traditional building skills.[72] Syed Mohamed Alatas, the owner of this mansion, was the leader of a Muslim society which teamed up with the dominant Chinese secret society in the Penang Riots of 1867.[73] Incidentally, Syed Mohamed Alatas also married the daughter of the leader of his Chinese ally. While the preservation of this building and location is seemingly motivated by the state's interests in promoting tourism, the signification of Malay identity in this project implies that the decision for preservation is also guided by larger nationalistic discourses concerning ethnicity. Given that Penang is a state with a predominantly Chinese identity and population, and that it needs to prove its commitment to the national project of modernity, the conservation of this Malay precinct is symbolic of the state and urban elite's desire to highlight Malayness as part of Penang's cultural life.[74]

UMNO politicians, Malay businessmen, and community leaders are not left out in this effort to register the Malay presence in Penang. These groups are responsible for the conservation of the Acheen Street Mosque, built in 1808, within the Acheen Street-Armenian Street heritage precinct. In 1993, a group of UMNO politicians, Malay businessmen and community leaders established a committee known as the Lebuh Acheh Malay Mosque Heritage Committee Association, in order to promote the history of the area as a center of Malay academics, writers, and prominent traders during the 1920s and 1930s.[75] Their aim was to restore the "glory" of this place and lobby for the continued existence of Malay communities in the center of Georgetown.[76] The project is being largely financed by the Penang UMNO branch and the public enterprise, PERNAS, but the state and federal governments also contribute financially. When completed, the conserved area is expected to house an art gallery, small museum, and pilgrimage office.

Following these contests for representation and control over urban space, various groups have championed the cause of urban conservation—mostly for their own ends. A local council, the Penang City Council, was one of these promoters of urban conservation. In 1993, the Penang City Council identified twenty "heritage" buildings located along Jalan Sultan Ahmad Shah, known locally as "Millionaire's Row." These buildings were to be preserved from the high-rise transformation affecting other properties along this road. In the context of the island's rapidly changing cityscape, the Penang City Council valued urban conservation as one way to instill a sense of identity and security in the local population.[77] However, the council's commitment to urban conservation was put in doubt when, on Christmas Day in 1993, an old hotel previously identified as a heritage building was

---

[72] Interview with the Secretary of PHT, October 5, 1993. The project was completed in 1996.

[73] In the riots, two Chinese secret societies, each with its own Muslim ally, fought for control of Georgetown. See Khoo Su Nin, *The Streets of Georgetown, Penang: An Illustrated Guide to Penang's City Streets and Historic Attractions* (Penang: Janus Print & Resources, 1993), pp. 31, 35, 156.

[74] See also Joel S. Kahn, "Culturalizing Malaysia: Globalism, Tourism, Heritage, and the City in Georgetown," in *Tourism, Ethnicity, and the State in Asian and Pacific Societies*, ed. Michel Picard and Robert E. Wood (Honolulu: University of Hawaii Press, 1987), pp. 99-127.

[75] Acheen Street is known as "Lebuh Acheh" in Malay.

[76] See *New Straits Times*, *City Extra Section*, May 26, 1993, p. 1.

[77] Interview with Mr. Tan Thien Siew, Planning Director of the Penang City Council, October 15, 1993.

demolished overnight by its new developer. It was revealed by the opposition political party that the President of the Penang City Council had been one of the previous owners of the hotel.[78] As a result of the ensuing political controversy, the developer was fined RM50,000 and ordered by the City Council to reconstruct the building within six months.[79] The company, however, never met this order, and plans to develop a thirty-nine story building on the site—with a reconstructed facade of the demolished hotel—were approved.[80]

Private capital has also, at times, purported to support the "heritage" movement. However, the intent here is usually not conservation but redevelopment. For example, property developers converted several colonial buildings in the city into offices, private colleges, fast food chains, and leisure clubs.[81] A famous example of this is the restoration of the historic Cheong Fatt Tze Mansion. This work was undertaken as a business venture by private capital, which saw potential in turning the restored mansion into a profitable tourist attraction.[82]

These various examples illustrate the number of groups with an interest in Penang's recent construction boom amidst the national push for modernization and urban development. The continued economic growth, a growing affluent class, and increasing consumption levels experienced in the state have been critical factors in spurring the activities of the construction industry. The recent transformation of Penang's urban landscape is the result of an intersection of economic growth with a number of political, class, and ethnic interests. The role of the state and its vision to turn Penang into an advanced industrial and cultured state is one important interest. Through its organizations and sphere of influence, the state encouraged the development of an infrastructure to support Penang's industrial, tourism, education, and cultural sectors. This resulted in a number of (competing) coalitions between private capital, state capital, class fractions, and community groups, all of which gave rise to heightened contests for the control of urban space and an intensification of discourses on ethnic and cultural distinctions. These contests are representative of the diverse economic, political, and cultural imperatives upheld by various social groups as they respond to, or are affected by, the forces of economic restructuring and rapid urban growth. The heritage movement provides a case in point. While originally pioneered by a privileged group of Penangites opposed to

---

[78] See *New Straits Times*, January 7, 1994, under caption, "Kit Siang probes Metropole sale." Information gathered from my interview with Mr. Chow Kon Yeow, a state legislative assemblyman from the Democratic Action Party, January 8, 1994.

[79] See *The Star*, January 8, 1994, p. 16.

[80] See *The Star*, August 2, 1996, p. 12.

[81] See Malaysia, *Property Market Report 1988* (Kuala Lumpur: Ministry of Finance, 1988), p. A-48. The new recreation clubs using converted colonial premises in Georgetown are the Maple Gold Club, the Club Tomorrow, and the Heritage Club.

[82] The Cheong Fatt Tze Mansion was built in the late 1800s by a famous Nanyang Chinese industrialist. See Khoo Su Nin, *The Streets of Georgetown*, pp. 106-107. This restored mansion was subsequently damaged when construction activities to expand a nearby hotel caused cracks in its walls. The damage led to a conflict between the owners of the mansion and the hotel proprietors, in which the former successfully applied for a court injunction to stop the hotel's expansion activities. See *The Star*, August 10, 1996, p. 18. The hotel proprietors later obtained an *ex parte* order, but the order was discharged by the Court of Appeal. The same fate might also befall the Syed Alatas Mansion. In 1996, the Penang City Council approved the development plan for a nine-story building next to the restored mansion. The City Council's decision met with protests from the Penang Heritage Trust. See *The Star*, July 31, 1996, p. 15.

the wholesale redevelopment of Georgetown, the notion of heritage was taken-up and put to new uses by state bodies, federal agencies, capitalists, and local community groups. The contradictions within the heritage movement are further testimony to the fact that the cityscape is a key site for the concrete expression of different class and cultural visions of a modern Penang.

These struggles had immediate repercussions on the spatial, political, and cultural conditions in the Pulau Tikus area, a particularly fast developing neighborhood in Georgetown City where Kampung Serani was located. In the next section we will see how the larger economic, political, and cultural dynamics operating in the Pulau Tikus area helped shaped the Church's and PEA's decisions in the Kampung Serani conflict.

PULAU TIKUS —THE NEW ADDRESS

Pulau Tikus has been a middle- and upper-middle-class residential town since the 1920s.[83] Until the 1970s, the area consisted largely of semi-detached and terrace houses, large "country bungalows," and commercial low-rises. The construction boom in the early 1980s saw the beginning of several high-rise residential projects there. It was only during the last property boom, which began around 1989, that a large number of upmarket condominiums and apartments sprang up in the Pulau Tikus area.

The reason for the concentration of high-rise development in Pulau Tikus was the availability of land and buildings not subject to the Rent Control Act. An additional attraction was the panorama offered from this area (in particular, views of the mainland across the Northern Channel, the northern tip of Penang Island, and the skyline of Georgetown).

All of these features made Pulau Tikus attractive to property developers and the new rich. There is a marked concentration of condominium projects in Pulau Tikus, in comparison with other areas of Penang. The first apartment project in Penang—the Sunrise Tower—was built in Pulau Tikus.[84] By 1993, Pulau Tikus was famous for two rows of prestigious condominiums along the shoreline of Gurney Drive (epitomized by the prestigious No. 1 Persiaran Gurney condominiums) and Cantonment Road (featuring the Mediterranean-style Cascadia project).

In order to gauge the intensity of condominium construction in Pulau Tikus, I compared the total number of existing (completed and on-going) schemes in the area with the number of schemes found in other metropolitan areas on Penang Island. As of December 1993, there were a total of eighty-nine schemes in metropolitan Penang. Pulau Tikus accounted for thirty four of these projects (see Table 7.7 below).[85] In making this comparison, I defined a condominium project as one or more

---

[83] Jesselton Heights, a residential suburb of large landed properties located along Western Road (Jalan Utama) in the vicinity of the Pulau Tikus area, has traditionally been known as the most exclusive residence in Penang.

[84] See Malaysia, *Property Market Report 1980* (Kuala Lumpur: Ministry of Finance, 1980), p. 52.

[85] I made this subjective count because there were no available statistics on the number of condominiums in Penang. The record of Strata Titles registration at the Penang Land and Mines Office reflects the total number of high-rises in Penang. Data from the Land and Mines Office reveal that a total of 196 high-rise schemes were built in Penang between June 1, 1985 and December 31, 1992. However, the record of Strata Registers does not reflect the number of

condo blocks within one development which contained individual units selling in excess of RM150,000 (for details, see Chapter Eight).[86] In order to understand the proximity of these projects to Kampung Serani, see Map 7.5 in Appendix R.

Table 7.7

**Fieldwork Compilation of Existing Condominium/Apartment Projects
on Penang Island as of December 31, 1993**

Area	Number of Condominium and Apartment Projects
Georgetown	10
Pulau Tikus	34
Northern Metropolitan	20
Western Metropolitan	10
Southern Metropolitan	15
Total	89

There was also a growth in the construction of high-rise commercial and retail complexes at this time. Their popularity in the Pulau Tikus area signified a growing preference on the part of businesses to relocate there. By December 31, 1993, there were a total of seven commercial projects in the immediate vicinity of Kampung Serani alone.[87] The largest of these projects was an "integrated development" called the Midlands One-Stop-Center, located a mere 300 meters from Kampung Serani.[88] This One-Stop-Center includes a retail complex, a water theme park, a hotel, and apartment towers. It was developed by a prominent—and, it has been said, politically well-connected—Penang property-development company, which I have called "Company Golden-Point." The two-hectare project was the result of the first privatization scheme of what was referred to as "underutilized" council land.[89] Under this privatization scheme, the site was leased from the Penang City Council for ninety-nine years for a sum of RM18.7 million. In addition, the Penang City Council anticipated collecting around RM7.5

---

condominium/apartment schemes, because it applies to low-cost housing and office complexes as well.

In Malaysia, all subdivided buildings are regulated by the Strata Titles Act, 1985 (enforced on June 1, 1985). This Act requires the original owner of a subdivided scheme on a land lot to make an application to the Director of Lands and Mines Office for the opening of a Strata Register. Before 1985, all subdivided schemes were registered under "Subsidiary Titles" according to provisions in the National Land Code 1965. A total of 133 Subsidiary Titles were opened in Penang. See Teo Keang Sood, *Strata Titles in Malaysia: Law and Practice* (Singapore: Butterworths & Co. [Asia] Pte Ltd., 1987), pp. 1, 2, 103.

[86] I found that developers were charging a minimum of RM250 per square foot in high-cost condominium schemes during 1993. In medium-cost schemes, the price per square foot varied from RM180 to RM249. In Penang, the size of a condominium unit usually ranges from between 1000 to 2030 square feet.

[87] See Map 7.5 in Appendix R.

[88] See Map 7.3 in Appendix P.

[89] This project was initiated in 1993 and was completed in 1995.

million per year in annual assessments from the development.[90]

The Midlands project had close connections to the property development company developing the Kampung Serani site, namely "Company Golden-Heights." Not only were the proprietors of the two companies siblings, but the owner of Company Golden-Heights had personally conceived and designed the Midlands project, in addition to making capital investment in the project through Company Golden-Point (see Chapter Eight).

These companies were also involved together in other property developments in the Pulau Tikus area. Together with Singaporean capital, they were involved in a joint venture with a Japanese supermarket chain to redevelop the almost 19-hectare site of the former Catholic College General Seminary. The development plans for this one billion RM "Gurney Park" project were submitted to the City Council in 1993, with construction beginning in 1996. When finished, "Gurney Park" will include a shopping mall, a five star hotel, apartments, and a "super-condominium" block, making it "Penang's largest condominium and commercial centre."[91] The redevelopment of the Catholic College General Seminary site began in 1982 when the Roman Catholic Church sold off the land to a local property development company for a reputed RM36 million (see Chapter Four). Upon purchase, the company immediately demolished the seminary building, which had been built in 1810. Despite protests from Penangites, the Penang City Council re-zoned the site from a religious to a residential-cum-commercial area within four months of the purchase.[92] But the project never materialized, as the company which bought the land went bankrupt in the recession of the mid-1980s . A Japanese real estate company bought the property for RM55 million when it was put up for auction in 1985,[93] but sold it to a Hong Kong tycoon who subsequently, in turn, sold it to a Japanese department store.[94]

Property developers were not the only ones promoting the Pulau Tikus as a prestigious address. Wealthy, long-term residents also sought to establish the exclusivity of Pulau Tikus. This was evident in the residents' protest over the seemingly innocuous renaming of Scott Road—an exclusive enclave of bungalow units in Pulau Tikus.[95] In 1990, the Penang City Council re-named Scott Road (which was named after the English businessman, James Scott, a friend of Francis Light, the founder of Penang) as D. S. Ramanathan Road after the deceased second mayor of Georgetown.[96] D. S. Ramanathan, who headed the Labor political party (which was latter banned), was Mayor of Penang from 1958 to 1960.[97] Ever since

---

[90] *The Star*, October 29, 1993, p. 16.

[91] *The Star*, Business Section, September 2, 1994, p. 1. This development plan came to a halt during the 1998 economic crisis.

[92] *New Straits Times*, December 20, 1988, p. 6.

[93] See Malaysia, *Property Market Report 1989*, p. A-78. This information was confirmed in my conversation with the lawyer who acted on behalf of the Japanese real estate company in this land transaction.

[94] *The Star*, October 31, 1993, p. 8; and *The Star*, Business Section, October 2, 1994, p. 1.

[95] For location of Scott Road, see Map 7.3 in Appendix P.

[96] Interestingly, Scott married a local Portuguese-Eurasian woman. See James F. Augustine, *Bygone Eurasia: The Life Story of the Eurasians of Malaya* (Kuala Lumpur: Rajiv Printers, 1981), p. 10.

[97] The Royal Charter by the British government that elevated Penang from municipality to city status in 1957 provided for a mayor to head the municipal council. See Choo Eng Guan, "A

this renaming, new road signs put up by the City Council were vandalized, whitewashed over, and pulled down, so much so that by 1993 at least twenty new road signs had been replaced.[98] This spate of vandalism coincided with strong protests from wealthy residents against the renaming of Scott Road, including residents of the nearby streets of Scott Avenue and Scott Crescent. According to the chairman of the protest panel, the residents' protest was based on the fact that: "Ramanathan is relatively unknown to the people in Scott Road. . . moreover, areas with a proliferation of British names should be maintained to sustain their uniqueness; like Brown, Park, Rose, Briggs and Wright. . ."[99] As part of their protest, the residents continued to use Scott Road as their postal address and deliberately wrote the words "Scott Road" on their letter boxes in defiance of the council's decision. Clearly, the name Scott Road symbolized the uniqueness of the British legacy in the area and the wealthy residents of Pulau Tikus wanted to maintain this prestigious identity.

But the class aspirations of the Scott Road residents had wider repercussions, especially among the Indian residents of Penang. Because after 1960 the late Ramanathan joined the Malaysian Indian Congress (after the abolition of local elections and the banning of the Labor Party) and was appointed as a Penang State Executive Councilor upon winning the 1964 State Election, the continuing defacement of the D. S. Ramanathan road sign led members of the Penang branch of the MIC to organize a *gotong-royong* (community effort) clean up of the road signs as a sign of protest.[100]

In the midst of this controversy, the Penang Malay Association, Pemenang,[101] announced that it had acquired a new headquarters and activity center on Cantonment Road in Pulau Tikus at a cost of RM600,000. According to the Association's president, the purchase of the building was a step towards realizing the Association's aspirations to see more Malay land ownership in Georgetown.[102] Ownership of a building in fashionable Pulau Tikus was thus a mark of distinction and presence for the Malay community in Penang.

The Penang Malay Association is a community organization akin to the PEA and heavily involved in promoting Malay participation in the urban economy and in pushing for Malay cultural representation. In 1992, it called on the state government to set up a Malay Cultural, Customs and Regalia Council and to construct a *Balai Istiadat* (ceremonial center) to revive "traditional Malay culture and ceremonial activities."[103] It argued that a Ceremonial Center was necessary because Penang Malays were left out of the state's year-round cultural programs that were heavily biased towards Chinese cultural activities. At the same time,

---

Study of the Administrative Process," p. 10. D. S. Ramanathan died in 1973.

[98] See *New Straits Times*, August 8, 1993, under the headline, "Penang 'road sign' vandals strike again."

[99] See *New Straits Times*, August 14, 1993, under the headline "Ramanathan deserves better." The latter roads are streets in the Scott Road vicinity.

[100] See *New Straits Times*, City Extra Section, August 28, 1993, under "Sri Tanjung" column.

[101] *Pemenang* literally means "winner" in the Malay language.

[102] See *New Straits Times*, City Extra Section, September 21, 1993, p. 1.

[103] See *New Straits Times*, August 29, 1992, under the headline, "Call for formation of cultural council." The president of the Penang Malay Association during this time happened to be an academic.

the Association also requested the state government to name roads after famous Penang Malay personalities, including the founding members of the Association.

In contrast to this inflow of wealthy residents and landowners, many of Pulau Tikus' poorer communities living in *kampung* enclaves, such as the Kampung Serani residents, faced imminent eviction as new building constructions encroached on their homes. Apart from the Eurasians of Kampung Serani, Pulau Tikus had a number of other ethnic communities within its boundaries, including groups of Burmese, Indian, Chinese, and Malays of South Indian, Arabic, and Javanese descent. One group of villagers which also found itself to be a reluctant participant of urban redevelopment was an enclave of three Malay *kampungs* located on the edge of Pulau Tikus bounded by Kelawei Road, Burma Road, Jones Road, and Edgecumbe Road.[104] The three *kampungs* in question are Kampung Tengah, Kampung Kopee Amah, and Kampung Palembang.[105] Kampung Tengah was the first to be affected, when a condominium project walled up its main entrance in the late 1980s.[106] The residents protested against this, and, with the help of the Consumers' Association of Penang (CAP), a compromise was reached between them and the condominium developer, who allowed the villagers common use of the condominium entrance. This arrangement resulted in a situation in which residents and visitors of Kampung Tengah are first screened at the guardhouse of the condominium project.

The villagers in Kampung Kopee Amah faced an even more pressing situation, as they lived on Muslim *wakaf* (endowment) land which had been earmarked for redevelopment. *Wakaf* land is held in trust for welfare or religious purposes, such as for the building of mosques, welfare homes, and orphanages.[107] The dilemma of Kampung Kopee Amah began in 1992, when the Penang State Islamic Religious Council made a decision to redevelop eighteen tracts of *wakaf* land located in the prime Northeast District, including Kampung Kopee Amah. The decision to redevelop *wakaf* property was made following a finding that these tracts of endowment land could fetch a market price of almost RM62 million.[108] After its decision, the Religious Council took over all of the *wakaf* land plots from their trustees and set up a private company to oversee their redevelopment.[109] The company planned to redevelop these lands into apartments, hotels, and office complexes. Not surprisingly, the communities living on these *wakaf* land tracts, including those in Kampung Kopee Amah, strongly opposed this move. This led the Religious Council to issue a warning that it would take legal action against any group obstructing its plans.[110] The conflict over the redevelopment of *wakaf* land

---

[104] See Map 7.3 in Appendix P.

[105] I would like to thank a former colleague, Ms. Zainab Wahidin, for introducing me to the residents in these Malay *kampungs*.

[106] Interviews with Encik Wahidin, Pak Syed, and Cik Molek on May 10, 1993.

[107] See Helen Fujimoto, *The South Indian Muslim Community and the Evolution of the Jawi Peranakan in Penang up to 1948*, Comparative Study in Multi-Ethnic Societies, Monograph Series No. 1 (Tokyo: Tokyo Gaikokugo Daigaku, 1988); and Nagata, *Malaysian Mosaic*, p. 107.

[108] See *New Straits Times*, September 3, 1992, under the caption "Sitting on a gold mine." Kampung Kopee Amah was said to be worth RM11.4 million at its 1992 market price.

[109] See *The Star*, January 9, 1993, p. 16; and *The Star*, March 15, 1993, p. 16.

[110] See *The Star*, May 11, 1993, p. 15.

remains unresolved and the future of the villagers in Kampung Kopee Amah depends on its eventual outcome.[111]

Reconciling the Church and PEA's Decisions in the Kampung Serani Conflict

Development pressure had always been strong in Pulau Tikus, largely because of the lack of rent-controlled premises in the area. But as the above discussion shows, since the mid-1980s, there has been a marked increase in the intensity of construction activities in Pulau Tikus as this area became a newly prestigious residential and business address. In part, the recent spate of condominium and commercial project developments is an outcome of the new material and cultural conditions created by the nationwide push for economic restructuring and modernization. The quest for modernization created a growing tendency to perceive land in financial terms and, in particular, as a resource or raw material which needs to be developed in order to both realize financial gain and contribute to Penang's future advancement. These perceptions and aspirations were reflected in the Penang City Council's decision to privatize its so called "underutilized" land. It is also evident in the Penang State Islamic Religious Council's decision to redevelop Kampung Kopee Amah and other endowment land.

The Catholic Church was one of the earliest non-commercial entities in the Pulau Tikus area to realize the financial potential of urban development. The Church made its initial deal with Company Dreamland as early as 1980, during the earlier development boom, to redevelop the Kampung Serani site. The Church's decision to form a joint venture with a private developer to redevelop this site is an indication of the Church's acquiescence to the pressure to treat land in financial terms. However, this decision should not be interpreted as motivated by simple greed. The Church faced two other dilemmas that contributed to its decision to redevelop the Kampung Serani site

Firstly, the Church was fearful of the land acquisition powers of the national Land Acquisition Act (1960). All three Church authorities I interviewed gave the Church's apprehension concerning the Land Acquisition Act as the main reason for the development of Kampung Serani. The Land Acquisition Act legislates compulsory land acquisition in Malaysia. At the time the Church made the decision to develop Kampung Serani in 1980, the Act provided state authorities with the power to acquire land on its own behalf or on behalf of a corporation undertaking work of a public utility (see Section 3 (b) of the Act).[112] The Church, as a large landowner in Penang, had good cause to fear the Act.[113]

---

[111] The economic crisis of the late 1990s appears to have placed the plan to redevelop *wakaf* land in Penang at a standstill.

[112] A government official determines the amount of compensation to be given for acquired land. The Land Acquisition Act does not make provisions for a right to a hearing in cases of dissatisfaction with the amount of compensation. See Teo Keang Sood and Khaw Lake Tee, *Land Law in Malaysia: Cases and Commentary* (Singapore: Butterworths & Co. [Asia] Pte Ltd., 1987), p. 420; and Wolfgang Senftleben, *Background to Agricultural Land Policy in Malaysia* (Wiesbaden: Otto Harrassowitz, 1976), pp. 99-100.

[113] A study on land ownership patterns in Penang identifies Christian churches as one of the largest land owners in Georgetown. See Goh Ban Lee, "Patterns of Landownership: Case Studies in Urban Inequalities," in *Malaysia: Some Contemporary Issues in Socio-Economic Development*, ed. Cheong Kee Cheok, Khoo Siew Mun, and R. Thillainathan (Kuala Lumpur: Malaysian Economic Society, 1979), p. 67. According to this study, in 1979 Christians owned

A major amendment to the Land Acquisition Act in 1991 gives infinite powers to state authorities concerning the compulsorily acquisition of private property for any use deemed to be economically beneficial to the country's development. With this amendment, the land acquired need not be confined to state use but may be used "by any person or corporation for any purpose which in the opinion of the State Authority is beneficial to the economic development of Malaysia, or any other thereof, or to the public generally, or any class of the public."[114] In addition, an insertion of Section 68A in the Act also makes it lawful for the state to subsequently change its mind about the development purpose of the acquired land or to dispose of it to other parties.

Responses from my three respondents revealed that the Church was exceptionally wary of the Act and anticipated that some of its land would be acquired for government projects. In my view, this pessimistic outlook was caused in part by the Church's insecure position in the country, in view of the uneasy relationship between Christianity and Islam in Malaysia.[115] No doubt the Church's prior experience with land acquisition also had an impact on its decision. In the past, for example, the state government had acquired Church land for the purposes of a state museum and public school.[116]

The second dilemma faced by the Church arises directly from the pro-modern aspirations of contemporary Malaysians. In this context, the vernacular and "non-modern" enclave of Kampung Serani posed an unhappy contrast to the adjoining new, "modern" high-rise projects. As argued in Chapter One, "urban *kampungs*" are increasingly seen as out of keeping with Malaysia's modern future and have been destroyed at an alarming rate in the name of development and national pride. The Church itself shared in this widespread negative assessment of the "urban *kampung*" and strong push for its redevelopment. The Church authorities gave the "dilapidated" condition of the "eye-sore" buildings in the "*lallang* covered" (weed-grown) Kampung Serani as a reason in favor of redevelopment (see Chapter Four). The Church's decision to redevelop the site may well have been a defensive move to prevent the government from acquiring the valuable site. The Church may well have feared that the *kampung's* position amidst new high-rise developments made it an obvious target for compulsory acquisition and redevelopment.

This leaves unexplained, however, the Penang Eurasian Association's position in the conflict and their final compromise in accepting a new heritage house. As noted earlier, the PEA first lobbied for the preservation of the Noah's Ark

---

9.1 percent of the land in the prime Northeast District. See Goh Ban Lee, "Urban Landownership by Capital in Penang" (PhD Dissertation, University of California, Los Angeles, 1981), p. 127.

[114] Section 3(b) 1991 Amendment of Land Acquisition Act.

[115] Regarding the Catholic Church's qualms over government policy on religious freedom in Malaysia, see John Rooney, *Khabar Gembira: A History of the Catholic Church in East Malaysia and Brunei (1880-1976)* (London and Kota Kinabalu: Burns & Oates Ltd., 1981). The strained relationship between the Catholic Church and Islamic groups was perhaps best demonstrated in a conflict over the construction of a parish building in a neighborhood in Shah Alam (the Federal Territory) in 1996. The building plan of the parish church not only had to be scaled down and altered several times, but construction work was subsequently stopped by the local council, due to growing protests from nearby Malay residents and Islamic groups. For details, see *Aliran* 16,4 (1996): 27.

[116] Interview with Brother M., August 3, 1993.

building, but quickly struck a deal with the developer, who offered in its place a Eurasian heritage house. As I have suggested, the PEA's enthusiasm for a heritage house arose out of a renewed focus on Portuguese-Eurasian cultural identity at the national level. However, the PEA's acceptance of this offer was also shaped by its ongoing political agenda amidst wider cultural-spatial politics in contemporary urban Penang.

The push to modernize Penang has seen the cityscape become an important site for the concrete expression of cultural visions of modernity. The rush to construct a new cityscape which symbolizes modernist and class aspirations, and the move to conserve historic buildings in order to maintain Penang's cultural identity, are two (conflicting) reflections of this tendency. The protests of the residents of Scott Road were also motivated by the perception that cultural values and social class aspirations were embodied in urban built forms. For these residents, Scott Road symbolized a British legacy of which they were proud. (Interestingly, the residents' protest in turn evoked objections from the Penang branch of the Malaysian Indian Congress as the new road name was in honor of a deceased MIC leader.)

During this time, the Penang Malay Association purchased an expensive building in Pulau Tikus as a sign of the Association's ability to assert a Malay presence and identity in modern Penang. It is not surprising then, that the PEA should seek to stamp a modern construction of Portuguese-Eurasian identity on the urban landscape. Although initially motivated by a desire to preserve the historic Noah's Ark building, the PEA's foremost concern—that is, the recognition of Portuguese-Eurasian cultural heritage and identity—was easily transferred to, and accommodated by, the promise of a new heritage house. The location of the heritage house within a new and expensive "modern" development was not seen to contradict the concerns and role of the PEA. Within the context of Penang's modernist aspirations, the professional and affluent PEA leaders may well have felt a degree of ambivalence towards the dilapidated wooden Noah's Ark. The opportunity to "landmark" Eurasian identity and culture within a "modern" development would have been doubly attractive to the PEA leaders.

Finally, it is imperative to understand the PEA's decision in terms of its leadership role and aspirations, along with the escalating cultural politics in the increasingly prestigious Pulau Tikus area. Its quick acceptance of the developer's offer may have been motivated by a fear that the Portuguese-Eurasian community might lose any concrete reference in the very area most associated with the Portuguese-Eurasian community in Penang. Given the scramble among various other community groups to maintain or acquire concrete expressions of their presence in the Pulau Tikus area (for example the Scott Road struggle and the Penang Malay Association's purchase of a property), it is likely that the PEA—which saw itself as the guardian of Eurasian cultural identity and heritage—seized the one opportunity offered to ensure a continued expression and recognition of Eurasian cultural identity in the area.

CONCLUSION

This chapter has illustrated that larger political economic forces and their class, cultural, and spatial correlatives had a direct effect on the Pulau Tikus neighborhood where Kampung Serani was located. The push for economic liberalization and the desire for capitalist development, international recognition, and modernity in Malaysia created a highly contested urban terrain in Penang as the state government, private capital, and community groups struggled to achieve their contrasting political, social, and cultural goals. These struggles had immediate repercussions on the spatial, class, and cultural conditions of the Pulau Tikus area, repercussions which affected the responses of the actors in the Kampung Serani conflict. I have shown that the wider economic, cultural, and spatial politics in modern, urban Penang exerted two political pressures on the Church which contributed to its decision to redevelop Kampung Serani: firstly, a heightened fear of compulsory land acquisition, and secondly, an increased negative assessment of "Kampung Serani" in the context of the pro-modern and upmarket aspirations in contemporary Penang. In addition, I have argued that the Penang Eurasian Association's desire for a heritage house on the *kampung* site was shaped, in part, by the intricate links between cultural politics and spatial processes by which the cityscape had become an important site for the concrete expression of ethnic and class presence or identity in modern Penang.

These findings illustrate this book's arguments that the material and cultural forces generated in the Malaysian aspiration for modernity posed particular contradictions, problems, and opportunities for the actors involved in the Kampung Serani conflict, forcing them into various responses as they struggled to cope and resist the conditions around them. Having established the interrelationships between these wider dynamics in the Kampung Serani conflict, we can also conclude that as much as the general picture is vital for understanding the Church's and the PEA's actions, our microanalysis of the Kampung Serani conflict has also demonstrated that insidious and long-standing power and class relations, local identities, histories, conceptions of place, and ways of life are equally important in shaping people's actions and aspirations. There is thus a constant need to dialectically balance the particular and the general, the micro and the macro in our investigations in order to better understand the Kampung Serani conflict. In the next chapter, in order to further understand the Kampung Serani conflict, we will examine the specific role of property developers in shaping modern urban Penang.

CHAPTER EIGHT

PROPERTY DEVELOPERS AND THE KAMPUNG SERANI CONFLICT

This chapter explores how the economic, political, and cultural imperatives of property developers in contemporary urban Penang contributed to the power struggle in the Kampung Serani conflict. I argue that it is only by understanding the priorities and modern visions of property developers and the consequences of their pursuits on the social landscape of Penang that we can explain the responses of Company Highview and Company Golden-Heights in the Kampung Serani conflict. In tracing the impacts of the exigencies of the property development industry on the two property development companies, I will offer an interpretation of two puzzling matters: firstly, why Company Highview denied the residents' demands for a low-cost flat but conceded to the Penang Eurasian Association's demands for a heritage house; and secondly, why Company Golden Heights was so interested in the Kampung Serani site that it offered a "clubhouse" to the PEA and supported the residents' fight.

This chapter is divided into three sections. First, I will provide a background to the legal and political structures within which property developers operate. Second, I will trace the particular goals of property developers as they compete with each other to transform urban space. Third, I will analyze how the actions of the two property developers in the Kampung Serani conflict were shaped by the material and cultural dynamics of the property development industry as they competed with each other in the Pulau Tikus area.

INTRODUCTION TO THE PROPERTY DEVELOPMENT INDUSTRY IN MALAYSIA: REGULATION AND REPRESENTATION

National Regulations

Malaysia has experienced four property booms since Independence. Property-development activities peaked during the following years: 1963-1964, 1973-1974, 1981-1983, and 1989-1993.[1] The most severe downturn in property development occurred in the mid-1980s as a result of a nationwide recession. This downturn forced

---

[1] There is a theory among economists and property consultants that the property development cycle in Malaysia peaks every eight years unless events disturb the cycle, in which case the cycle lengthens to ten or twelve years. See Kamal Salih, "The Malaysian Economy in the 1990s: Alternative Scenarios," in *The Malaysian Economy Beyond 1990: International & Domestic Perspectives*, ed. Lee Kiong Hock and Shyamala Nagaraj (Kuala Lumpur: Persatuan Ekonomi Malaysia, 1991), p. 51; and Aloysius B. Marbeck, "Investing in Residential Property," *Property Malaysia* (June-July 1993): 62.

many developers into bankruptcy, and as a result a total of 428 housing projects, involving 83,542 houses, were abandoned throughout the country.[2] In Penang alone, a total of thirty-seven development schemes, involving 6,729 houses, were abandoned.[3]

Given the risks involved and the political importance of housing, it is not surprising that the activities of property developers are highly regulated by both the national and local governments. At the national level, the Minister of Housing and Local Government is empowered by the Housing Developers (Control and Licensing) Act, 1966 (Revised 1973), to control the industry. The Act has been updated via two sets of Regulations to control specific problem areas of the housing industry: the Housing Developers (Housing and Licensing) Regulations, 1989; and the Housing Developers (Housing Development Account) Regulations, 1991. These regulations determine basic functioning structures for property developers.

Among other things, the Housing Developers (Housing and Licensing) Regulations, 1989, require property developers to obtain licenses from the Ministry of Housing and Local Government before they can engage in development activities, to procure advertising permits from the same Ministry before they can advertise and sell their projects,[4] and to enter into contracts of sale with purchasers in the form of the Sales and Purchase Agreement.[5] The Sales and Purchase Agreement determines that, once a property developer enters into a contract with the purchaser, a development project should be completed within twenty-four months in the case of non-subdivided buildings, and thirty-six months in the case of subdivided buildings.[6] This contract requires purchasers to pay an initial payment amounting to 10 percent of the purchase price upon the signing of the agreement, and subsequent payments corresponding to the different stages of construction progress. This means that property developers in Malaysia are actually financed by purchasers throughout the construction period—an unusual feature when compared to many other countries.

On the other hand, the Housing Developers (Housing Development Account) Regulations, 1991, were introduced to prevent housing developers from absconding with the purchasers' payments. This regulation makes it mandatory for property developers to open a Housing Development Account,[7] or, if failing to do so, to face the possibility of a fine between RM10,000 to RM100,000, or a three-year jail sentence. All monies collected from purchasers and loans for each scheme must be deposited into these accounts and can only be withdrawn at specific phases of development.[8]

---

[2] See *New Straits Times*, July 17, 1993, p. 5.

[3] Ibid.

[4] Developers can start selling their projects once they have procured the necessary permissions from the Ministry of Housing and Local government and from the local authority.

[5] Two types of Sales and Purchase Agreements are provided to cater to subdivided and non-subdivided buildings.

[6] For details, see Section 20(1) of Sale and Purchase Agreement (Land and Building) and Section 22(1) of Sale and Purchase Agreement (Subdivided Building). The developer must pay damages to the purchaser if the project is not completed on time.

[7] Due to tax and financial purposes, property developers set up a new (subsidiary) company each time they begin a fresh development scheme.

[8] Property developers undertaking construction activities (most developers contract out their construction work) are further controlled by the Ministry of Works under the Construction

Penang State Regulations

At the state level, property developers are subject to the planning regulations made by local authorities. In Penang, these authorities are the Penang City Council and the Seberang Perai City Council (see Chapter Seven).[9] Property developers must have their building plans approved by the two local councils before commencing construction work.[10] The processing of building plans can be tedious and time consuming, as approvals from a vast number of related government departments are needed.[11] (For an illustration of the complexity of the development process in Penang, see Chart 8.1 in Appendix H.)

Property developers must adhere to the Penang state housing policy, also regulated by the two local councils.[12] The state housing policy stipulates terms and conditions on the provision of low-cost housing and *bumiputera* privileges in housing.[13] The state requires property developers involved in any housing development schemes exceeding 150 units in the metropolitan region and a hundred units outside the metropolitan region to ensure that 30 percent of the units are low-cost houses.[14] Enacted in 1985, the ruling originally required the low-cost units to be

Industry Development Board Act, 1994, which regulates the standards and efficiency of the construction industry. For details, see Pawancheek Marican, "New Law on Construction Industry in Malaysia," *International Business Lawyer*, (April 1995): 180-183. In addition, property developers building subdivided units are regulated by the Land and Mines Office under the Strata Titles Act, 1985 (STA 1985). The STA 1985 requires property developers to apply to the Director of Lands and Mines Office for the opening of a Strata Register and to manage the completed property for a specific period. For details, see Teo Keang Sood, *Strata Titles in Malaysia: Law and Practice* (Singapore: Butterworths & Co [Asia] Pte Ltd., 1987) and Cheah Gaik Lean, "Strata Titles: Some Insights into the Law and the Problems Encountered," paper presented at the Seminar on Malaysia Land Laws organized by Persatuan Pengurusan Tanah Semenanjung Malaysia and Pejabat Pengarah Tanah dan Galian Pulau Pinang, May 3, 1993.

[9] All local planning rules are guided by the Town and Country Planning Act, 1976; the Street, Drainage and Building Act, 1974; and the Uniform Building By-laws, 1980.

[10] This requirement is imposed by Section 18(1) of the Town and Country Planning Act, 1976. Only a local authority is allowed to commence, undertake, or carry out any development without the need to obtain planning permission.

[11] Apart from the need to obtain planning permission, developers must obtain Occupation Certificates from the local authority before releasing their properties to purchasers.

[12] The policy is made by the State Housing, Environment, Culture and Civic Amenities Committee.

[13] The Penang state government uses a minimum size of forty-six square feet and a price range from RM25,000 to RM50,000 to define a low-cost housing unit. Property developers must sell the completed low-cost units to the state government, which allocates units to low-cost housing applicants. Penang adopts the following ethnic quotas in its low-cost housing allocation: 45 percent for Malays, 45 percent for Chinese, and 10 percent for Indians.

Under the national government's Special Low-Cost Housing Scheme, introduced in 1986, a low-cost house is defined as a unit costing no more than RM25,000 with a minimum floor space of forty-three square feet. In October 1996, a new definition allows price variation according to location.

[14] There is a national Special Low-Cost Housing Scheme that makes the private sector wholly responsible to deliver a target of 84,000 low-cost units per year. Property developers participate in this low-cost housing project through the Penang state's privatization scheme, in which state land is granted to developers at a nominal rate. Developers must then construct and

built on the affected development site, but currently allows developers to construct them at other sites.[15] In addition, the state makes it compulsory for developers to allocate 30 percent of their developed units for *bumiputera* purchasers and to sell these units at a 5 percent discounted rate.[16] Under a 1996 policy, developers must pay the 5 percent discount offered to *bumiputera* purchasers into a State Bumiputera Fund if these units remain unsold after six months and only then can they be released to non-*bumiputera* purchasers.[17]

Given the weight of these bureaucratic controls on the property development industry, it is not surprising that property developers have formed an association to represent their interests. The national body of the Housing Developers' Association Malaysia (HDAM) was set up in 1970 to promote the development of land in line with national objectives, to improve methods of construction, to seek representation in relevant government authorities and organizations concerned with the development of land, and to protect the legitimate interests of its members.[18]

Property developers in Penang are represented by the Penang branch of the HDAM, which was set up in 1985. It had a total membership of forty-nine companies in 1993. Because property developers in Penang have historically had an uneasy relationship with the local councils due to the latter's inefficiency and unclear planning policies,[19] the Penang branch of the HDAM has been lobbying the state to exert its planning authority to make local councils more efficient and to ensure clear and stable local planning rules. Likewise, the HDAM has been pushing the state to draft a long-term state housing policy.[20]

In the early 1990s, the Penang branch of the HDAM witnessed developments as a result of its long-standing lobbying efforts. A change of leadership within the local councils brought about significant improvements in the local planning process. For instance, in 1993 property developers received their first assurance that they would get a response from the Penang City Council within two weeks of submitting their building applications. In addition, the Penang City Council set up a special ad hoc Committee to expedite building plan processing.[21] Comprising senior council officials and representatives from the Penang branch of the HDAM, the Malaysian

---

sell the low-cost units back to the state. Various concessions, such as exemptions from development charges and infrastructure provisions, are given in the development of low-cost housing.

[15] Developers can be exempted on a case-by-case basis from fulfilling this requirement.

[16] Property development companies with a majority *bumiputera* equity share are given an additional 30 percent building density concession in their development projects.

[17] See *The Star*, July 2, 1996, p. 16.

[18] The Housing Developers' Association Malaysia represents the interests of about five hundred property developers in the country.

[19] It was only in 1996 that the Penang City Council produced a comprehensive Development Control Policy in which land-use zones on the island are clearly demarcated. See *The Star*, October 3, 1996, p. 12. However, building height regulations remain unclear and are decided on a case-by-case basis.

[20] Interview with Datuk Eddy Choong, President of the Penang branch of the HDAM, October 13, 1993.

[21] This ad hoc committee is known as SPEAD. SPEAD is an acronym for the types of representatives in this committee that comprised surveyors, planners, engineers, architects, and developers.

Institute of Planners, and the Malaysian Builders Association, this committee meets fortnightly to review building applications.

Of late, the Penang branch of the HDAM has taken on new tasks. It has placed more emphasis on promoting its own image. According to its president, the Association wanted to establish itself as a "professional body" known for its "honest and transparent dealings."[22] Besides this effort, it has taken an active interest in national policy and has joined a nation-wide lobby, which during the early 1990s opposed the Foreign Investment Committee's restrictions on foreign purchases of local properties.

It is evident that national and local regulations have established the basic operating conditions for the property development industry. These regulations aim not merely to standardize the industry and protect consumers, but are also designed to impose obligations on property developers to contribute to national goals by providing low-cost housing and extending privileges to *bumiputera* purchasers. However, property developers are not simply passive in the face of these regulations. Instead, they actively negotiate with state authorities through their representative bodies. The fact that property developers remain a driving force behind the current urban expansion suggests their agility in responding to regulatory constraints, as well as to the demands of the modern era. Using my research findings, I will explore this issue in the next section.

SHAPING MODERN URBAN PENANG: ECONOMIC, POLITICAL, AND SOCIO-CULTURAL IMPERATIVES

General Profile of the Companies Studied

The main aim of my study of property developers was to investigate their economic, political, and cultural priorities in order to understand the actions of the two property development companies in the Kampung Serani conflict. Over the course of my fieldwork, I studied twenty property development companies which, according to my own estimation, represented about 35 percent of the total property development companies active in Penang during 1993.

The companies I studied consisted of eighteen private limited companies and two public limited companies listed on the Kuala Lumpur Stock Exchange (KLSE).[23] Included in the private limited companies were five local-foreign joint ventures involving Japanese, Taiwanese, Kuwaiti, and Sino-Indonesian capital. One private limited company was wholly owned by Taiwanese capital.[24] The company representatives interviewed consisted of five executive directors, twelve general managers, a project manager, a marketing manager, a marketing executive,

---

[22] Interview with Datuk Eddy Choong, the President of the Penang branch of the HDAM, October 13, 1993.

[23] Publicly limited companies offer their shares to the public and can be listed on the KLSE. On the other hand, private limited companies restrict the right to transfer shares, limit their membership to no more than fifty stockholders and prohibit public sale of their shares. In a private limited company, members restrict their liability in two ways: first, by shares (or a specific amount owned); and second, by guarantee (or a specific amount undertaken to be contributed to assets after a company's termination).

[24] This company was granted a three year period to incorporate at least 40 percent *bumiputera* partnership. Interview with Executive Director, November 30, 1993.

and a technical and planning advisor.[25] A profile of the types of capitalization and capital base of the twenty companies is provided in Table 8.1.

While I will refer to these companies by the numbers allocated to them in Table 8.1, I will retain the pseudonyms of the two companies involved in the Kampung Serani conflict—that is, Company Highview and Company Golden-Heights. However, as an analysis of Company Golden-Heights must take into account its connection with Company Golden-Point (see Chapter Seven), because they shared the same capital base and carried out similar development projects, I will treat them as one company and call them "Company Golden-Heights and Golden-Point."

Speculating on Condominiums and Commercial Complexes

> Throughout my experience in property development for over twelve years, you can do feasibility studies, et cetera, but the last straw is still gut feeling. The most important thing is to trust your gut feeling in knowing when to go in, what price to sell, who to target, and when to get out.[26]

> I say the recession will not occur now. This is because property development has about a eight-year cycle in it. When it occurs again, it will not be so bad as before because the government has very good fiscal policies now. The government steps in to boost the market by having public works such as the North-South Highway, the Kuala Lumpur Tower, and other infrastructure. All these will stimulate the market and boost the property development sector.[27]

Thirteen companies have been set up since 1988 to take advantage of the recent property boom. Encouraged by the economic boom and the government's pro-growth policy, these developers were highly optimistic about the demand for condominiums and commercial complexes, as illustrated in their following conjectures.

> On the island there is still a very strong demand for commercial space as businesses are expanding.[28]

---

[25] All executive directors were proprietors while some general managers were share-holding partners. I interviewed a total of twenty-one respondents as there were two representatives from Company Golden-Heights and Golden-Point.

[26] Interview, General Manager, Company III, October 19, 1993.

[27] Interview, General Manager, Company XI, September 11, 1993.

[28] Interview, Executive Director, Company Golden-Heights and Golden-Point, December 1, 1993.

Table 8.1
Profiles of the Twenty Companies Studied

COMPANY NAME	DATE SET UP	TYPE OF COMPANY/TYPE OF CAPITAL (CAPITAL BASE)
I	1982	Local capital: Became publicly listed in 1986 (originally a construction subsidiary of a publicly listed company in property development, plantations, and palm oil processing)
II	1990	Private Company: Local capital (business and trade)
III	1989	Private Company: Local capital (trade and construction)
IV (Golden-Heights & Golden-Point)	1988	Private Company: Local capital (jewelry manufacturing)
V (Highview)	1986	Private Company: Local-Indonesian capital (business, merchant, pharmaceuticals and supermarket chain)
VI	1956	Private Company: Local capital (established as construction company but ventured into property development in 1987)
VII	1993	Private Company: 100 percent Taiwanese ownership (property development)
VIII	1990	Private Company: Local-Kuwaiti capital (diamond manufacturing)
IX	1987	Private Company: Local-Japanese capital (Company I had 20 percent share equity. Other partners: sugar and food manufacturing, real estate and construction)
X	1991	Private Company: Local-Indonesian capital (trade and business)
XI	1988	Private Company: Local capital (trade and real estate)
XII	1988	Private Company: Subsidiary of a publicly listed company in plantations, palm oil processing, rubber products, hotel and property development
XIII	1988	Private Company: Local capital: financed by a publicly listed company in credit and financial services and the leisure industry, which manages a listed Property Trust Fund
XIV	1979	Private Company: Subsidiary of a Penang-based banking group
XV	1978	Local capital: became publicly listed in 1982 (originally a subsidiary of a publicly listed company in steel manufacturing and financial services)
XVI	1988	Private Company: Local-Taiwanese capital (trade and leisure industry)
XVII	1988	Private company: Local capital (leisure industry)
XVIII	1988	Private company: Local capital (trade, construction, and leisure); company was formerly owned by the Japanese Kumagai Gumi group. Current owners purchased company in 1988.
XIX	1966	Private company: Local capital (established as construction company but ventured into property development in 1988)
XX	1970	Private company: Subsidiary of a publicly listed company in tin-mining, plantation, palm oil processing, and commodity trading

Some people say the high-cost condominium market is now saturated. But we believe that it is still sustainable as the manufacturing and its downstream industries are growing.[29]

We believe that the condominium market is mobile. You see, people upgrade themselves and move from a project to another. Also, a lot of people living in terrace houses would want to buy condos. In this way, demand is generated.[30]

As a result of this optimism, all companies speculated heavily on condominiums and commercial property. All the companies were involved in condominium construction. Among them, eight companies were solely involved in building condominiums (see Table 8.2). There was a strong preference for building high-cost condominiums. A total of seventeen companies were developing such schemes, and among these, ten placed their stakes entirely on high-cost condominiums, while

Table 8.2
Companies Studied and Details of Development Activities

DEVELOPMENT DETAILS	COMPANIES INVOLVED	TOTAL NUMBER
TYPE OF PROPERTIES DEVELOPED i. Condominium	II, III, IX, X, XII, XVIII, XIX	7
ii. Condominium and Commercial	VI, Highview, XIII	3
iii. Condominium and Leisure	IX, XV	2
iv. Condominium, Commercial and Leisure	VII, Golden-Heights & Golden-Point, XIV, XVI	4
v. Condominium, Commercial and Industrial	XVII, XX	2
vi. Condominium, Commercial, and Education Center	I	1
vii. Condominium, Leisure and Industrial	VIII	1 (Total = 20)
TYPES OF CONDOMINIUM/APARTMENT PROJECTS i. High-cost only	II, III, Highview, VII, VIII, IX, X, XI, XII, XV	10
ii. High-cost and Medium-cost	XVI, Golden-Heights & Golden-Point, XVIII	3
iii. High-cost, Medium-cost and Low-cost	I, XIII, XIV, XX	4
iv. Medium-cost only	VI	1
v. Medium-cost and Low-cost	XVII, XIX	2 (Total = 20)

---

[29] Interview, General Manager, Company III, October 19, 1993.

[30] Interview, General Manager, Company Highview, October 7, 1993.

seven played it safer by developing both high- and medium-cost condominiums (see Table 8.2).[31]   The preference for building high-cost condominiums suggests that it was a lucrative venture. Indeed, one developer revealed that his company was making a "three-figure percentage profit" from each high-cost condominium scheme.[32] Inevitably, the focus on high-cost condominiums meant that these developers were targeting the upper-middle income group as their purchasers. Although they were also selling to foreigners, the shrinking foreign market, due to restrictions imposed by the Foreign Investment Committee since 1990, made them more dependent on local purchasers, as illustrated in these responses:[33]

> We target the upper-income group and expatriates. This is one sector which we feel more comfortable with. We have been involved with this sector and our property has been selling very well.[34]

> We built this condominium for the high-class people here and for Taiwanese expatriates.[35]

> Our project is a luxurious upper-market condo. The people who buy it are basically those who live in bungalows, but their children are grown up or those who do traveling and worry about the security of their bungalows when they are away.[36]

> We are planning to build the first retirement village in Penang. It will be a low-rise condo which will cater to a small niche of people. These are the cosmopolitan- and metropolitan-type of people here who have lived overseas.[37]

Commercial property was the second most important development scheme for these twenty companies. Eleven companies were developing commercial projects such as retail outlets, office, and commercial complexes as well as integrated developments (see Table 8.2).

---

[31] In 1993, housing in Penang was commonly defined according to the following price categories: a) Low-cost housing (not exceeding RM25,000); b) Low-medium-cost housing (around RM50,000); c) Medium-cost housing (around RM100,000); d) High-cost housing (RM150,000 to RM250,000); e) Up-market housing (above RM300,000). See Ooi Poay Lum, "An Overview of the Housing Industry in Penang: From a Private Developer's Perspective," paper presented at the International Conference on Penang 2002: Into the 21st Century, Penang, July 26-27, 1994, p. 2.

[32] Interview, Technical and Planning Advisor, Company XVIII, July 12, 1993.

[33] A classic case was Company IX—a local-Japanese venture set up in 1987 during the heyday of liberalization—which sold 88 percent of its first condominium scheme to Japanese purchasers during 1989, but had to switch to focus on the local market in the 1990s. (The Foreign Investment Committee later restricted foreign ownership to 30 percent of total units in a condominium scheme.) This information was obtained during my interview with the General Manager of Company IX, August 13, 1993.

[34] Interview, General Manager, Company Highview, September 7, 1993.

[35] Interview, Executive Director, Company VII, November 30, 1993.

[36] Interview, Executive Director, Company VIII, September 8, 1993.

[37] Interview, General Manager, Company I, September 16, 1993.

Besides these two types of property, seven of the larger companies ventured into developing and managing leisure, industrial, and education-related properties as a strategy to ensure sustainable income during property downturns (see Table 8.2).[38] However, these developers were reluctant to build low-cost housing, claiming that they would have to subsidize such developments, due to the high land costs in Penang. All the six companies building low-cost housing were compelled to do so by state requirements.

The heavy speculation on high-cost condominiums and commercial property made these two activities highly competitive. Given the uncertainty of the property development industry, it was not surprising that the developers adopted a variety of strategies to ensure that their condominium and commercial projects would sell.

CREATING CULTURAL DIFFERENCES: LOCATION, TECHNOLOGY, AND CULTURE

Location

There was a common trend among developers to use location to sell their projects as represented in their promotions:

> Enjoy high living on a hill crest, directly overlooking the picturesque Penang Bridge. . . . Each apartment has a panoramic view of the scenic coast. . . to Georgetown's graceful skyline. . . .[39]

> Located at the helm of the commercial neighbourhood of Pulau Tikus . . . [this commercial center] is developed with astute investment sensibilities in mind. With its excellent road frontage position. . . , proximity to Georgetown, Batu Ferringhi, and other major localities in Penang, . . . [it] offers a conducive setting for retail outlets and corporate offices.[40]

As illustrated in Table 8.3 below, there was a concentration of commercial and high-cost condominium schemes in the city and a predominance of high-cost condominium projects in the scenic northern metropolitan area. In turn, medium- and low-cost condominiums and industrial developments were concentrated in the western and southern metropolitan areas.

Inevitably, the preference for building particular types of properties in certain localities had several consequences. First, as developers transformed chosen localities into prestigious commercial centers and exclusive condominium addresses, and turned other areas into medium- and low-cost housing suburbs, they created class and status distinctions between localities in urban Penang. Second, the concentration of particular development activities in certain localities meant that developers active in the same areas were in the stiffest competition with each

---

[38] Companies VI, XII, XIV, and XX were also developing townhouses and terrace houses.

[39] Advertisement of Company Golden-Heights and Golden-Point, in *The Star*, March 5, 1993, p. 10.

[40] Advertisement of Company Highview for the commercial center on the Kampung Serani site, in *The Star, Section Two*, December 15, 1993, p. 55.

Table 8.3
Profile of Companies Studied and Location of Development Activities

COMPANY	LOCATION AND NUMBER OF DEVELOPMENT PROJECTS ON ISLAND				
	CITY CORE		GREATER METROPOLITAN		
	PULAU TIKUS	GEORGETOWN	NORTH	WEST	SOUTH
#I	1 high-cost condo 1 commercial complex	3 commercial complexes 1 high-cost condo 1 heritage park	2 high-cost condos 1 condotel		2 medium-cost condos 1 low-cost flat 1 commercial complex 1 educational Center 2 new townships
II	1 high-cost condo		2 high-cost condos		
III	1 commercial complex	1 high-cost condo			
IV (Golden-Heights & Golden-Point)	6 high-cost condos 2 integrated developments	1 integrated development	1 condotel 2 high-cost condos 1 service apt*		1 service apt
V (Highview)	6 high-cost condos 1 commercial complex	1 high-cost condo	1 commercial complex		
# VI		2 medium-cost condos 1 bank building			
VII		1 high-cost condo 1 office complex	1 service apartment*		
VIII		1 conservation scheme	2 high-cost condos		2 industrial complexes
IX			2 high-cost condos 1 condotel		
X			2 high-cost condos		
XI			1 high-cost condo		
XII			1 high-cost condo 1 townhouse		
XIII				1 high-cost condo 3 medium-cost condos 1 commercial complex 2 low-cost flats	
XIV				1 high-cost condo 2 medium-cost condos 1 commercial complex 1 sports center	
XV			1 service apt		3 high-cost condos
XVI		1 office complex	1 high-cost condo		3 medium-cost condos 1 country club
XVII					2 medium-cost condos 2 low-cost flats 1 commercial complex 1 industrial complex
XVIII					1 high-cost condo 1 medium-cost condo
# XIX					1 medium-cost condo
# XX			1 high-cost condo		1 high-cost condo 1 medium-cost condo 1 low-cost flat 2 terrace housing 1 commercial complex 1 industrial complex

also developing residential properties in Seberang Perai/mainland
* joint ventures among developers

other. Indeed, this explains why Companies XV, XVI, XVII, XVIII, XIX, and XX, active in the southern metropolitan region, were most agitated by the Penang Development Corporation's move to build medium-cost apartments, since this property was in their development niche. Their irritation toward PDC is conveyed in a comment by Company XVI:

> There is no point for PDC to compete with private developers. It should instead build more low-cost housing and public amenities like parks and gardens.[41]

Apart from location, these developers were trying to outdo each other by using technology and cultural influences to enhance the prestige of their projects.

Security, Heritage, and Feng Shui

A salient feature of condominium and apartment living is security—the reputedly "hi-tech" intercom systems and twenty-four hour security maintenance these projects offer. While a closer examination of projects quickly reveals more hype than actual surveillance (their "hi-tech" communication system was sometimes no more than a buzz button for communication and their security guards were reported to fall asleep on duty), I found in my interviews with condominium dwellers that the selling of security appealed strongly to purchasers.

In addition, under the rubric of a "modern lifestyle", developers chose romantic, exotic, exclusive, and auspicious names for their projects. Some examples are: Bella Vista, Belle Vue, Bellisa Court, Seri Emas, Desa Mas, Mutiara Villa, Noble Villa, Diamond Villa, Desa Mar Vista, Seri York, Sunnyville, Silverton, Bukit Awana, Horizon Towers, and Ratu Mutiara.[42]

In line with the vogue for "heritage" among the urban middle classes, there was a trend for the trappings of "colonial architecture," particularly rooftops and window designs found in "heritage buildings."[43] According to one respondent:

> There is a nostalgia of late in Penang for the beauty of the past, especially for the more affluent Penangites who appreciate things like cultural environment and architecture.[44]

Among the developers studied, Companies I, Golden-Heights and Golden-Point, Highview, and VIII were interested in what they termed "bungalow" or "colonial" architecture in a rather big way. Company I incorporated heritage designs in its super-exclusive condominium near the historic Suffolk house—built around 1790 by

---

[41] Interview, Marketing Manager, Company XVI, June 26, 1993.

[42] *Emas* or *mas* means gold; *Seri* means shining; *Desa* is another word for *kampung*, but it is often used by developers to mean villa; *Mutiara* means pearl; *Bukit Awana* literally means "Hill in the clouds"; and *Ratu* means Queen. (Penang is also referred to as the "Pearl of the Orient.") Since 1991, the Ministry of Housing and Local Government has imposed a ruling requiring developers to use Malay names for their projects. However, developers circumvented this ruling by using Malay names when they applied for advertising permission from the Ministry, but switched to non-Malay names when they promoted their projects.

[43] Companies VII, VIII, and Golden-Heights and Golden-Point restored and converted colonial buildings into their offices.

[44] Interview, General Manager, Company I, September 16, 1993.

Francis Light, the founder of Penang—and promoted this project as "the renaissance of the timeless Penang lifestyle." To further accentuate the historic value of the project, Company I developed a four-hectare "Heritage Park" where trees indigenous to Penang were planted. Company VIII's "heritage project" was to convert the area surrounding the famed Khoo Kongsi—a major tourist attraction in the Armenian-Acheen Street heritage precinct—into a modern center with hotel and residential facilities. Not surprisingly, Company Highview appropriated the heritage theme in its development on the Kampung Serani site. Its General Manager described the project in the following manner:

> The commercial row will be something very unique, special, and nice for Penang. We are using colonial architecture. We will copy some of the architectural elements from heritage buildings, such as the repeated roofs, but incorporate modern facilities and air conditioning to make it a more conducive place to shop in. The residential units will be clustered around a courtyard system. The courtyard will have a very water-based landscape with undulating grounds. We basically came up with the idea and the design brief. The architects interpret it for us into models. You see we are in touch with the market and purchasers and know what they want.[45]

Another popular theme used to promote projects was *feng shui. Feng shui*, the practice of Chinese geomancy, literally means "wind and water" and has its origins in ancient folk beliefs.[46] The practice of *feng shui* incorporates beliefs in:

> the power of the natural environment: the wind and the airs of the mountains and hills; the streams and the rain; and more than that: the composite influence of natural processes. . . . By placing oneself well in the environment feng shui will bring good fortune. Conversely, an analysis of the site of any building or grave with knowledge of the metaphysics of feng shui will tell the fortune of the site owner. This analysis and the art of good siting we call Chinese geomancy.[47]

Nineteen of the companies studied revealed that they designed their condominium and commercial projects with *feng shui* considerations in mind.[48] However, I found that they had two different motivations for using *feng shui*.

---

[45] Interview, General Manager, Company Highview, September 7, 1993.

[46] Charles F. Emmons, "Hong Kong's Feng Shui: Popular Magic in a Modern Urban Setting," *Journal of Popular Culture* 26,1 (1992): 39.

[47] Stephan D. R. Feuchtwang, *An Anthropological Analysis of Chinese Geomancy*, first edition (Vientiane, Laos: Vithagna, 1974), p. 2. A study by Emily Ahern shows that among a group of Taiwanese villagers, *feng shui* refers only to the geomancy of graves. Ahern explains that in the geomancy of graves, it is the ancestor, and not abstract natural forces, who determines the *feng shui*. According to this belief, good *feng shui* means that the ancestor is happy and at ease, while bad *feng shui* means that the ancestor is uncomfortable or unsatisfied. See Emily M. Ahern, *The Cult of the Dead in a Chinese Village* (Stanford: Stanford University Press, 1973). For a contrasting view that argues the ancestor is a passive agent and merely a conductor of the power exhibited by natural forces, see Maurice Freedman, *Lineage Organisation in Southeastern China* (London: The Athlone Press, 1958).

[48] Only Company III, whose proprietors were all born-again Christians, did not observe this practice.

First, thirteen companies merely incorporated "basic *feng shui* logic" in their project designs in order to attract buyers. These developers explained that "basic *feng shui* logic" meant having building designs which avoided several features: measurements of four feet,[49] triangular designs, roof ridges facing windows, doors aligned in parallel lines, and so on. As a sales gimmick, Company XIV even engaged a *feng shui* expert from Singapore to give free advice to interested buyers. These developers reported that *feng shui* was most important among business clients, as they placed more emphasis on *feng shui* in their commercial projects.

Second, five developers (Companies I, II, IX, XVI, XVIII) engaged *feng shui* experts to help shape their projects because they believed that good *feng shui* would augur well for their own enterprises and ensure continued prosperity for their companies. Among them, Company XVIII, whose proprietors were "staunch believers of *feng shui*," had a large water-retention pool specially built to ensure that water running down from the hills behind its condominium project flowed through the scheme for *feng shui* purposes upon the advice of *feng shui* experts.[50]

While at first glance the use of *feng shui* might seem contradictory to a modern lifestyle, several scholars have noted the persistence of *feng shui* practices in contemporary Asian societies.[51] For example, Stephan Feuchtwang argues that the amoral code of *feng shui*, a practice that expresses individual hope for wealth and honor in the future and which assumes that benefits are to be had by divining laws of natural and cosmic forces, facilitates differentiation and competition.[52] He observes that it is often only those who possess some degree of wealth who are concerned with this practice, as the very essence of *feng shui* manipulation is to lessen the anxiety of maintaining wealth.

Confirming Feuchtwang's observation, a geomancer practicing in Malaysia and Singapore has noted a new interest in *feng shui* among the region's economic elites such as "bankers, accountants, medical doctors, architects or businessmen."[53] The *feng shui* master I interviewed also revealed that his clients consisted largely of

---

[49] There is a local superstition that the number four brings ill luck.

[50] This company engaged the services of a *feng shui* expert from Thailand.

[51] These scholars have explained *feng shui*'s current popularity by treating it as either a practice that enables modern society to deal with uncertainty, anxiety, and the unpredictable or, alternately, as a practice that offers opportunities for differentiation, competition, and conflict. See Emmons, "Hong Kong's Feng Shui"; and Jack Goody, "East and West: Rationality in Review," *Ethnos* 58,1-2 (1993): 6-36). For the alternate approach, see Rubie S. Watson, "Remembering the Dead: Graves and Politics in Southeastern China," in *Death Ritual in Late Imperial and Modern China*, ed. James L. Watson and Evelyn S. Rawski (Berkeley: University of California Press, 1988), pp. 203-227; Martin K. Whyte, "Death in the People's Republic of China," in *Death Ritual in Late Imperial and Modern China*, pp. 289-316; and Vincent S. R. Brandt, *A Korean Village: Between Farm and Sea* (Cambridge, MA: Harvard University Press, 1971). Others have illustrated how *feng shui* offers opportunities for urban conflicts. See Stephen Boyden, Millar Sheelah, Ken Newcombe, and Beverley O'Neil, *The Ecology of a City and its People: The Case of Hong Kong* (Canberra: Australian National University Press, 1981); and James Hayes, *The Rural Communities of Hong Kong: Studies and Themes* (Hong Kong: Oxford University Press, 1983).

[52] Feuchtwang, *An Anthropological Analysis of Chinese Geomancy*, pp. 212, 220.

[53] Peter Gwee Kim Woon, *Fengshui: The Geomancy and Economy of Singapore* (Singapore: Shinglee Publishers, 1991), p. 79.

the wealthy and of businessmen, professionals, and developers.[54] Attesting to the revived interest in *feng shui* in Malaysia is the appearance of numerous books by local authors on this subject.[55] Given this, we can reasonably presume that *feng shui* is a reworking of "tradition" among the wealthier groups to express their aspirations for high class status and wealth.

The use of *feng shui* by the developers I studied suggests that their appropriation of this cultural discourse into the building aesthetics and designs of their projects was a means to appeal to the desires, ideals, and demands of richer and upper-income groups who are able to purchase condominiums. However, their differing responses suggest that this appropriation was also due to their own need to cope with the anxiety of maintaining success in a highly uncertain and competitive industry, for they also saw *feng shui* as a means to insure their company's continued well-being and success.

While these developers had their own imperatives as they pursued their goals in urban Penang, they also faced checks and balances.

Responses to Political and Cultural Constraints

Given the pervasive government regulation of the property development industry, it was inevitable that state laws posed a major hindrance to the pursuits of developers. I found that developers considered the state's ruling on low-cost housing provision to be a major constraint. Reluctant to build low-cost housing, they were constantly trying to outwit the local council by building just short of the mandatory quota of low-cost housing. While many got away with this, one firm, Company I, was caught because it pushed its luck too far. In 1993, Company I submitted building plans for a 148 unit medium-cost apartment on the mainland— just two units short of the mandatory quota for metropolitan areas. But this incurred the wrath of the municipal councilors on the mainland, who withheld approval for the project.

Property developers have to contend with planning constraints, as well as the power of federal agencies such as the Penang Regional Development Authority (PERDA). For example, the Taiwanese-owned Company VII not only had a building plan for a commercial tower in Georgetown rejected by the local council, but its twenty-six acre piece of land in the southern metropolitan town of Teluk Kumbar was also acquired by the government for PERDA's use after Company VII turned down a partnership request from the federal authority, which wanted to be a joint developer on the project. The Executive Director of Company VII interpreted things in the following way:

> The State is so powerful that developers need to have the right contacts. This is the only way to ensure that their projects get on. That is why some developers are in the favor of state officials. It is a game. Everyone knows how

---

[54] According to this *feng shui* master, about 30 percent of developers in Penang used the services of geomancers. Interview with Mr. Tung Leong Chye on September 27, 1993.

[55] See Evelyn Lip, *Feng Shui for the Home* (Singapore: Times Books International, 1986); Lilian Too, *Feng Shui* (Kuala Lumpur: Konsep Lagenda Sdn Bhd., 1993); Peter Gwee Kim Woon, *Fengshui*. During my interviews, three developers reported that they were reading books on *feng shui* by Evelyn Lip and Lilian Too.

to play it and to do what is needed. We have found local Malays as our partners. I think we have made the right connections now.[56]

Clearly, this corporate manager saw political connections as an effective means of evading regulation, a view shared by others who have tried to forge links with important political figures in order to mitigate government control. For instance, Companies I and VIII had partners who were ex-senior federal government officials; Company Highview took on a member of Negeri Sembilan royalty as a partner; and Company Golden-Heights and Golden-Point made the brother of the Deputy Prime Minister (who is also the Finance Minister) its Executive Chairman. Companies VIII, XVIII, and XX took on ex-senior staff from the local councils and the Penang Development Corporation as their partners or executive staff.

Needless to say, objections from ground tenants were another common obstacle to the development process. Eager to take advantage of the property boom while it lasted, developers explained that they tried to reach "peaceful" settlements with their ground tenants as quickly as possible. Six companies provided ground tenants on their sites with compensatory low-cost flats or medium-cost apartments.[57] Company XX, which entered into a joint venture with a landowner to develop a private estate, gave the best compensation deal.[58] This was because the landowner had required the company to provide the ground tenants with double-story terrace houses on the development site, as well as to allocate to each ground tenant family RM60,000 worth of shares from the joint enterprise between the developer and landowner in compensation for their eviction.[59]

While these developers were able to negotiate such impediments, another problem was more difficult. I refer here to the effective use, by devotees who come from various ethnic groups, of the power of the *keramat* and Indian and Chinese "gods" to thwart developers. *Keramat* are "tombs or reputed tombs of saints that are believed to be wonder working shrines."[60] A specifically Malayan institution, the worship of innumerable saints arises from Indian-derived Shia' beliefs and practices in local Islam. This worship involves making offerings at the graves of ancestors, founders of settlements, rulers, religious teachers, and even rocks or stones.[61] It is said that the Malays, who are otherwise Sunni Muslims of the School of Shafie, adopted the institution of the *keramat* to continue, under the guise of Islam, some of their former animistic practices.[62] As a result, *keramat* shrines are commonly found in Penang, even in the city center. While *keramat* worship was originally a Malay practice, members of the Chinese and Indian communities have also adopted it.[63] In addition, Chinese and Indians have their own assortment of

---

[56] Interview, Executive Director, Company VII, November 30, 1993.

[57] These were Companies VI, VIII, XIII, XVII, XVIII, and XX.

[58] This landowner (an English woman living in Perth, Australia) is the descendant of a famous colonial businessman in Penang who owned large land tracts in the southern metropolitan area.

[59] Interview, General Manager, Company XX, September 24, 1993.

[60] Abdul Kahar bin Yusoff, et al., "Historical Survey of the Mosques and Kramats on Penang Island." Research Paper of the Malayan Teachers College, Penang, 1974, p. 14.

[61] Ibid.

[62] Ibid.

[63] Since the Islamic resurgence in the early 1980s, Malays have increasingly abandoned *keramat* worship. For a discussion on how Malays became ritual mediators upon their abandonment of

"deities" and have also built a proliferating number of shrines all over Penang.[64] There persists a folk belief that *keramats* and the various religious "deities" worshiped at shrines do not only have the power to heal, protect, and bless devotees, but also the ability to admonish, punish, and torment individuals, should disrespect be shown to them or their abodes disturbed.

As a consequence, developers often face the task of "evicting" "spirits" in the development process.[65] Akin to the process of evicting ground tenants, a series of negotiations with the worshippers of these "spirits" or shrines is needed for such evictions, except that the negotiation is done through a spirit "medium"—often a devotee upon whom the *keramat* or "god" descends.

Six of the developers studied had to build new shrines for *keramat* and Indian and Chinese "gods" within the compound of their condominium projects. These developers explained that they conceded to these demands by shrine devotees because they were reluctant to incur the wrath of these spirits lest "bad luck" should strike them.[66] Among them, Company XVIII (whose directors were fervent believers in *feng shui*) had to build two new shrines on its condominium site—one for a *keramat* and the other for a popular Chinese "god" known as Toa-peh-kong.[67] In relocating an Indian shrine, the Executive Director of the problem-ridden Company VII was even required by the "god" to participate in a ritual of relocation in which he had to don a *dhoti* and move the "picture of the Indian god" to its new shrine personally.[68] As the submission to "spiritual" powers among developers generally stemmed from a desire to avoid "bad luck," these actions can be seen as an attempt to control the uncertainties of the property-development industry. All my respondents considered "luck" to be an essential part of achieving success in the highly unpredictable property-development industry.

Having traced the priorities and responses among developers, let me conclude this section by highlighting how their entrepreneurial pursuits and strategic choices affect spatial changes and local politics. We have seen how developers speculated heavily in high-cost condominiums and commercial property as they took advantage of the property boom created by the economic liberalization accompanying the nationalist agenda of modernizing Malaysia. Their speculative choices meant that they were dependent upon the upper-middle classes and economic elite as their clientele. As developers competed with each other, they used geographical, technological, and cultural arguments reflecting the status and cultural aspirations of their anticipated customers to stimulate consumption and promote their projects. In this process, they created an idealized concept of the

---

this practice as the Chinese took over, see Mohd. Razha Rashid and Wazir-Jahan Karim, "Ritual, Ethnicity, and Transculturalism in Penang," *Sojourn* 3,1 (1984): 62-77.

[64] For an introduction to the Chinese folk belief in spirits, see Alan J. A. Elliot, *Chinese Spirit-Medium Cults in Singapore* (Singapore: Donald Moore Books, 1964).

[65] In Malaysia, it is also common for building contractors to erect *keramat* shrines on construction sites to appease local "spirits" as a measure to avoid mishaps during the construction period.

[66] These developers were Companies Golden-Heights and Golden-Point, VII, XII, XVII, XVIII, and XIX.

[67] This "god" is supposed to guard the area where pioneers settled. See Elliot, *Chinese Spirit-Medium Cults in Singapore*, p. 78.

[68] A *dhoti* is the loincloth worn by male Hindus. Interview, Executive Director, Company VII, November 3, 1993.

modern lifestyle, which confirmed these elites' class identity and their aspirations for increasing wealth, physical security, and architectural aesthetics. However, in the course of achieving their objectives, developers faced impediments in the form of government regulations and challenges by communities, religious groups, and individuals. Developers were forced to meet national requirements on ethnic quotas in terms of their capital equity, sales volume, and the provision of low-cost housing. In addition, an eagerness to evade ill luck in a highly competitive and volatile industry made developers susceptible to demands for relocation made in the name of "spirits" or local religious "deities" perceived to have mystical powers of punishment should their dwelling spaces be disturbed. Hence, while the activities of property developers are to a large extent determined by economic interests and conditions, they become inevitably intertwined with cultural and identity politics in these contests for control over urban space. In the next section, we shall see how this general feature of Penang's property development industry was played out in the Kampung Serani conflict.

COMPETITION IN PULAU TIKUS: COMPANY HIGHVIEW AND COMPANY GOLDEN-HEIGHTS AND GOLDEN-POINT

At the time of my study, there were five companies developing properties in the Pulau Tikus area. These were Companies I, II, III, Golden-Heights and Golden-Point, and Highview. Among them, Companies Golden-Heights and Golden-Point and Highview were the two dominant developers during 1993. Company I is a large property development company and hence was a serious competitor with Company Golden-Heights and Golden-Point and Company Highview. On the other hand, Companies II and III represented the many small property development companies that were able only to construct single small condominium schemes in the area. A brief look at their development activities in the area will provide us with an insight into the nature of competition between developers in Pulau Tikus.

Company I

Company I is one of the largest property development companies in Malaysia. Active nationally and involved in developing properties overseas,[69] Company I was formed in 1982 when a publicly listed property development company (started by a tin-mining family from Ipoh)[70] acquired two major construction companies. Four years after its establishment, Company I was publicly listed. Among its board of directors were former senior federal government officials.

Company I's motto was "excellence through quality" and it aimed to be a "trend setter and a market leader" in the property scene in Penang. Indeed, Company I set several precedents when it became the first developer in the state to develop and

---

[69] Among its overseas projects were: the Southfork residential development in Orlando, Florida, United States of America; the Crendon Holdings' Industrial Park in Long Crendon, England; the Lincoln Lodge Condo, the Astrid Meadows Condo, and the Alkaff Mansion in Singapore; the Hong Kong Villa in Hong Kong; and the St. George Headquarters Building in Sydney, Australia.

[70] Ipoh is located in the state of Perak—a neighboring state just south of Penang's mainland. Company I had fifteen subsidiary companies (which had another fourteen branch companies) and fifteen associate companies.

manage an education center, to use the heritage theme for its condominium scheme, and to develop a retirement village.

It had several projects in the city and the northern and southern metropolitan areas. In Georgetown, Company I developed two commercial towers along the famed "Millionaire's Row" (or Jalan Sultan Ahmad Shah), a commercial complex in the city center, and a luxurious "heritage condominium-cum-heritage park" project on the periphery of the city (see Table 8.4). In the northern metropolitan area, it collaborated with Company IX to develop a condotel and two condominium projects. In the southern metropolitan area, it developed a flyover near the Penang state Mosque, the Penang International Higher Education and Information Technology Center joint venture with the Penang Development Corporation (PDC) and the Penang Bumiputera Foundation (see Chapter Seven), a ninety-seven hectare new township project, and two state-privatized medium-cost apartment townships (see Table 8.4).

Company I entered Pulau Tikus in 1993 to develop a condominium tower and a low-rise condominium row at the corner of Pangkor Road and "Millionaire's Row." Its entry into Pulau Tikus was an expansion of its earlier development activities along "Millionaire's Row." With its performance record, Company I's incursion into Pulau Tikus marked the entry of a large and aggressive player who had the potential to challenge existing major players in this highly valued location.

Company II

Company II was set up by a Chinese trader in 1990.[71] During my fieldwork, it was only developing high-cost condominiums and had three small condominium schemes—two of which were located in the northern metropolitan town of Tanjung Tokong and one in Pulau Tikus (see Table 8.4). Its project in Pulau Tikus was a seven-story condominium of twenty units, located along Cantonment Road. This condominium was built on a bungalow site that, according to the company's Marketing Executive, was bought for an "expensive amount" in 1989.[72] Apart from this project, Company II had no other development plans in Pulau Tikus; it was deterred from looking for more locations due to high land costs. However, Company II owned several small land plots in the northern metropolitan town of Tanjung Tokong for future developments.

Inevitably, high land costs and the scarcity of land in Pulau Tikus meant that smaller companies like Company II found it harder to compete with larger companies which, with their higher capitalization and reputation, were in a better position either to buy land or strike deals with landowners.

Company III

Company III was about the same size as Company II. It was set up in 1989 by a group of born-again Christians engaged in various business ventures, including construction. By 1993, it had only one condominium scheme, a six-story luxury condominium of fifteen units in a wealthy bungalow enclave in Georgetown. In Pulau Tikus, it was developing a commercial complex along Kelawei Road,

---

[71] The owner was also a partner in Company XVIII.

[72] Interview, Marketing Executive, Company II, June 29, 1993.

opposite the former College General site (see Table 8.4). Like Company II, it did not own any other land in Pulau Tikus. Indeed, Company III did not have further plans and admitted that, as a small company, it had to follow market leaders in the area.

Company Golden-Heights and Golden-Point

Company Golden-Heights and Golden-Point were together viewed as a shining success among those who turned to property development during the recent property boom. It was set up in 1988 by three brothers, all in their thirties. Their business careers began when they set up a cottage industry producing jewelry in 1981. By 1984, they were doing so well that they established a factory in the Free Trade Zone to export jewelry to the global market.[73]

They ventured into property development in 1988 by setting up two separate but linked companies: Company Golden-Heights and Company Golden-Point. They began by building properties in Pulau Tikus. By 1991, they had completed two high-cost condominiums and two commercial buildings in this locality. By 1993, these brothers had a total of thirteen existing and on-going projects in Penang (see Table 8.4). Eight of these projects were located in Pulau Tikus, while the rest were located in the northern and southern metropolitan areas. In the northern metropolitan area, Company Golden-Heights and Golden-Point had built two high-cost condominium schemes and a condotel. In addition, during 1993 it entered into a joint venture with Company VII to turn a five-acre site into a major recreation and service apartment project. In the southern metropolitan area, it had developed a service apartment scheme.

In Pulau Tikus, the company developed three condominiums, two commercial buildings, and three integrated developments. Among these condominium projects was a thirty-six-story "super-luxurious condominium" scheme along Gurney Drive.[74] According to one brother, they targeted the *datuks* and the *datins* for this condominium scheme.[75] Interestingly, this project stood on a ex-bungalow site rented by the Consumer Association of Penang (CAP)—a non-government organization known, among other things, as a defender of ground tenants against developers which also played a role in the Kampung Serani conflict (see Chapter Four).[76]

Company Golden-Heights and Golden-Point's largest projects in the Pulau Tikus area were the Midlands One-Stop-Center on the 4.5 acres of land leased from the Penang City Council and the 18.6 acre Gurney Park project on the ex-College General site.[77] With the One-Stop-Center development, Company Golden-Heights and Golden Point became the dominant developer in Pulau Tikus. Strengthening their position was their joint venture to develop the Gurney Park project.

---

[73] In 1993, its jewelry factory was processing 500 kilograms of gold per month and catering to markets in the Middle East, Singapore, Australia, Europe, and Japan.

[74] This condominium was sold at over RM1 million per unit.

[75] *Datuk* is an honorary title conferred by either the state or federal government. Recipients of this award are often politicians, famous business personalities, or community leaders. The female spouse of a *Datuk* automatically becomes a *Datin*.

[76] The two parties reached an amicable agreement with CAP moving out after a settlement.

[77] It also had a plan to develop a thirty-story commercial tower along "Millionaire's Row."

Their successful and aggressive ventures made these brothers famous personalities in Penang. Their success was often attributed to their "political connections." During my fieldwork, rumors claimed that they had established connections with UMNO. The fact that the brother of the former Deputy Prime Minister, Dr. Anwar Ibrahim, was one of their executive directors reinforced this impression.[78]

In the One-Stop-Center development, Company Golden-Heights and Golden-Point faced public protests from nearby residents who were worried about the potential noise levels and traffic congestion. However, backed by the local council, Company Golden-Heights and Golden-Point efficiently dealt with these protests by holding a series of dialogues with residents.[79]

Company Golden-Heights and Golden-Point's performance reached new heights in 1996 when its construction subsidiary company became a publicly listed company.[80] Along with its listing on the Kuala Lumpur Stock Exchange, the company expanded its construction activities to the Federal Territory and Johore.

Company Highview

Company Highview was set up in 1984 by a Chinese businessman (holding a 51 percent equity share) and his Sino-Indonesian wife (holding a 49 percent equity share). However, its establishment coincided with the onset of the mid-1980s recession and Company Highview had to sit out the recession, only able to begin its construction in Pulau Tikus in 1986. It completed its first condominium scheme along Kelawei Road in Pulau Tikus at the beginning of the recent property boom.

By 1991, Company Highview had completed two high-cost condominium projects and was in the process of launching a thirty-story condominium scheme of 102 units in Pulau Tikus. By 1993, it had built a total of five projects, comprising four condominiums and a seven-story commercial complex on the island (see Table 8.4). Three of its condominium projects were located in Pulau Tikus, one of which was featured as an example of quality housing in the *Penang Investment Guide*—an annual guide to investors published by the PDC.[81]

Encouraged by its success in Pulau Tikus, Company Highview bought into Company Dreamland in 1991 and took over the development of the Kampung Serani site. By acquiring the 4.8 acre *kampung* site, Company Highview was able to establish itself as a major player in Pulau Tikus. Indeed, its condominium-cum-commercial scheme on the Kampung Serani site, comprising seventy units of retail

[78] When Company Golden-Heights and Golden-Point won the Penang City Council's land privatization deal, a political controversy erupted as the opposition political party (the Democratic Action Party) accused the local council of giving special treatment to the company because the latter was exempted from providing low-cost housing in this project. Apparently, the local council had waived the low-cost housing regulation in this project in order to procure a higher tender price.

[79] In 1996 Company Golden-Heights and Golden-Point again faced community protests in a massive commercial and residential project it was developing in the southern metropolitan area.

[80] Its construction vehicle was listed in the Kuala Lumpur Stock Exchange's Second Board Index in November 1996. (The Kuala Lumpur Stock Exchange's Second Board Index was launched on January 2, 1991.)

[81] Penang Development Corporation, *Penang Investment Guide* (Penang: Penang Development Corporation, 1993), p. 20.

and office lots and 130 condominium units, was Company Highview's largest development since its formation. As noted earlier, Company Highview also appropriated the heritage significance of Kampung Serani to build its first project incorporating "heritage design," which became a source of architectural pride for the company.

Table 8.4

Companies Active in the Pulau Tikus Area: Details of Development Projects

Company	No. of Projects	Details of Projects	Site
I	1	1 Super-exclusive condominium: - Thirty-two story condominium tower - One Condominium Row	Pangkor Road & Kelawei Road
II	1	1 High-cost condominium: - Seven-story scheme of 20 units	Cantonment Road
III	1	1 commercial row	Kelawei Road
Golden-Heights and Golden-Point	8	3 Condominiums: - Eight-story high-cost scheme of 14 units (Golden-Point only) - Eight-story high-cost scheme of 80 units (Golden-Point only) - Thirty-six story super-exclusive scheme of 68 units (Golden-Point only) 5 Commercial projects: - Five-story office headquarters (Golden-Point only) - Eight-story commercial building (Golden-Heights only) - One Integrated development (Golden-Heights only) - One-Stop-Center (two twenty-story towers of hotel and 260 apartment units) (joint development) - Gurney Park Integrated development of 600 units of "super-condominium block" and hotel, retail on ex-College General site (a joint development with other companies)	Cantonment Road Kelawei Road Gurney Drive Gurney Drive Cantonment Road Burmah Road Burmah Road Kelawei Road & Gurney Drive
Highview	6	4 Condominiums: - Seven-story scheme of 24 units - Eight-story scheme of 26 units - Thirty-story scheme of 102 units - Three to eleven-story super-exclusive condominium of 130 units 2 Commercial projects: - Seven-story podium block - Four-story scheme of 70 units	Kelawei Road Gurney Drive Bagan Jermal Road & Kelawei Road Kampung Serani site Tanjung Tokong Kampung Serani site

However, this joint development was also significant for Company Highview because, by buying into Company Dreamland, it was able to forge connections with Negeri Sembilan royalty. This was because in 1984, the original owners of

Company Dreamland took control of a publicly listed company dealing with medical supplies and pharmaceuticals that was chaired by a member of the Negeri Sembilan royal family. In the joint venture between Companies Highview and Dreamland to develop Kampung Serani, the medical and pharmaceutical company eventually obtained a 50 percent share in the company (see Chapter Four).

We have established that Company Golden-Heights and Golden-Point and Company Highview were the two dominant players in Pulau Tikus during the early 1990s. On the other hand, Company I, a large developer that had established dominance in other areas in Penang, represented a threat to this dominance. In turn, Companies II and III represented the many small-scale speculators in the area. With their small capital bases, relatively unknown reputations and a lack of powerful connections, they were unable to effectively compete with the larger players.

Thus, there was a highly competitive and volatile property market in Pulau Tikus in which dominant players like Company Golden-Heights and Golden-Point and Company Highview not only faced threats from each other but also from larger companies. Bearing this in mind, I will offer an interpretation of why Company Highview denied the residents' demands for low-cost flats, but conceded to the PEA's demands for a heritage house, and why Company Golden-Heights was so interested in the Kampung Serani site that it offered a clubhouse to the PEA to solicit support from the residents.

ANALYZING COMPANY RESPONSES IN THE KAMPUNG SERANI CONFLICT

As dominant developers in Pulau Tikus, it was not surprising that Company Highview and Company Golden-Heights were keen to look for land to expand their development activities in this increasingly fashionable area. With their expansionist plans, a prime 4.8-acre site of *kampung* land situated in the hub of development activities in Pulau Tikus would have caught their attention. Already well established, gaining control of such a site would undoubtedly confirm them as dominant players there.

The site was, however, encumbered by a development deal between the Church and Company Dreamland. As we know, Company Highview effectively bought into Company Dreamland to take over the development of Kampung Serani. We have also remarked on the importance of "heritage" design to the Company's image. Given the need for developers to forge political connections and to incorporate popular aspirations such as heritage into their development projects to remain competitive, the Kampung Serani project would have been vitally important for Company Highview.

On the other hand, the ambitious Company Golden-Heights did not give up its interest in the Kampung Serani development. Company Golden-Heights' persistence was not surprising, as the Kampung Serani conflict was not settled when Highview took over the development project. Thus, Golden-Heights' move to solicit support from the PEA and even funding of the kampung residents' court injunction proceedings against the Church and Highview was a strategic attempt to stall the development of Kampung Serani in the hope that they themselves could negotiate a deal with the Church.

Having established their specific interests on the *kampung* site, I will first explore why Company Golden-Heights specifically offered the PEA a "clubhouse" in recognition of Eurasian heritage in Kampung Serani in order to win support from the Association and the villagers.

I argue that Company Golden-Heights' response was shaped by the necessity for developers, desiring to compete in the property development industry, to stay in tune with the status and cultural aspirations of the upper-middle classes. Given this imperative, an aggressive developer like Golden-Heights would have been alert to the heritage aspirations among urban middle classes in Penang, as well as to the PEA's heritage interests in Pulau Tikus. It would have known that the offer of a clubhouse to represent Eurasian identity on the *kampung* site would have been a proposal attractive enough to win PEA support for its cause. While Company Golden-Heights failed to win the right to develop the Kampung Serani site, its proposed offer of a building to validate the heritage significance of Pulau Tikus's Portuguese-Eurasian community provided the PEA with leverage to make such a demand to the Church and Company Highview.

But why did Company Highview concede to the PEA's demands for a heritage house but deny the residents' request for low-cost housing? We need to bear in mind that the Association leaders were members of the upper-middle classes. We must equally remember that the PEA's evocations of cultural preservation and representation in the Kampung Serani conflict gained the attention and sympathy of the elites and upper-middle classes of Penang as a whole.

Due to the upper-middle class interest in the Kampung Serani conflict, we can argue that as a supplier of high-cost condominiums that thrived by catering to the status and cultural aspirations of this class, Company Highview would be concerned to protect its image among its potential clientele. By denying PEA's demands for a heritage house, Company Highview could risk damaging this image. But by giving in to the PEA's demands, it could protect its image as well as gain a reputation as the first developer in Penang to build a "heritage house" for a community group. Indeed, Company Highview's concern for its image was confirmed during my interview with its General Manager, who told me that the company aimed to be "a responsible developer who does not go to extremes to maximize profit."[82]

Moreover, Company Highview could tolerate the demands for a heritage house because it was perfectly in keeping with a prestigious condominium-cum-commercial center. A modern heritage house could blend in with a modern condominium-cum-commercial project as such "heritage" structures had come into vogue in urban Penang. We have pointed out that this company even exploited the "heritage" theme to incorporate trappings of "heritage" architecture in the project to highlight its uniqueness. This reaffirms our argument about the shared values of developers and the upper-middle classes in their conceptions of a modern lifestyle.

In denying the *kampung* residents' requests for low-cost flats, Company Highview's imperatives as a builder of prestigious condominiums and commercial centers again came into play. The plan to build an exclusive and architecturally unique condominium-cum-commercial center would explain why the company did not want low-cost flats nearby. As it was a norm among developers to separate high-cost condominiums from medium- and low-cost developments in order to symbolize exclusivity, the inclusion of low-cost flats on the redeveloped *kampung* site would certainly affect the prestige of this project. There were, therefore,

---

[82] Interview, General Manager, Company Highview, September 7, 1993.

contrasting conceptions of urban space between the developer and the *kampung* residents.

Furthermore, we must remember that Highview had nothing to lose from denying the *kampung* residents' demands, as the residents, besides being a working-class population of little interest to Company Highview, had after all been stripped of their negotiation rights by their own elite.

From our analysis, we can surmise that the actions and decisions of Company Highview and Company Golden-Heights and Golden-Point were shaped by a combination of their economic, political, and cultural priorities as they competed in the Pulau Tikus area. Our analysis also reveals that Company Highview had more in common with the aspirations of the PEA than it did with the *kampung* residents.

CONCLUSION

In this chapter, I have illustrated how the decisions of two developers in the Kampung Serani conflict can be explained by reference to the economic, political, and cultural prerogatives of property developers as they competed with each other in Pulau Tikus. My findings affirm that as much as the Kampung Serani conflict was about the contrasting cultural arguments between the villagers and the Penang Eurasian Association, it was also about the contrasting visions of modernity between the developers, the Church, the PEA, and the *kampung* residents. As developers attempted to realize their goals, they created a particular vision of a modern lifestyle that expressed status, wealth, and class aspirations. The developers' conception of a modern, urban lifestyle resonated with the aspirations and aesthetics of the upper-income and wealthier classes, although they might each have their own distinctive material interests in the urban arena. As a consequence of these specific conceptions of modern life, developers were not only transforming urban space but also polarizing society by inscribing class, status, and cultural differences upon the urban terrain. In the course of excavating and redeveloping the urban landscape, developers became embroiled in the politics of ethnic identity representations. In the course of their activities, they were compelled by state regulations to conform and contribute to a nationalist agenda of ethnic redistribution. In addition, their pursuits were also impeded by cultural politics as community and ethnic groups affected by their development activities articulated religious or cultural arguments demanding compensation or relocation in the face of the threat of eviction. The volatility and highly competitive nature of Penang's property development industry rendered developers amenable to some of these demands in order to ensure success for their projects. The larger spatial and cultural politics in a rapidly modernizing Penang recurred in Pulau Tikus as this area experienced fast-paced urban renewal and development. Clearly, as developers transformed urban Penang and stepped up their construction activities in the Pulau Tikus area, Kampung Serani became the site of contrasting political, economic, and cultural ambitions, with the groups involved fighting to realize their own interests on the same terrain. In short, this chapter has demonstrated that company priorities, as well as the imperatives of the property development industry, shaped the actions of the two property developers in the Kampung Serani conflict and that their responses contributed to the cultural politics and spatial transformation of the Kampung Serani site.

CHAPTER NINE

CONCLUSION

This book opened with an overview of the Kampung Serani conflict and the complex set of political, economic, cultural, and spatial forces that are forging a modern Malaysia. In the subsequent chapters I introduced my theoretical framework which sought to recognize the agency of local agents by uncovering their specific cultural contexts and historical priorities. Through this approach I sought to understand differing conceptions of the nation, ethnicity, class, and modernity in Malaysia within the complex intermingling of local, national, and global forces. In particular, however, I analyzed the contrasting cultural imaginaries of local actors that combined to shape the politics and spatial consequences of the Kampung Serani conflict. In this final chapter, I explore how the empirical findings presented in the preceding chapters can contribute to a rethinking of Malaysian modernity.

As previously explained, Malaysian society has experienced a series of unprecedented changes in the 1990s. Two of the most fundamental transformations involved, on the one hand, the restructuring and liberalization of the economic base in the push to turn Malaysia into a fully industrialized country in the twenty-first century, and, on the other, a push towards reorganizing cultural subjectivities. These new conditions have in turn affected the nature of the urban experience as various fractions of the state, capital, classes, and community groups struggled to achieve their contrasting cultural visions of a modern Malaysia. These struggles gave rise to a highly contested urban arena and a rapidly changing cityscape. The resulting diverse changes at the national level have had a direct impact on regional and local political authorities which assiduously draft their own developmental plans in line with this national vision of progress. The rapid urban growth ignited by the push for economic and cultural modernization at the national and state levels resulted in a series of local conflicts over contrasting political, economic, and cultural interests, as was the case in Kampung Serani.

My analysis of the Kampung Serani conflict seeks to understand how national and global political, economic, cultural, and spatial forces shaped the reactions of the local players and how their responses combined to characterize the cultural politics of the conflict and determine transformations in the associated cityscape. My argument throughout has been that the actions of the *kampung* residents, the Penang Eurasian Association, the Church, and the developers can only be understood in terms of the intersection between each of their particular circumstances and ambitions and the state's endorsement of the national drive for modernization and urban development. The rapid and continued urban growth in Penang created a contested urban terrain within which private capital, state capital, and community groups each strove to achieve their own economic, political, and cultural imperatives. The impetus behind the ensuing drama was the transformation of the Pulau Tikus area into a prestigious residential and commercial address in response to the wider forces of urban development and modernization. The Kampung Serani residents were the first to be affected, as reluctant participants of urban development, when their village became a site for urban renewal. Facing the threat of eviction, the villagers drew on the historical particularity of the *kampung* to assert their rights as the descendants of pioneer Portuguese-Eurasian settlement in Penang in order to demand compensatory low-cost housing.

The tension between the villagers, the Church, and the developer, in turn, provided the Penang Eurasian Association with the opportunity to further its own agenda of promoting a distinct Portuguese-Eurasian identity in Penang. Drawing on national and regional debates on the topic of Malayness and indigenousness, the Association constructed the rhetoric of a unique Portuguese-Eurasian identity (with historical roots in the Portuguese Settlement in Melaka) to give political weight to its demands for a heritage house and to quench opposition from the *kampung* residents. The combination of local identity politics and the escalating land pressure in the Pulau Tikus area created a sense of urgency for the Penang Eurasian Association, which seized this opportunity to procure a heritage house and ensure a continued expression and concrete recognition of Eurasian cultural identity in Pulau Tikus.

For the Church, the development pressure in Pulau Tikus heightened its fears of compulsory land acquisition, prompting it to quickly redevelop Kampung Serani as the village increasingly became an "eyesore" in the fast modernizing precinct. On the other hand, driven by the economic, political, and cultural imperatives of the property development industry, Company Golden-Heights and Company Highview had more to gain from supporting and conceding to the Penang Eurasian Association's demands for a heritage house than the villagers' request for low-cost housing.

As demonstrated, each of the local actors in the Kampung Serani conflict had his or her own set of particular politics, circumstances, and hopes which significantly shaped that person's or that organization's responses to the challenges raised by the conflict over the *kampung* site. Each party's particular circumstances and experiences helped and hindered that party, both limiting and empowering them at the same time. As a result, the conflict gave rise to a series of shifting and sometimes inconsistent, sometimes ambiguous, discourses about culture and ethnicity. In sum, the diverging constructions of Portuguese-Eurasian cultural identity and the concrete changes to the Pulau Tikus cityscape in the Kampung Serani conflict were the consequence of a complex articulation between the larger forces of modernity and the power politics of the local players. Everyone involved—the state, *kampung* residents, developers, the Church, community leaders, and others—were contending with vicious economic, social, urban, and symbolic transformations which established an overarching framework of constraints and possibilities within which they could pursue their specific material and cultural interests.

The series of transformations associated with the Kampung Serani conflict reveal that ongoing conflicts over nationality, ethnicity, class, and urban change—problems which engage everyone from the most common resident to the highest bureaucratic echelons of the state—were fundamentally about how individuals and groups are captured by, as well as cope with, the promise of "modernity." The fundamental question then is how do we understand modernity, in the Malaysian or Southeast Asian context?

Given the evidence from my investigations, it is not sufficient to consider Malaysian "modernity" as merely ideological or as simply the product of state or capitalist domination. Rather, what we see is that while domination and social upheaval are central to the experience of "modernity," the latter also facilitates the empowerment of people. The experience of modernity should be differentiated from "modernization," which in the Malaysian case refers to an official mission of national material progress organized by a state-sponsored project of national identity formation. Malaysian modernity should be understood less as a state-initiated, top-down project and more as a response by specific, local actors to existing social conditions. It needs to be pointed out that the initiation of a top-down official project of modernization, as represented in the National Economic Policy of the 1970s, was itself a riposte to the tumultuous and fluid social conditions of that time. While official Malaysian modernity has clear goals, its implementation and reception are much more ambiguous, characterized as they are by shifting economic policies and the changing meanings of nation, ethnicity, and class, and as these objectives are contested, appropriated, and reworked by various non-state actors.

Consequently, a much more ambiguous unfolding of "modernity" is experienced by individuals in everyday life, particularly in urban arenas. In the 1990s the urban terrain of Malaysia became an important location for the expression of a "modern society." Cityscapes were particularly affected by the changing policies of economic liberalization and consequently became a stage upon which contests over the meaning of nation, ethnicity, and class were played out as urban space was intensively transformed. As previously demonstrated, the struggles over new subjectivities in the Malaysian pursuit of modernity are closely associated with the categories of nation, ethnicity, and class. Recent constructions of nation, ethnicity, class, and urban development reveal a deep-seated ambivalence at all levels of society over the colonial and the postcolonial, East and West, the new and the traditional, Islam and Malay, class and ethnicity. This unsettled modernity arises from an indecisive stance by the national state, as well as from the contestation and conciliation over the meanings and manifestations of the modern among various institutions and communities outside the state. Modernity in Malaysia is unmistakably associated with processes of domination and violence over urban space, as well as the constitution of political consciousness, class, and identity politics. Yet despite the state's greater power, it cannot enforce a hegemonic vision of modernity. Local identities, aspirations, notions of place, and lived experiences, such as the ones that unfolded in the Kampung Serani conflict, can rework and resist the state's vision of development and its interpretations of ethnicity, class, and urban modernization. The state doesn't have complete power over people, because cultural meanings and political identities are never determined by one source alone but, rather, arise from a complicated quilt of interests, contexts, and representations.

In sum, this book has demonstrated that the experience of modernity in Malaysia begins with the everyday processes of urban eviction and the accompanying upheavals of social, political, and economic behavior, which unfolds within a complex intertwining of local, national, and global dynamics. The tumultuous everyday experience of Malaysian modernity, entailing rapid spatial, material, and symbolic changes, is unavoidably associated with ethnic identity formation and reformulation. While modernity is analogous with the processes of domination and violence, it also brings about the constitution of identity. It is precisely the processes of domination, violence, and change that provide a space for the articulation of human agency and the reworking of cultural/identity politics. As such, the Malaysian experience of modernity cannot be simply understood in terms of state domination or the transforming power of capitalism. Rather, a meaningful conception of the Malaysian modern experience must take into consideration how people struggle to derive power, class, and ethnic status from their positions within the nation-state's modernizing practices, which are, in turn, framed by a complex interaction between local and global forces of transformation. These struggles, in turn, can powerfully reshape the foundational material and cultural conditions of contemporary Malaysian society. This scenario suggests that it is most appropriate to understand modernity as a process of conversion, negotiation, and translation between internal group dynamics and the larger national and global forces of change. The imperative, then, is to investigate further the existing social-structural and cultural orders that limit as well as empower ordinary Malaysians and help to determine the consequences of their actions. What we learn from the Kampung Serani conflict is that people are never passive recipients of external initiatives, but rather always struggle within their own immediate contexts of constraints and opportunities to produce a meaningful life in accordance with their own particular values and goals.

LETTER OF REQUEST FOR INTERVIEW

Date:

The Executive Director
Company Name

Dear Sir/Madam
Re: Request for Interview

I am a Malaysian who is currently pursuing a PhD degree in Anthropology a t Monash University, Melbourne, Australia. I would like to request for an interview with you regarding your company's development projects in Penang.

Let me first introduce my research plans. I am writing a thesis on the "modernity" of Penang Island with a focus on its urban growth since the late 1980s. One of my interests is to investigate into the emergence of a distinct modern lifestyle in Penang especially with the construction of high-rise condominiums, apartments, resorts and new commercial centers. Property developers are one of my targeted respondent groups. I would like to look at how developers create a new concept of living and to understand the nature of the property development industry.

I have collected some information about your company through your various advertisements in the local press and would like to know more about the nature of your development projects. I enclose herewith a copy of my intended questionnaire for your perusal.

As my interview might take up to at least forty minutes of your time, I am ready to interview you after working hours, if that is of no inconvenience to you. Information gathered from the interview will be treated as confidential and I will use pseudonyms should I refer to your company in my thesis.

I thank you for your attention and look forward to a positive reply from you.

Yours Sincerely,

Benglan Goh

QUESTIONNAIRE FOR DEVELOPERS

HISTORY OF COMPANY

1) Please provide your company details (e.g., type of capital, shareholders, et cetera). When and why did you venture into property development?

2) Please list existing development projects, their price range and location.

3) Do you intend to diversify into other economic activities? Why?

NATURE OF THE CONSTRUCTION/DEVELOPMENT INDUSTRY.

4) What are your strategies to minimize risks and to ensure success?

5) Were you affected by the property slump in the mid-1980s? What lessons have you learnt from it? What do you think of the current property boom?

6) Why do you develop properties at the locations selected? Does location have an effect on the type of properties developed? Please explain.

7) What kind of preparations do you undertake before implementing a project? Do you carry out market research? What are your priorities when designing and launching a project?

8) Who are your targeted purchaser groups? Please explain the reasons behind your choice/s.

9) How well do your projects sell? Why is this so? Are your purchasers mainly locals or are they foreigners? What is the percentage distribution between local and foreign buyers in each of your projects?

10) What do you think of the competition posed by foreign property developers in Penang? Please comment.

CONCEPTS USED

11) What concepts (for example, modern living, security, technology, exclusivity, costs considerations, architectural concepts, and so on) do you sell in each of your projects? How are these concepts created? Who are the producers of these ideas?

12) Do you obtain your ideas from research or from following development trends in the other Asian cities or from other countries? Please explain.

13) What is your foremost concern when planning a new project? Please elaborate.

14) Which of your projects would you consider to be the pride of your company? Why?

15) In what ways has your company contributed to the modernization of Penang and its urban landscape alterations? Is this an important consideration to your company?

16) Do you encounter problems in evicting ground tenants? How do you resolve them? Please provide examples. What is your company-policy on compensation when evicting ground tenants and squatters? What is your opinion on the relationship between property developers, ground tenants and squatters in Penang?

17) What are your future development plans?

GOVERNMENT REGULATION

18) Is your company affected by the restrictions on foreign purchasers imposed by the Foreign Investment Committee (FIC)? How do you view the FIC rulings?

19) How is your company affected by the regulations imposed by the Ministry of Housing? Please comment.

20) Has your company encountered problems with the local council, the Penang Development Corporation (PDC) and federal bodies such as the Penang Regional Development Authority (PERDA) in the course of your development projects? Please elaborate.

21) What is your response to the state's ruling on private developers to provide low-cost housing? What is your opinion on the special allocations for *bumiputera* purchasers?

22) What do you think of the current regulations on the property development industry? How do you cope with these government controls?

23) What is your view on the role of the Housing Developers' Association, Malaysia?

FENG SHUI AND "KERAMAT"

24) How important is *feng shui* to the development process? Why? Do you personally believe in *feng shui*? Please explain.

25) Do you engage the services of any *"feng shui"* experts? Explain.

26) Are special rituals related to *"keramat"* worship or any other religious rituals performed at your development sites? Why? Please elaborate.

REAL PROPERTY GAINS TAX REVISIONS FROM 1984 TO 1987

Date of Disposal (since date of acquisition)	From October 23, 1981	From October 19, 1984 Indiv.	Co.	From October 24, 1986 to December 31, 1993 Indiv.	Co.	From October 27, 1997 Indiv.	Co.
Within 2 years	40%	40%	40%	20%	20%	30%	30%
In 3rd year	30%	30%	30%	15%	15%	20%	20%
In 4th year	20%	20%	20%	10%	10%	15%	15%
In 5th year	10%	10%	10%	5%	5%	5%	5%
In 6th year	5%	5%	5%	Nil	5%	5%	Nil
After 6 years	Nil	Nil	5%	Nil	5%	5%	Nil

(Source: Infoline, Malaysia, January 1991, and October 1997)

APPENDIX D

GUIDELINES ON FOREIGN OWNERSHIP OF LAND IN MALAYSIA ISSUED BY THE FOREIGN INVESTMENT COMMITTEE (FIC), 1992-2000

Housing Type	1992 * Prior to March 11, 1992 # Dated December 17, 1992	Dated January 11, 1993	Dated June 24, 1995	December 12, 1998-January 12, 1999 (home ownership campaign period)	2000 Guidelines
ALL HOUSING	* # Units less than RM80,000: ownership not allowed except for a foreign company purchasing for workers' use	No change	No change	No restrictions on purchase of properties more than RM125,000 50 percent margin of financing from Malaysian banks allowed	Units less than RM250,000 not allowed except for foreign company purchasing for workers' use, subject to conditions: a) financing must be from external sources, b) properties must be more than 50 percent completed
CONDOMINIUM	* Units less than RM500,000: ownership allowed if owner occupied and no resale within five years. * Units more than RM500,000: no conditions imposed # Units RM80,000-RM300,000: ownership allowed (if owner-occupied, no resale within three years; if rented out, no resale within five years) # Units more than RM300,000: no conditions imposed	No change from guidelines dated December 17, 1992	Units more than RM-250,000: owner-ship allowed.		Units more than RM250,000: ownership allowed

Housing Type	1992 * Prior to March 11, 1992 # Dated December, 17 1992	Dated January 11, 1993	Dated June 24, 1995	December 12, 1998- January 12, 1999 (home ownership campaign period)	2000 Guidelines
CONDOMINIUM HOLIDAY HOME	* # Generally 30 percent of total units in each project, but flexibility to increase to 51 percent	No change from guidelines dated December 17, 1992	Not more than 30 percent of the total units in each block		Not more than 49 percent of total units in each block
TERRACE HOUSE	*Units RM80,000-RM200,000: ownership allowed for owner occupancy only and no resale within three years. # Units more than RM200,000: ownership allowed (if owner-occupied, no resale after three years; if rented out, no resale within five years)	No change from guidelines dated December 17, 1992	Ownership allowed only for units more than RM250,000		Ownership allowed only for units more than RM250,000
BUNGALOW	* # Units RM80,000-RM500,000: ownership allowed (if owner-occupied, no resale within three years; if rented out, no resale after five years)	No change from guidelines dated December 17, 1992	Ownership allowed if more than RM250,000 but subject to 10 percent quota from each housing project		Ownership allowed if more than RM250,000

Housing Type	1992 *Prior to March 11, 1992 #Dated December 17, 1992	Dated January 11, 1993	Dated June 24, 1995	December 12, 1998 – January 12, 1999 (home ownership campaign period)	2000 Guidelimes
SHOPHOUSE	Ownership allowed for companies with 70 percent local equity (30 percent *bumiputera*)	No change	Ownership allowed for units taller than three stories with conditions: a) Not more than 20 percent of units in a project b) Ownership through setting up local company with at least 49 percent local equity (40 percent *bumiputera*)		Ownership allowed for units taller than three stories with conditions: Not more than 49 percent of units in a project

(Sources: FIC circulars procured from Lim Kean Siew & Co., Advocates & Solicitors, Penang, *The Star*, December 25, 1995, p. 19; *The Star*, May 1, 1998, p. 1; and personal communication with Mr. Lim Hooi Siang.)

A SYNOPSIS OF AMENDMENTS PERTAINING TO DISPOSAL OF LAND TO FOREIGNERS IN THE NATIONAL LAND CODE, 1985-2000

YEAR AMENDED AND YEAR OF EFFECT	NATURE OF AMENDMENTS
Prior to 1984	No stipulations on disposal of land to foreigners
Amended in 1984 (came into effect on March 25, 1985)	Act 587 : totally prohibited disposal and transfer of agricultural and building land to foreigners (Section 433A-E created)
Amended in 1985 (came into effect on September 13, 1985)	Act 624 : enabled banks (which were largely foreign-owned at that time) to create charges and liens on agricultural and building land but disallowed them to bid in case the land was put up for auction (Section 433A-E amended)
Amended in 1986 (came into effect on January 1, 1987)	Act 658 : lifted all restrictions on foreign disposal and transfer of agricultural and building land (Section 433A-E deleted)
Amended in 1992 (came into effect on January 1, 1993)	Act 832 : required a prior written approval from respective state authorities in disposal and transfer of agriculture and building land (Section 433A-E amended)
Amended in 1995 (came into effect on February 16, 1996)	Act 941 : required prior written approval from respective state authorities and specific terms and conditions could be imposed by the state authorities. A levy was imposed on all disposal and transfer of land to foreigners executed on or after October 27, 1995 (Section 433A-E amended and Section 433F-H created)

CHART 4.1: SEQUENCE OF EVENTS IN THE KAMPUNG SERANI CONFLICT

1979	Church entered into joint venture with Company Dreamland to redevelop Kampung Serani.
1980 (coincided with 1981-1983 property boom in Malaysia)	Commencement of Kampung Serani conflict Residents received eviction notices from the Church and established Residents' Association. Residents had first and only meeting with the Bishop, and subsequently searched for political patronage. Residents used local media for public support and evoked a local discourse on the Eurasian heritage of Kampung Serani.
1983	Notification by the Penang City Council of plan to rezone Kampung Serani into a semi-residential-cum-commercial zone. Residents sought help from the Consumers' Association of Penang.
1984	Residents' Association invited the Penang Eurasian Association (PEA) to mediate on their behalf.
1985-1987	Tranquility due to economic recession. Residents revived the Residents' Association upon receiving eviction notices again in 1987.
1991 (coincided with the peak of a property boom which began around 1989)	Company Highview bought into Company Dreamland and became an active partner in pursuing development plans at the Kampung Serani site. Company Highview began persuading sub-tenants in Kampung Serani to settle for cash compensation.
	PEA approached by competing developer Company Golden-Heights with an offer of a clubhouse in recognition of the Eurasian heritage and identity of Kampung Serani. PEA used Company Golden-Heights' offer to persuade the Church to consider Company Golden-Heights as the new developer of Kampung Serani.
1992	Tensions escalated in the Kampung Serani conflict. PEA re-approached the Church and used Company Golden-Heights' readiness to recognize the Eurasian heritage and identity in

Kampung Serani to pressurize Company Highview to provide a compensatory clubhouse for the Association. PEA used Company Golden-Heights' offer to get support from the *kampung* residents.

March 12, 1992   Company Highview sent in a bulldozer to partially demolish Mary Carrier's house before compensation terms were settled.

PEA initiated a campaign to save the Noah's Ark building. A PEA leader writes an article, "Preserve Noah's Ark," which introduced three new arguments:

i)   the identification of a distinct Eurasian contribution to modern education in Malaysia

ii)   that the Eurasians from Kampung Serani and the Pulau Tikus area once spoke Malay

iii)   that the ancestry of the Eurasians in Kampung Serani could be traced to the earliest Eurasian community in Melaka

March 15, 1992   PEA organized "Coffee Morning-cum-Protest" in front of the Noah's Ark building (joined by residents, the media, and members of the Penang Heritage Trust). The event received support from the public and seven articles appeared in the local presses the next day.

Company Highview responded by calling the PEA for a meeting at which it expressed sympathy for the PEA's cause but indicated that the final decision lay with the Church. Company Highview began negotiating with remaining subtenants in Kampung Serani to settle for cash compensation.

PEA leaders used their role as Church leaders to pressure the Bishop into making a commitment to support the Association's request for a compensatory building on the *kampung* site. The leaders also revealed that their first priority was to get a reconstructed Noah's Ark and not alternative accommodation for the residents. PEA leaders met with *kampung* spokesperson but the meeting became strained as residents insisted on being provided with alternative accommodation. The Association leaders reacted by challenging the *kampung* spokesperson's rights to represent the residents on the grounds of his Indian ethnic origins.

March 26, 1992   Company Highview sent a bulldozer again to Kampung Serani and completely demolished Mary Carrier's house. Residents reacted by applying for a court injunction to restrain the Church and Company Highview from entering the *kampung* land.

March 28, 1992	The Penang High Court granted the residents' application for a court injunction.
	Company Highview turned to negotiate seriously with the PEA and in the process agreed to provide a compensatory building for the Association in recognition of the Eurasian heritage of Kampung Serani.
	PEA used the existence of a court injunction to declare that it could no longer represent the residents and would only negotiate for itself from this point on. Having struck a deal with Company Highview, the PEA changed the language of clubhouse to "heritage house."
July 10, 1992	Court injunction lifted following Company Highview's *ex parte* appeal.
	Company Highview demolished the Noah's Ark building.
End of 1992	Church initiated court proceedings on behalf of Company Highview to evict Kampung Serani residents by claiming that they were illegal squatters.
	Residents re-approached the Consumers' Association of Penang for legal representation.
July 5, 1993	The Church and Company Highview won first court case against the remaining shed in Kampung Serani which was found by the courts to be an illegal structure.
August 5, 1993	Company Highview demolished the remaining shed in Kampung Serani.
February 7, 1994	*Kampung* spokesperson won his defense when the court found him not to be an illegal squatter but a lawful tenant holding on after termination of tenancy.
February 9, 1994	Four *kampung* resident-families won their defense when the courts similarly found them to be lawful tenants holding on after termination of tenancy.
October 15, 1994	PEA signed a Memorandum of Understanding with the Church for the latter to execute a ninety-year lease on the *kampung* site for the construction of a Eurasian heritage house.
End of October, 1994	Kampung Serani ceased to exist as the last resident-family settled for cash compensation and moved out of the *kampung* site.

CHART 5.1 : FAMILY TREE OF GUNASEKARAN, D'MELLO, AND PESTANA FAMILIES IN KAMPUNG SERANI

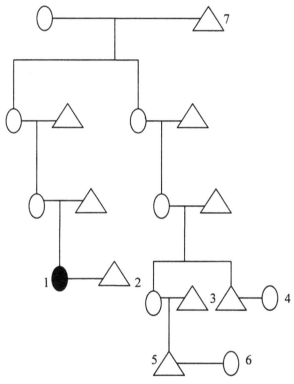

1 = Pauline D'Aranjo
2 = Paul Gunasekaran
3 = Anthony D'Mello
4 = Agnes Ling
5 = Colin Pestana
6 = Marie Pestana
7 = F. Pasqual

APPENDIX H

CHART 8.1: HOUSING DEVELOPMENT PROCESS ON PENANG ISLAND

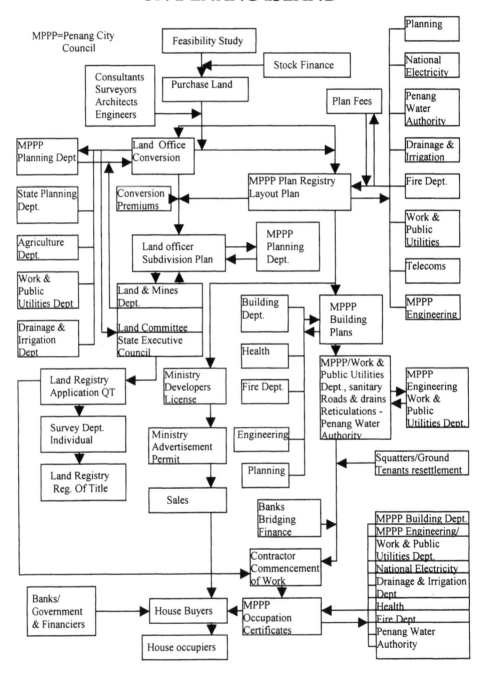

PLATE 4.1: HOUSE AT 356C LEANDROS LANE, KAMPUNG SERANI

PLATE 4.2: HOUSE AT 350B LEANDROS LANE, KAMPUNG SERANI

PLATE 4.3: VIEW OF THE NEW COMMERCIAL PROJECT AND
CONDOMINIUM ON THE KAMPUNG SERANI SITE

PLATE 4.4: VIEW OF THE EURASIAN "HERITAGE HOUSE" ON
THE KAMPUNG SERANI SITE

LAY-OUT PLAN OF BUILDINGS IN KAMPUNG SERANI

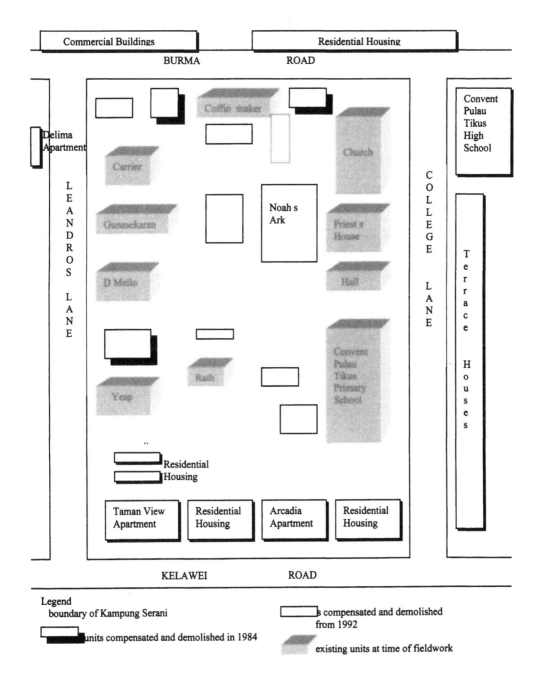

Commercial Buildings

Residential Housing

BURMA ROAD

Delima Apartment

LEANDROS LANE

Coffin maker

Carrer

Gunasekaran

D Mello

Yeap

Bath

Noah s Ark

Church

Priest s House

Hall

Convent Pulau Tikus Primary School

COLLEGE LANE

Convent Pulau Tikus High School

Terrace Houses

Residential Housing

Taman View Apartment

Residential Housing

Arcadia Apartment

Residential Housing

KELAWEI ROAD

Legend
boundary of Kampung Serani

units compensated and demolished in 1984

s compensated and demolished from 1992

existing units at time of fieldwork

MAP 7.1: BOUNDARIES OF METROPOLITAN GEORGETOWN AND ADMINISTRATIVE DISTRICTS IN PENANG

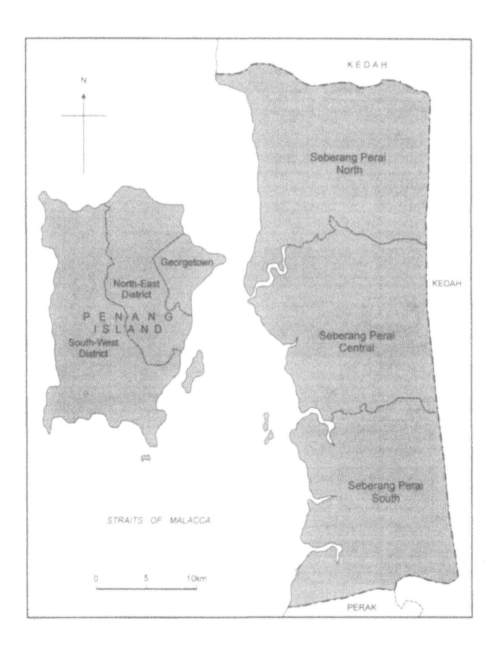

MAP 7.2: LOCATION OF PULAU TIKUS WITHIN THE GEORGETOWN METROPOLITAN AREA

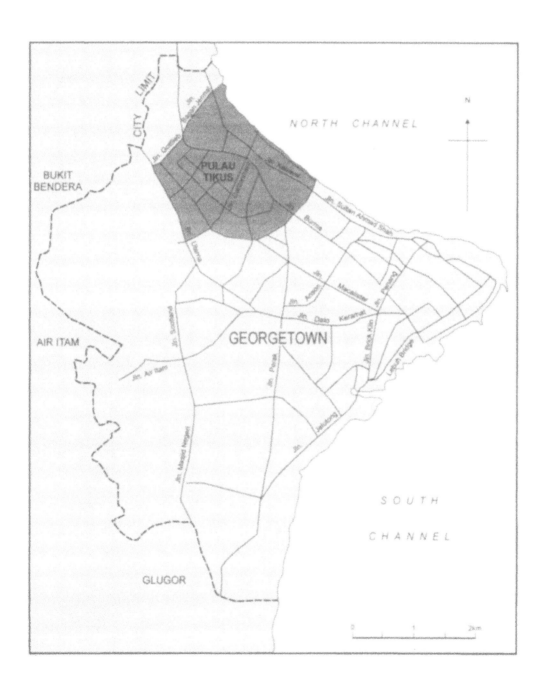

MAP 7.3: MAJOR ROADS AND LANDMARKS IN THE PULAU TIKUS AREA

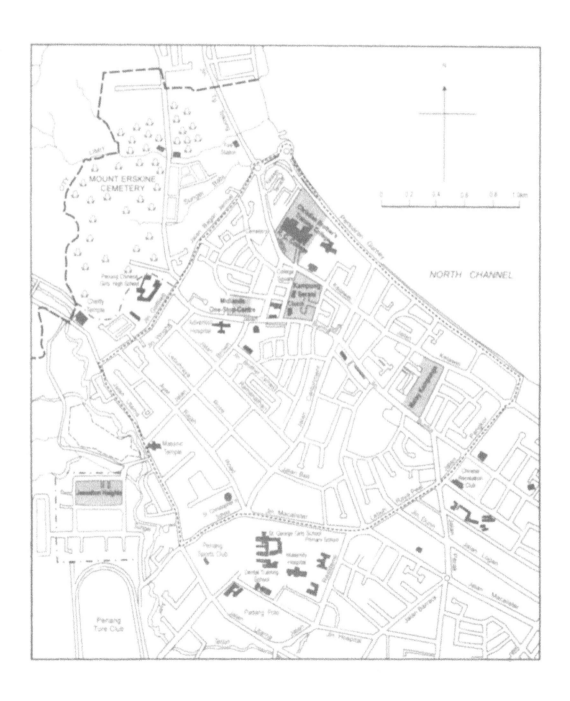

MAP 7.4: LOCATION OF MAJOR TOWNS ON PENANG ISLAND

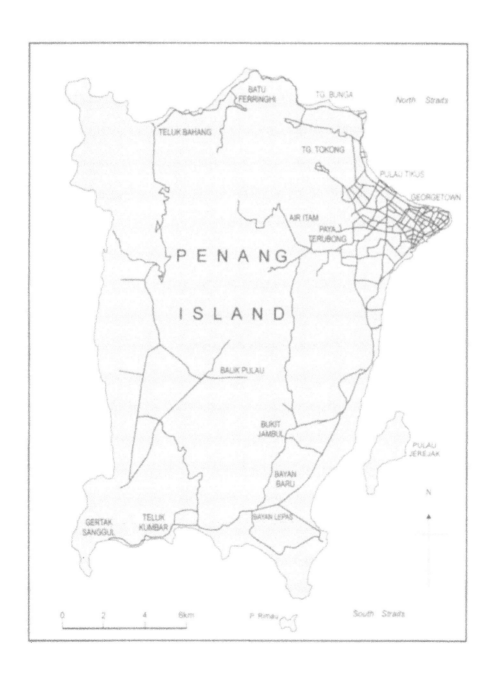

MAP 7.5: CONDOMINIUMS/APARTMENTS AND COMMERCIAL COMPLEXES IN THE VICINITY OF KAMPUNG SERANI AS OF DECEMBER 31, 1993

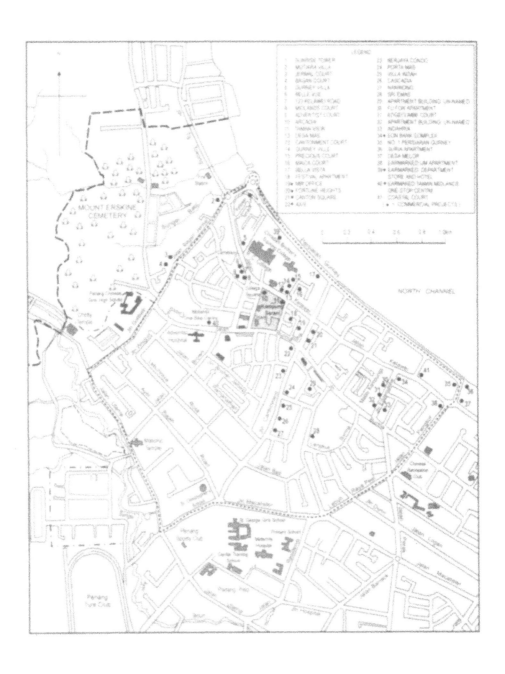

SOUTHEAST ASIA PROGRAM PUBLICATIONS

Cornell University

Studies on Southeast Asia

Number 32   *Fear and Sanctuary: Burmese Refugees in Thailand*, Hazel J. Lang. 2002.
204 pp. ISBN 0-87727-731-1.

Number 31   *Modern Dreams: An Inquiry into Power, Cultural Production, and the
Cityscape in Contemporary Urban Penang, Malaysia*, Beng-Lan Goh. 2002.
225 pp. ISBN 0-87727-730-3.

Number 30   *Violence and the State in Suharto's Indonesia*, ed. Benedict R. O'G.
Anderson. 2001. 247 pp. ISBN 0-87727-729-X.

Number 29   *Studies in Southeast Asian Art: Essays in Honor of Stanley J. O'Connor*, ed.
Nora A. Taylor. 2000. 243 pp. Illustrations. ISBN 0-87727-728-1.

Number 28   *The Hadrami Awakening: Community and Identity in the Netherlands East
Indies, 1900-1942*, Natalie Mobini-Kesheh. 1999. 174 pp.
ISBN 0-87727-727-3.

Number 27   *Tales from Djakarta: Caricatures of Circumstances and their Human Beings*,
Pramoedya Ananta Toer. 1999. 145 pp. ISBN 0-87727-726-5.

Number 26   *History, Culture, and Region in Southeast Asian Perspectives*, rev. ed.,
O. W. Wolters. 1999. 275 pp. ISBN 0-87727-725-7.

Number 25   *Figures of Criminality in Indonesia, the Philippines, and Colonial Vietnam*,
ed. Vicente L. Rafael. 1999. 259 pp. ISBN 0-87727-724-9.

Number 24   *Paths to Conflagration: Fifty Years of Diplomacy and Warfare in Laos,
Thailand, and Vietnam, 1778-1828*, Mayoury Ngaosyvathn and
Pheuiphanh Ngaosyvathn. 1998. 268 pp. ISBN 0-87727-723-0.

Number 23   *Nguyễn Cochinchina: Southern Vietnam in the Seventeenth and Eighteenth
Centuries*, Li Tana. 1998. 194 pp. ISBN 0-87727-722-2.

Number 22   *Young Heroes: The Indonesian Family in Politics*, Saya S. Shiraishi. 1997.
183 pp. ISBN 0-87727-721-4.

Number 21   *Interpreting Development: Capitalism, Democracy, and the Middle Class in
Thailand*, John Girling. 1996. 95 pp. ISBN 0-87727-720-6.

Number 20   *Making Indonesia*, ed. Daniel S. Lev, Ruth McVey. 1996. 201 pp.
ISBN 0-87727-719-2.

Number 19   *Essays into Vietnamese Pasts*, ed. K. W. Taylor, John K. Whitmore. 1995.
288 pp. ISBN 0-87727-718-4.

Number 18   *In the Land of Lady White Blood: Southern Thailand and the Meaning of
History*, Lorraine M. Gesick. 1995. 106 pp. ISBN 0-87727-717-6.

Number 17   *The Vernacular Press and the Emergence of Modern Indonesian
Consciousness*, Ahmat Adam. 1995. 220 pp. ISBN 0-87727-716-8.

Number 16   *The Nan Chronicle*, trans., ed. David K. Wyatt. 1994. 158 pp.
ISBN 0-87727-715-X.

Number 15   *Selective Judicial Competence: The Cirebon-Priangan Legal Administration,
1680–1792*, Mason C. Hoadley. 1994. 185 pp. ISBN 0-87727-714-1.

Number 14   *Sjahrir: Politics and Exile in Indonesia*, Rudolf Mrázek. 1994. 536 pp.
ISBN 0-87727-713-3.

Number 13   *Fair Land Sarawak: Some Recollections of an Expatriate Officer*, Alastair Morrison. 1993. 196 pp. ISBN 0-87727-712-5.

Number 12   *Fields from the Sea: Chinese Junk Trade with Siam during the Late Eighteenth and Early Nineteenth Centuries*, Jennifer Cushman. 1993. 206 pp. ISBN 0-87727-711-7.

Number 11   *Money, Markets, and Trade in Early Southeast Asia: The Development of Indigenous Monetary Systems to AD 1400*, Robert S. Wicks. 1992. 2nd printing 1996. 354 pp., 78 tables, illus., maps. ISBN 0-87727-710-9.

Number 10   *Tai Ahoms and the Stars: Three Ritual Texts to Ward Off Danger*, trans., ed. B. J. Terwiel, Ranoo Wichasin. 1992. 170 pp. ISBN 0-87727-709-5.

Number 9   *Southeast Asian Capitalists*, ed. Ruth McVey. 1992. 2nd printing 1993. 220 pp. ISBN 0-87727-708-7.

Number 8   *The Politics of Colonial Exploitation: Java, the Dutch, and the Cultivation System*, Cornelis Fasseur, ed. R. E. Elson, trans. R. E. Elson, Ary Kraal. 1992. 2nd printing 1994. 266 pp. ISBN 0-87727-707-9.

Number 7   *A Malay Frontier: Unity and Duality in a Sumatran Kingdom*, Jane Drakard. 1990. 215 pp. ISBN 0-87727-706-0.

Number 6   *Trends in Khmer Art*, Jean Boisselier, ed. Natasha Eilenberg, trans. Natasha Eilenberg, Melvin Elliott. 1989. 124 pp., 24 plates. ISBN 0-87727-705-2.

Number 5   *Southeast Asian Ephemeris: Solar and Planetary Positions, A.D. 638–2000*, J. C. Eade. 1989. 175 pp. ISBN 0-87727-704-4.

Number 3   *Thai Radical Discourse: The Real Face of Thai Feudalism Today*, Craig J. Reynolds. 1987. 2nd printing 1994. 186 pp. ISBN 0-87727-702-8.

Number 1   *The Symbolism of the Stupa*, Adrian Snodgrass. 1985. Revised with index, 1988. 3rd printing 1998. 469 pp. ISBN 0-87727-700-1.

SEAP Series

Number 19   *Gender, Household, State: Đổi Mới in Việt Nam*, ed. Jayne Werner and Danièle Bélanger. 2002. 153 pp. ISBN 0-87727-137-2.

Number 18   *Culture and Power in Traditional Siamese Government*, Neil A. Englehart. 2001. 130 pp. ISBN 0-87727-135-6.

Number 17   *Gangsters, Democracy, and the State*, ed. Carl A. Trocki. 1998. 94 pp. ISBN 0-87727-134-8.

Number 16   *Cutting across the Lands: An Annotated Bibliography on Natural Resource Management and Community Development in Indonesia, the Philippines, and Malaysia*, ed. Eveline Ferretti. 1997. 329 pp. ISBN 0-87727-133-X.

Number 15   *The Revolution Falters: The Left in Philippine Politics after 1986*, ed. Patricio N. Abinales. 1996. 182 pp. ISBN 0-87727-132-1.

Number 14   *Being Kammu: My Village, My Life*, Damrong Tayanin. 1994. 138 pp., 22 tables, illus., maps. ISBN 0-87727-130-5.

Number 13   *The American War in Vietnam*, ed. Jayne Werner, David Hunt. 1993. 132 pp. ISBN 0-87727-131-3.

Number 12   *The Political Legacy of Aung San*, ed. Josef Silverstein. Revised edition 1993. 169 pp. ISBN 0-87727-128-3.

Number 10   *Studies on Vietnamese Language and Literature: A Preliminary Bibliography*, Nguyen Dinh Tham. 1992. 227 pp. ISBN 0-87727-127-5.

Number 9   *A Secret Past*, Dokmaisot, trans. Ted Strehlow. 1992. 2nd printing 1997. 72 pp. ISBN 0-87727-126-7.

Number 8   *From PKI to the Comintern, 1924–1941: The Apprenticeship of the Malayan Communist Party*, Cheah Boon Kheng. 1992. 147 pp. ISBN 0-87727-125-9.

Number 7   *Intellectual Property and US Relations with Indonesia, Malaysia, Singapore, and Thailand*, Elisabeth Uphoff. 1991. 67 pp. ISBN 0-87727-124-0.

Number 6   *The Rise and Fall of the Communist Party of Burma (CPB)*, Bertil Lintner. 1990. 124 pp. 26 illus., 14 maps. ISBN 0-87727-123-2.

Number 5   *Japanese Relations with Vietnam: 1951–1987*, Masaya Shiraishi. 1990. 174 pp. ISBN 0-87727-122-4.

Number 3   *Postwar Vietnam: Dilemmas in Socialist Development*, ed. Christine White, David Marr. 1988. 2nd printing 1993. 260 pp. ISBN 0-87727-120-8.

Number 2   *The Dobama Movement in Burma (1930–1938)*, Khin Yi. 1988. 160 pp. ISBN 0-87727-118-6.

Translation Series

Volume 4   *Approaching Suharto's Indonesia from the Margins*, ed. Takashi Shiraishi. 1994. 153 pp. ISBN 0-87727-403-7.

Volume 3   *The Japanese in Colonial Southeast Asia*, ed. Saya Shiraishi, Takashi Shiraishi. 1993. 172 pp. ISBN 0-87727-402-9.

Volume 2   *Indochina in the 1940s and 1950s*, ed. Takashi Shiraishi, Motoo Furuta. 1992. 196 pp. ISBN 0-87727-401-0.

Volume 1   *Reading Southeast Asia*, ed. Takashi Shiraishi. 1990. 188 pp. ISBN 0-87727-400-2.

CORNELL MODERN INDONESIA PROJECT PUBLICATIONS
Cornell University

Number 75   *A Tour of Duty: Changing Patterns of Military Politics in Indonesia in the 1990s*. Douglas Kammen and Siddharth Chandra. 1999. 99 pp. ISBN 0-87763-049-6.

Number 74   *The Roots of Acehnese Rebellion 1989–1992*, Tim Kell. 1995. 103 pp. ISBN 0-87763-040-2.

Number 73   *"White Book" on the 1992 General Election in Indonesia*, trans. Dwight King. 1994. 72 pp. ISBN 0-87763-039-9.

Number 72   *Popular Indonesian Literature of the Qur'an*, Howard M. Federspiel. 1994. 170 pp. ISBN 0-87763-038-0.

Number 71   *A Javanese Memoir of Sumatra, 1945–1946: Love and Hatred in the Liberation War*, Takao Fusayama. 1993. 150 pp. ISBN 0-87763-037-2.

Number 70   *East Kalimantan: The Decline of a Commercial Aristocracy*, Burhan Magenda. 1991. 120 pp. ISBN 0-87763-036-4.

Number 69   *The Road to Madiun: The Indonesian Communist Uprising of 1948*, Elizabeth Ann Swift. 1989. 120 pp. ISBN 0-87763-035-6.

Number 68   *Intellectuals and Nationalism in Indonesia: A Study of the Following Recruited by Sutan Sjahrir in Occupation Jakarta*, J. D. Legge. 1988. 159 pp. ISBN 0-87763-034-8.

Number 67   *Indonesia Free: A Biography of Mohammad Hatta*, Mavis Rose. 1987. 252 pp. ISBN 0-87763-033-X.

Number 66   *Prisoners at Kota Cane*, Leon Salim, trans. Audrey Kahin. 1986. 112 pp. ISBN 0-87763-032-1.

Number 65   *The Kenpeitai in Java and Sumatra*, trans. Barbara G. Shimer, Guy Hobbs, intro. Theodore Friend. 1986. 80 pp. ISBN 0-87763-031-3.

Number 64   *Suharto and His Generals: Indonesia's Military Politics, 1975–1983*, David Jenkins. 1984. 4th printing 1997. 300 pp. ISBN 0-87763-030-5.

Number 62   *Interpreting Indonesian Politics: Thirteen Contributions to the Debate, 1964–1981*, ed. Benedict Anderson, Audrey Kahin, intro. Daniel S. Lev. 1982. 3rd printing 1991. 172 pp. ISBN 0-87763-028-3.

Number 61   *Sickle and Crescent: The Communist Revolt of 1926 in Banten*, Michael C. Williams. 1982. 81 pp. ISBN 0-87763-027-5.

Number 60   *The Minangkabau Response to Dutch Colonial Rule in the Nineteenth Century*, Elizabeth E. Graves. 1981. 157 pp. ISBN 0-87763-000-3.

Number 59   *Breaking the Chains of Oppression of the Indonesian People: Defense Statement at His Trial on Charges of Insulting the Head of State, Bandung, June 7–10, 1979*, Heri Akhmadi. 1981. 201 pp. ISBN 0-87763-001-1.

Number 58   *Administration of Islam in Indonesia*, Deliar Noer. 1978. 82 pp. ISBN 0-87763-002-X.

Number 57   *Permesta: Half a Rebellion*, Barbara S. Harvey. 1977. 174 pp. ISBN 0-87763-003-8.

Number 55   *Report from Banaran: The Story of the Experiences of a Soldier during the War of Independence*, Maj. Gen. T. B. Simatupang. 1972. 186 pp. ISBN 0-87763-005-4.

Number 52   *A Preliminary Analysis of the October 1 1965, Coup in Indonesia (Prepared in January 1966)*, Benedict R. Anderson, Ruth T. McVey, assist. Frederick P. Bunnell. 1971. 3rd printing 1990. 174 pp. ISBN 0-87763-008-9.

Number 51   *The Putera Reports: Problems in Indonesian-Japanese War-Time Cooperation*, Mohammad Hatta, trans., intro. William H. Frederick. 1971. 114 pp. ISBN 0-87763-009-7.

Number 50   *Schools and Politics: The Kaum Muda Movement in West Sumatra (1927–1933)*, Taufik Abdullah. 1971. 257 pp. ISBN 0-87763-010-0.

Number 49   *The Foundation of the Partai Muslimin Indonesia*, K. E. Ward. 1970. 75 pp. ISBN 0-87763-011-9.

Number 48   *Nationalism, Islam and Marxism*, Soekarno, intro. Ruth T. McVey. 1970. 2nd printing 1984. 62 pp. ISBN 0-87763-012-7.

Number 43   *State and Statecraft in Old Java: A Study of the Later Mataram Period, 16th to 19th Century*, Soemarsaid Moertono. Revised edition 1981. 180 pp. ISBN 0-87763-017-8.

Number 37   *Mythology and the Tolerance of the Javanese*, Benedict R. O'G. Anderson. 2nd edition 1997. 104 pp., 65 illus. ISBN 0-87763-041-0.

Number 25   *The Communist Uprisings of 1926–1927 in Indonesia: Key Documents*, ed., intro. Harry J. Benda, Ruth T. McVey. 1960. 2nd printing 1969. 177 pp. ISBN 0-87763-024-0.

Number 7   *The Soviet View of the Indonesian Revolution*, Ruth T. McVey. 1957. 3rd printing 1969. 90 pp. ISBN 0-87763-018-6.

Number 6   *The Indonesian Elections of 1955*, Herbert Feith. 1957. 2nd printing 1971. 91 pp. ISBN 0-87763-020-8.

LANGUAGE TEXTS

INDONESIAN

Beginning Indonesian through Self-Instruction, John U. Wolff, Dédé Oetomo, Daniel Fietkiewicz. 3rd revised edition 1992. Vol. 1. 115 pp. ISBN 0-87727-529-7. Vol. 2. 434 pp. ISBN 0-87727-530-0. Vol. 3. 473 pp. ISBN 0-87727-531-9.

Indonesian Readings, John U. Wolff. 1978. 4th printing 1992. 480 pp. ISBN 0-87727-517-3

Indonesian Conversations, John U. Wolff. 1978. 3rd printing 1991. 297 pp. ISBN 0-87727-516-5

Formal Indonesian, John U. Wolff. 2nd revised edition 1986. 446 pp. ISBN 0-87727-515-7

TAGALOG

Pilipino through Self-Instruction, John U. Wolff, Maria Theresa C. Centano, Der-Hwa V. Rau. 1991. Vol. 1. 342 pp. ISBN 0-87727—525-4. Vol. 2. 378 pp. ISBN 0-87727-526-2. Vol 3. 431 pp. ISBN 0-87727-527-0. Vol. 4. 306 pp. ISBN 0-87727-528-9.

THAI

A. U. A. Language Center Thai Course Book 1, J. Marvin Brown. Originally published by the American University Alumni Association Language Center, 1974. Reissued by Cornell Southeast Asia Program, 1991. 267 pp. ISBN 0-87727-506-8.

A. U. A. Language Center Thai Course Book 2, 1992. 288 pp. ISBN 0-87727-507-6.

A. U. A. Language Center Thai Course Book 3, 1992. 247 pp. ISBN 0-87727-508-4.

A. U. A. Language Center Thai Course, Reading and Writing Text (mostly reading), 1979. Reissued 1997. 164 pp. ISBN 0-87727-511-4.

A. U. A. Language Center Thai Course, Reading and Writing Workbook (mostly writing), 1979. Reissued 1997. 99 pp. ISBN 0-87727-512-2.

KHMER

Cambodian System of Writing and Beginning Reader, Franklin E. Huffman. Originally published by Yale University Press, 1970. Reissued by Cornell Southeast Asia Program, 3rd printing 1992. 365 pp. ISBN 0-300-01314-0.

Modern Spoken Cambodian, Franklin E. Huffman, assist. Charan Promchan, Chhom-Rak Thong Lambert. Originally published by Yale University Press, 1970. Reissued by Cornell Southeast Asia Program, 3rd printing 1991. 451 pp. ISBN 0-300-01316-7.

Intermediate Cambodian Reader, ed. Franklin E. Huffman, assist. Im Proum. Originally published by Yale University Press, 1972. Reissued by Cornell Southeast Asia Program, 1988. 499 pp. ISBN 0-300-01552-6.

Cambodian Literary Reader and Glossary, Franklin E. Huffman, Im Proum. Originally published by Yale University Press, 1977. Reissued by Cornell Southeast Asia Program, 1988. 494 pp. ISBN 0-300-02069-4.

HMONG

White Hmong-English Dictionary, Ernest E. Heimbach. 1969. 7th printing 1997. 523 pp. ISBN 0-87727-075-9.

VIETNAMESE

Intermediate Spoken Vietnamese, Franklin E. Huffman, Tran Trong Hai. 1980. 3rd printing 1994. ISBN 0-87727-500-9.

* * *

Southeast Asian Studies: Reorientations. Craig J. Reynolds and Ruth McVey. Frank H. Golay Lectures 2 & 3. 70 pp. ISBN 0-87727-301-4.

Javanese Literature in Surakarta Manuscripts, Nancy K. Florida. Vol. 1, *Introduction and Manuscripts of the Karaton Surakarta.* 1993. 410 pp. Frontispiece, illustrations. Hard cover, ISBN 0-87727-602-1, Paperback, ISBN 0-87727-603-X. Vol. 2, *Manuscripts of the Mangkunagaran Palace.* 2000. 576 pp. Frontispiece, illustrations. Paperback, ISBN 0-87727-604-8.

Sbek Thom: Khmer Shadow Theater. Pech Tum Kravel, trans. Sos Kem, ed. Thavro Phim, Sos Kem, Martin Hatch. 1996. 363 pp., 153 photographs. ISBN 0-87727-620-X.

In the Mirror, Literature and Politics in Siam in the American Era, ed. Benedict R. O'G. Anderson, trans. Benedict R. O'G. Anderson, Ruchira Mendiones. 1985. 2nd printing 1991. 303 pp. Paperback. ISBN 974-210-380-1.

To order, please contact:

Cornell University
SEAP Distribution Center
369 Pine Tree Rd.
Ithaca, NY 14850-2819 USA

Tel: 1-877-865-2432 (Toll free – U.S.)
Fax: (607) 255-7534

E-mail: SEAP-Pubs@cornell.edu

Orders must be prepaid by check or credit card (VISA, MasterCard, Discover).

Lightning Source UK Ltd.
Milton Keynes UK
UKHW031816260123
416025UK00010B/789